BY MICHAEL LALLY

What Withers (1970)

The Lines Are Drawn (1970)

MCMLXVI Poem (1970)

Stupid Rabbits (1971)

The South Orange Sonnets (1972)

Late Sleepers (1973)

Malenkov Takes Over (1974)

Rocky Dies Yellow (1975, 1977)

Dues (1975)

Sex/The Swing Era (1975)

Mentally, He's a Sick Man (1975)

My Life (1975)

Oomaloom (1975)

Charisma (1976)

Catch My Breath (1978, 1995)

In the Mood (1978)

Just Let Me Do It (1978)

White Life (1980)

Attitude (1982)

Hollywood Magic (1982)

What You Find There (compact disc, 1994)

Cant Be Wrong (1996)

Of (1999)

It's Not Nostalgia: Poetry & Prose (1999)

MICHAEL LALLY

IT'S NOT NOSTALGIA

POETRY & PROSE

BLACK SPARROW PRESS

SANTA ROSA
1999

ACKNOWLEDGMENTS

Some of the work in this collection has appeared in the following periodicals and anthologies: *American Review, Barney, The Big House, Blasts!, Bomb, Editor's Choice, Face of the Poet* (Brooke Alexander Gallery: Alex Katz catalogue), *The Hollywood Review, Hot Water Review, Journal: A Contemporary Art Magazine, Little Caesar, New York Sex, None of the Above, Outlaw Poetry, Poetry Loves Poetry, Salk Lick, Shiny, SoHo Arts Weekly, Washington Review of the Arts, ZZZ*; and in the plays, *Hollywood Magic*, first performed at Stages Theater in Hollywood, CA, 1983, and *The Rhythm of Torn Stars*, first performed at The Pacific Theater in Venice, CA, 1989.

Thanks to Karen Allen, Eve Brandstein, Jim Haining, Joan Hartgens, Hubert Selby, Jr., Terence Winch, and especially to Geoffrey Young and John Martin. And as always to Caitlin and Miles and now Jaina and Flynn.

And to the memory of my parents, my brother Jim and sister Joan, my first wife Lee, and my friends Joan Baribeault, Ted Berrigan, Joe Brainard, Ed Cox, Ralphy Dickey, Tim Dlugos, Cliff Heard, Mel Johnson, Sissie Johnson, Etheridge Knight, Greg Millard, Elio Schneeman, and James Schuyler.

LIBRARY OF CONGRESS CATALOGING-IN-PUBLICATION DATA

Lally, Michael, 1942–
   It's not nostalgia : poetry & prose / Michael Lally.
     p.   cm.
   ISBN 1-57423-111-1 (paperback)
   ISBN 1-57423-112-X (cloth trade)
   ISBN 1-57423-113-8 (signed cloth)
    I. Title.
   PS3562.A414I87   1999
   818'.5407—dc21   99-51344

for Jaina and Flynn

TABLE OF CONTENTS

1960-1970

1970-1975 (*Washington, DC*)

1975-1982 (*New York City*)

It's Not Nostalgia

Poetry & Prose

1960-1970

"It's like a man being born in a little place, just a bend in the road somewhere. After a while he begins to travel the road. He travels all the road there is and then he comes back. That man, he understands something when he gets back. He knows the road goes away and he knows the road comes back. He knows the road comes back just the same way it goes away."

—*Sidney Bechet*

T*he south orange sonnets*

1   In books it was the Lackawanna Valley.
The Lackawanna Railroad ran through it
separating those on the hill from us.
Lackawanna Place was the toughest block
in the neighborhood until 1952 when
the temptations and reputation moved
to Church Street where THE PINK DEVILS
had roses tattooed between their thumbs
and forefingers, wore delicate gold
crucifixes on chains around their
brown Italian necks, and carried porno
playing cards from Newark, the city
where parades got lost and statues
died. Newark, where we all had lived.

2   My brother brought the moon back from
Okinawa. I mean, there they learned of
the surrender three days late and then
they danced all night. My brother played
the saxophone. Junkman Willy did a one
step that most girls didn't want to do.
They called him that for all the old cars
he worked on till he was old enough to
drive. He was a paddy cat like me and we
lived on Cabbage Hill till we were old
enough to live anywhere. We believed
Italians and Jews ran THE SYNDICATE
maybe the world. In West Orange a man
hung himself higher than he could reach.

3   The girls liked to dance with Eddie
     we believed. He came back from jail
     with big muscles and, it was rumored
     bleached blonde hair. He had a tattoo
     with the name crossed out and dimples.
     One girl's father sent Eddie to school
     in Las Vegas to learn to be a shill.
     The girl's father was a big man in Las
     Vegas it was rumored. Eddie was a big
     man in South Orange. While he was gone
     I met an Italian girl with hair on her
     chest and poured beer out my side of
     Junkman's truck when nobody was looking.
     After only two weeks Eddie came back.

4   In East Orange Carol Robinson decided I
     was her boyfriend. Her father found out
     before I did. Told his friends and neigh-
     bors how he didn't want no white boy hang-
     ing around his little girl. One asked me
     not to pass the time at his house anymore
     listening to his son's Clifford Browns or
     talking to his twin daughters. Walking
     home that night three teenagers sitting
     on a stoop on Halstead Street yelled: Hey
     white boy, whatchu doin around here? You
     know where you are? Where you from? When
     I answered South Orange this fat girl said
     Shoot, that muss be Carol Rob's turkey.

5   Little Robert called himself a sporting man
     at fourteen. Came by Charlie's house talking
     about being a gambling fool and losing a
     hundred dollars a minute and who has got
     the playing cards. A friend of Charlie's wife
     laughed and said Ain't you too old for card
     games now? Charlie's wife made most men turn
     around. When I was fourteen I watched her
     walk by the store where I swept the floor.
     Seven years later Charlie's cousin told me I
     danced too close to Charlie's wife. My father
     figured Charlie, Kenny, Bobby and the other
     friends I loved were lazy 'cause they didn't
     have good jobs. Kenny didn't even have a job.

14

6   In 1959 I thought of myself as NEVER
     FEAR and liked to talk about a door
     that when you walked through it you were
     dancing. My father thought we had to be
     up to no good out till two o'clock in the
     morning. We rode around in Charlie's car
     and talked. We decided one difference
     between white girls and black girls was
     the way you danced with them. White girls
     you held around the waist with your right
     arm. You put the same arm over a black
     girl's shoulder. That was in 1959. Did you
     ever have a woman's cunt wrapped around
     your head asked Eddie. That was in 1956.

7   One year our people refused to buy Christmas
     cards that said SEASON'S GREETINGS. A year
     later we christened the new homes on the hill
     JEWSTEAD. Three years later we sang Guns for
     the Arabs, bicycles and sneakers for the Jews.
     Then a year came when the Jewish girls turned
     soft and ripe and full of round things we
     longed to hold. That was the year we all wanted
     to be Jewish. We wanted to kiss the thing
     they hung on their doors. We wanted to dip
     our fingers into whatever holy water was theirs.
     But most of all we didn't want to wait to be
     the forbidden goyim they would sneak down
     from their hill three years later to sample.

8   A sign across the street said WATCH
     CHILDREN. The street ended at the top
     with the house where the man lived
     who sang opera on his front stoop at
     three or four in the morning when he
     came home drunk. Sober he repaired
     telephones. At the bottom it crossed
     what passed for a highway in 1942
     only to dead end into the railroad
     tracks. It had eighteen houses on it
     a bowling alley a gas station the
     back of a supermarket and a practice
     football field where we played Ring-
     a-lario the night Babe Ruth died.

9   When my mother died two Irish great aunts
     came over from New York. The brassy one
     wore her hat tilted and always sat with
     her legs wide apart. At the wake she told
     me loud You look like your grandfather
     the cop, if you ever get like him shoot
     yourself. The other one waited till after
     the funeral to pull my ear down to her
     level and whisper You're a good looking
     young man but if you don't shave off them
     side boards people will mistake you for
     a Puerto Rican. We had so many cousins
     in our neighborhood everybody called my
     mother Aunt Irene. Even the Italians.

10   My uncle shot himself before I was born.
     My grandfather who carried an old petri-
     fied potato in his pocket for his arth-
     ritis got up and walked out of the funeral.
     His sons slipped out of their pews as
     piously as they knew how and went to find
     him. He was buttoning up his fly as they
     came through the big oak doors of the
     church and caught the reflection of the
     sunlight on his piss. He used to open the
     door of a fast moving vehicle which the
     driver would hysterically beg to a stop
     squeezing everything. He'd say It's time
     to shake a little water off the potatoes.

11   In the morning people read *The Daily News*.
     I pored over the cheesecake in the center
     spread and in the newsreels in my head was
     Eddie only more like me escorting one of
     those women to the opening night of the in-
     ternationally renowned BIG APPLE CLUB.
     The older kids built their clubhouse in the
     vacant lot where we played in the 1938 Olds
     mobile with the miniature pin up of Betty
     Grable in the suicide knob on the steering
     wheel or in the open sewer we called The
     Brook. One cousin made a coop for a sick
     pigeon he was nursing. When the pigeon flew
     away we made that coop our little club house.

16

12 The Lackawanna Railroad was an electric commuter
special that cut off the head of a ten year old
Boy Scout one summer. He was listening to the
tracks to hear if the train was coming. His
cousin saw it happen and was sick for a week.
He was seven. In bed when I was a kid listening
to the sound of the Lackawanna rolling by I'd
dream of the places it would take me someday.
And it did. It took me to all the places it goes
to like Jersey City Belleville Maplewood Movies
West Orange Newark and New York. Some times
we jumped off halfway home to avoid paying.
One year somebody got a plate in his head from
jumping off onto something hard like my cousins.

13 Junkman was the oldest of fourteen kids. My
father called him a bum when he quit school
to work construction. My father quit school
in 1910 to work in a hardware store. Junkman's younger brothers went to the Catholic
Prep School. One was crushed by his locker
his first year there and died. A family of
eleven lived on one side of us. Once my
brother the cop pulled up to a couple in a
car making out. He put his light on them
and saw it was one of the girls next door.
She was with another girl. When Junkman began his own construction company my father
asked me why I wasn't ambitious like that.

14 The tree between the sidewalk and the curb
attracted me. The leaves turning up in the
breeze before a summer storm revealed a side
that glowed, flashed like the palms of a
dark woman shaping castles in the air. My
father didn't like it. He'd ask why a boy sat
on the stoop staring at trees when he could
be watching TV learning the things a boy
should know to be well liked by the men who
could help him. Golfing terms, starting line
ups, some news. Too much thinking can ruin
you he'd say. When we were alone my mother
would ask Don't you think there might be
something wrong with having no white friends.

15 My cousin was an artist but no one knew.
    They thought he was only a work of art
    like a pinball machine made out of marble.
    When someone deliberately broke the first
    two letters of the ESSEX HOUSE sign, my
    cousin did the same to a new kid's head.
    He grew bigger than any cousin and more
    gentle. Eddie no, I said, I never did
    have a lady's cunt wrapped around my head.
    I knew Eddie was an artist when he ate
    the aspirin. Girls from THE CRAZY KITTENS
    played "Eddie My Love" eighteen times in a
    row that night. Eddie looked at me and
    said Whadja do, kid, come out of a horse's ass?

16 They say prospectors saved their scalps
    by acting crazy. I acted as crazy as I
    could when white guys asked me what it
    was like with a, didn't want to say it
    but afraid to look like they didn't want
    to say it, said it: *nigger*. I hit them.
    Or I told them Fine as 400 wine. Like
    laying under that tree before a storm
    watching the leaves turn over and shine.
    Like getting it steady and nice. Like
    the first time twice. Like standing in
    the rain laughing. Like sitting at Broad
    and Market, spitting at the moon and
    hitting it. The word I wanted to marry.

17 There is some music you have to listen to.
    In South Orange there were rich Catholics
    rich Protestants and rich Jews. My cousin
    became a cop. His brother was stabbed by
    an Italian called Lemon Drop. Across the
    street lived two brothers called Loaf and
    Half a Loaf. My brother became a cop. On
    St. Patrick's Day 1958 I came home drunk. My
    mother said He's only fifteen. My father:
    It had to happen once. My grandfather was
    a cop. One cousin won a beauty contest at
    thirteen. My sister married a cop. By 1959
    I knew I was going to be a jazz musician.
    My father joined AA before I was even born.

18

18   At first the world's great heroes were FDR
      Churchill and Uncle Joe Stalin. The block
      hero was FLYING ACE who shot down Krauts
      on a seven inch screen. One brother served
      with the Navy band, one with the Army
      Air Corps. Before TV we sat through Sunday
      matinees with newsreel footage of Nazi war
      crimes. The boarder in our house had been
      a doughboy in World War I. We called him
      uncle. My third brother worked on tanks in
      Germany during the Korean thing. I joined
      the Air Force on February eighth 1962. I
      went AWOL July fourth 1962. For a long time
      no one we knew ever went away a civilian.

19   There were people who didn't need nick-
      names. Love I'd say to myself walking
      those streets under the old gas lights.
      The woman on Valley Street who waited
      after her friend went home. The eyes of
      pretty Italian girls as their boyfriends
      pulled up to the curb. The voice on the
      phone from West Orange saying love the
      first time saying what saying wait saying
      Say it again. Or like getting on the bus
      to Newark six thirty in the morning
      with a beautiful black girl in a party
      dress and all of the people going to work.
      In 1960 you could star in South Orange.

20   My father lost the store, we all went to
      work when I was ten. Then he became a
      ward heeler. My grandfather was dead before
      I knew he spoke Gaelic. My father could
      remember when they had mules instead of
      automobiles and you had to remove your cap
      and step to the curb to let the rich walk
      by. My grandfather was glad to die in the
      USA. He'd say if you can't find a job within
      thirty miles of New York City there aren't
      any jobs to be found. My father would say
      You can write all the poetry you want to
      when you're a millionaire. Eddie would say
      You got to try a shoe on before you buy it.

                                      (1960-69)

1959: gave all my Frankie Lyman records to my cousin to keep for me while I'm away.

1960: wrote a poem about a dark-skinned girl whose hands are like the leaves before a storm, contrast, light under dark, flashing, turning over gently. I love her. They call her Bambi. Smoked some tea for the first time while drinking a lot of Gallo half & half. Tried to write a story about a kid addicted to heroin. The day Curtis Powell took me to meet Bob Kaufman he wasn't home.

1961: lost virginity for the third time since 1956, to a woman I can dig but everybody else says what are you doing with that ugly pitch black street running two timing jiving funny time dyke. But Princess is okay. We like each other, and leave each other alone. Borrowed the rubber, the second one I ever used, from Lex Humphreys, Slide Hampton's drummer, who was smoking some boo with some other boots & a couple of sheets, three white girls from the South who follow jazz musicians around all week long until they get them up to their Brooklyn apartment on weekends to smoke some gage and do that thing. I think I've never been to Brooklyn in the daytime. Smoking seems to make everybody unsociable. I dig it with a few friends but with new people in large groups, you know, 10 to 40, it just makes for sleepy eyes and bull-shit. So me and Princess made it in the bathroom after we tried the roof, which was too slanted, and after I got the rubber because she swore she would give me all kinds of creeping shit. I didn't get anything. And the next time we made it, in Clifford's bathroom, we didn't use no rubber, that was just after she threatened to commit suicide by jumping out Clifford's bathroom window which is seven stories high on West Fourth Street but has bars on it and is too small for anything larger than a big cat to get through anyway.

1962: now I'm in Texas and this lame sergeant gave me a bunch of shit for looking at the sky while marching. I told him I just real-ized I'd been here 3 days and hadn't really dug the fact that this was Texas and a whole different sky. The guys I joined with think I'm a little weird. When we left from Newark the guy I sat with on the plane explained that everybody figured I was some kind of throwback from "The Pineys" which is like Jersey's Ozarks, on account of my long wild tangled hair and my old surplus Salvation Army clothes. They took all the clothes away my first day. They told me They burned them because they smelled so bad. They took all the hair away too. A lot of these cats are complaining because they haven't had any women in a week. I know they're jive because I'm enjoying the vacation from it. The night before I left the city Al asked this Irish chick to take me out from the bar when they closed and she went ahead and took me home. She lived with Pauline the mulatto hooker. Pauline didn't want to see me. Probably sick of men which I can understand too. But I didn't want to see her either. I was skunky drunk feeling sad about Bambi and then I passed out. When I came to I was on one of the twin beds and the two of them were on the other. Hookers are usually good people like that, strippers too. When I stood up I saw Pauline's box sort of hanging out from under the slip she was sleeping in. My first three nights at basic I had nightmares about that pussy. I love women. I love life sometimes. I hate machines and systems and this goddam service but I got to admit I'm enjoying the respite. Gimme a week to get myself back in shape.

When we came up on Denver I knew it was too late to go back. Had to see Frisco, though hip people tell me hip people don't call it Frisco anymore, but I dug Frisco anyway. Bucks wanted to get a hotel room right away. He drove all the way, except for about an hour in Utah when I guess I scared the piss out of him. When we got to Frisco I just leaned out a window and asked a dude where North Beach was. Bucks got a cheap Chinese hotel anyway and I went walking. Found the Hot Dog Palace where they had a box with real "jazz" on it. They also had chocolate cake. Couldn't make up my mind what to drop my last quarter on. Did the music and pulled a chair up close to the speaker. Had my action-back French cut Klein's-on-the-Square in Newark special sport coat on. Hadn't shaved since we left the base in Illinois, a cap over my eyes, and my military ID in my shoe. Somebody slaps me on the shoulder and I turn around the other way thinking I'm still in the movies. It's Andre the spade junkie with the effeminate rap from the city. My first time West of the Mississippi and here's some street partner from New York. He seems okay, turns out he's taking the cure in the California sun and doesn't seem impressed with the fact I'm AWOL. We get Bucks' car and split to a party in Berkeley. Andre knows everybody just like New York. We move in with this crazy musician and his beautiful old lady who starts talking to me. She's crazy too but gentle. After a week the dude throws us all out getting paranoid about me and his old lady but he gets too nasty so Andre drops his phony accent and does him up right with a lot of motherfuckers and a few bounces on the dude's head. I wish we could take the girl with us. Bucks sells the car and splits leaving me some coin. Andre finds a French hooker who is in the country illegally and balls her in this hotel room somebody lets us use. Finally I go up to go to sleep. They're still fucking but when Andre hears my hacking cough he goes out for some bourbon for me. While he's gone the French girl tries to turn me on. I tell her I got another woman on my mind. She can't get it so I tell her I don't like white meat. It's so stupid. Andre comes back and lays the bourbon on me which I demolish in a matter of minutes and am out nicely. Wake up to a cackling landlady chasing about seven weird looking beatnik dudes out the door who must have come in to sleep on the floor after I conked out. The French chick splits with them. Me and Andre have five minutes to get our shit together. When the landlady goes out Andre pisses in the sink and does a few ballerina turns in front of the mirror. He was actually a rich kid once. He says ain't it weird he likes white women and I like black. Talks me into proposing to Dolores on the phone collect later that night all the way back in Jersey. He doesn't know it's Bambi who is causing all the trouble, who really has my nose open. Dolores is a friend and bedmate but. Back in Illinois I take a court martial and get out of the stockade by exaggerating some. I tell this major it was a bind because my first sergeant is a Southerner and I needed leave to see my pregnant girl who is black. The major is a liberal who admires my courage but not my lack of responsibility. What is this shit. So I'm busted fined restricted to the base and put on extra work duty again. Bucks is dragged back by the gestapo from the Colorado hills and gets off with a simple bust. Six months later he gets his stripes back. It takes me a year and a half. He's from Darien, Connecticut. I get sent to Greenville, South Carolina.

1963: I celebrate my 21st birthday on leave with a party at Lois Flemings' sister's, who says she doesn't believe I'm only 21. That I've done too much dirt to be that young. Me and Dolores argue about kids and I get to take back my proposal. Bambi has a ten pound baby boy at St. Michael's hospital on High Street in Newark with me standing by but it ain't mine.

1964: got married. Lee introduces me to Dylan albums. I realize we met once, me and him, in the Fat Black Pussycat when we didn't know who he was gonna be. I fall outa my tree listening to him, as the fringies say, living on the fringes of society I guess in the university district of Seattle, the nearest big city a day's ride away. We are all spaced out getting together an underground newspaper which I try to write a column for. Before my getting married Sandy and her husband ball in the same bed with me after me and Sandy ball and we all discuss free love and sexual hang ups. Everybody's smoking boo now and popping some new pill that turns you inside out. I want to paint the old Willys with some scenes from Manhattan 'cause I'm homesick. We hear of similar scenes down the coast and a farm commune outside the city named after Tolstoy. I argue a lot with college kids, get called on special duty the night of Tonkin Bay to chart weather maps for Northern China, SAC bombers need wind estimates to drop their atomic load. I remember the Cuban scare when I was stationed in South Carolina and how they took "expendables" for the First Assault Group so that they wouldn't lose valuable fighters in the first wave. Lord Buckley albums get scarce and valuable. I argue with Sandy that *Playboy* is shit, she thinks it's hip. She and Billy get put away for contributing to the delinquency of a minor. Joy gets put away for shoplifting. Jimmy, my drummer, tells the cops everything because he is afraid. And doesn't realize what happened. I split. Get married. Jimmy gets married. Tom gets married. Our wives get married too.

1965: I stop drinking and hanging around. Average of two fights a week dwindles to one every three months. Lose Jimmy to a slick sax player from Georgia who starts a new group and takes over Al Jackson's job at the East Side Club. I realize my music's getting no better. Think about doing something else. Argue with more college kids. Continue to love William Saroyan.

1966: liberation. Home from the war. Travel through Oregon down to SF. A lot of new kids around the streets looking spaced saying wow, and yeah yeah yeah. Get flack from every gas station owner across the country after we leave the Chinese hotel in Frisco where Lee was a little put out by sharing the bathroom with some old dude next door who would take horribly loud, wet, and unendurably long shits in the middle of the night and wake us up. Try growing a beard, walking around Manhattan living in Brooklyn. Everything we own fits into my '56 Pontiac hard top. I sell it for 60 bucks. Can't take the Lower East Side or Coney Island McDougal Street anymore, same hustlers. Run into Curtis Powell in the Cooper Union post office. He's back from Europe. Watch the cops beat the shit out of a guy on 33rd Street. Crowd doesn't dig it. Watch my mother die. Shave the beard. Take a gig in Overbrook Hospital in Jersey where James Moody wrote *Last Train From Overbrook* before he was discharged. The patients like me but I quit. Rent a van and make it to Iowa City in 20 hours and try to push my way into the work shop based on a few little mag publications. They say I need a BA first. Nowhere to go. We stay. I get the GI bill and 3 part time jobs. Read about 3,000 books. Sit in class with 18 year olds who talk like some of the books. Quit smoking. Work odd jobs as always. Unload trucks. Wash windows. Lee finally gets a job as a telephone operator. I start seeing through e.e. cummings. Wonder about Saroyan but defend him anyway. Discover millions more. Tell people about old favorites, not many interested. Who's Coltrane they say. Who is this Cecil Taylor or Eric Dolphy. One or two have been into them but then they don't want to remember Little Richard or Chuck Berry, Diane DiPrima or Nina Simone who I used to write "poems" to sitting in the old basement Village Gate when I first left home because I loved her then when everyone said she was "too ugly" and because she married a cop. Watch Lee march in a demonstration. Can't believe the cops and counterdemonstrators. Kill! Kill! Kill! they scream. One guy spots a MAKE LOVE NOT WAR sign and freaks out calling the woman carrying it a whore and slavering. I catch a dude I've seen around moving through the crowd telling people to throw rocks at the demonstrators. Some of them do. Some people bleed. I go home and get sick. Start a veterans against the war group.

1967: make speeches. March. Picket. Leaflet. Get punched out. Get busted with 107 others. Try non-violence but can't get into it. Jim Tate says I can't write poetry, well, says I won't win any prizes. Nathan Whiting encourages me. I haven't written any fiction since getting here and getting shot down. Howard Stein likes my first play written the night before it was due for his class. Albert Ayler's music knocks me out.

1968: Peace & Freedom Party forms. SDS squabbles a lot and papers keep calling me an SDS leader. Me and Wessels never even join but laugh about how I used to tell him SDS was full of commies just like the goddam straights said it was. Lee worries about me becoming a commie and what it means. I stop writing record reviews and write political raps about what's going down. Introduce the Panthers to Iowa City in an article and get called on to talk about them but they start up in Des Moines and do their own talking. P&F nominates me for sheriff candidate of Johnson County. I turn it down arguing we should run the whole party. Fuck individualism. They nominate me again arguing that running the whole party is illegal and stupid. I turn it down again. One more time around and I accept on the condition anybody in the party can speak for me and will, must. Naturally it doesn't work out that way. At the national convention Cleaver has me thrown out of a caucus because I back Peggy Terry for his vice presidential candidate, a revolutionary middle-aged beautiful white Southern lower class woman, over his choice of Jerry Rubin. Some national publication calls me from New York after an article on the front page of *The Wall Street Journal* mentions my candidacy. I tell them to fuck off. See my picture in the papers too much and realize I'm getting to like it. Try to back away from it. Cait was born and Lee quit work before I even noticed it. We are poor as usual.

1969: finally back away for good. Haven't had a drink in several years, or a cigarette in 3, or played piano since coming to Iowa. Got a lot of poems published, some other stuff. Nobody really digs it though, either too political, which means when I say I love it's a speech, when he says it it's poetry, or too private, meaning my particulars ain't as universal as theirs. Everybody has problems. SDS in Chicago does it up for good this time. Me and Wessels get treated like enemies by everybody except Mike James and his people who I dig for real and Mike's idea of a street greaser paper. Don't like the way Weather People talk at parties about PLers and each other. Has nothing to do with making the world livable. Sounds like personal squabbles as usual. Everybody thinks they're smarter than the people. And all these white kids want some spade to kick their ass and get rid of the guilt. Can't dig any of it. But the goals are mine too, and the criticisms are right on target and who else to change the world with? Split for DC and discover long hairs can be as ruthless and fucked up as o shit we all knew that from the first time in '66 I got jumped for long hair and everybody said too bad but TS 'cause it is your problem, or the way politicos said the freak thing was later or the freaks said the political thing was. I was digging Sun Ra back on the Lower East Side and wondering what all those white cats in Detroit thought they were doing saying we should read Mao because it pisses off the straights. I remembered rejection slips from John Sinclair and wondered why he didn't trust the people. Mark Rudd shakes hands like an elitist.

1970: didn't cry when my mother died. Came close when Trane did but really haven't dropped tears since I stopped drinking. But Kent State and this crazy FM disc jockey who kept playing these heavy sounds and between cuts just kept repeating the four names of the murdered over and over again got to me. From the back window watched the tear gas hanging over the University of Maryland. Wrote stuff for all the undergrounds that could still dig it and wondered what I was doing here with Nixon and the other piggies. Tried to start a reading up for the November deal last year and Ed Sanders and Bly came across fine but others were too busy, like Ginsberg. Want to hang it up but can't because it ain't over yet and there ain't no mass exodus of blacks to the farms and rural communes and besides I really *dig* cities, like Snyder couldn't understand, having no room for me then in his world. Got two kids now anyway, can't move if we wanted to. So many good people have died. We try to deal with our relationship and the roles we've been forced to play. So do a lot of other people.

1970-1975
Washington, DC

"the only thing to do is simply continue
is that simple
yes, it is simple because it is the only thing to do
can you do it
yes, you can because it is the only thing to do"

—*Frank O'Hara*
"Adieu to Norman"

"…no rules, no secret equipment no anything
except the conviction of the artist, his challenge to
the world and his own identity."

—David Smith
David Smith

"You are what you look for"
—Ronald Johnson
Eyes & Objects

L ATE BLOOMER

I was living in a "commune" at the time. It was 1972, and most of us were veterans of the various "movements" of the 1960s. We had come to Washington, D.C. for demonstrations—anti-war rallies usually—and had stayed on. A few people in the house belonged to actual "parties" or leftist factions. But most of us were just well-intentioned, left-leaning do-gooders. Out of the ten adults and two children—both of them mine—one was openly "gay." He was my best friend.

My kids considered him an "uncle." My wife considered him a model for me to fashion myself after, because he was gentle, open to the point of constantly confessing his confusion and sexual encounters, and devoted to her. The feminist movement had been the latest force to influence us as a group. My wife was in the forefront, and with her, several women we all once knew as sexy, pretty hippies. They were rapidly becoming short-haired, pants wearing, macho lesbians. My wife would be one of them eventually. But before that happened, they worked on me.

There were several "communes" in D.C. at that time all informally linked by shared political perspectives. We often worked on the same projects together. Usually these had to do with demonstrations and publications against the war. More and more they were having to do with demonstrations and publications against sexism. One commune was made up entirely of gay men, all of whom had been involved in a demonstration against the war a few years earlier, then stayed on after they all got involved in the same court case.

It seems two of them—a little, white, lower-class man from Chicago and his Puerto Rican lover—had entered a bar in North-west D.C. and been asked to leave. In the discussion that surrounded the circumstances of their leaving, several anti-fag remarks were made and threats exchanged. Within an hour the two had returned with a force of thirteen "revolutionary faggots," as they styled themselves at the time. Together they tore up the bar, managing to subdue the crowd of supposedly macho rednecks who were regulars there, as well as put the bouncer in the hospital. The case was reported in the papers and I read it avidly. They were a new phenomenon to me: tough, fearless, kick-ass sissies.

I was thirty years old at the time. My wife and I had long since grown tired of our marriage, but were working hard on our "political consciousness" and maintaining the semblance of some sort of relationship by living in separate rooms in the "commune" and sharing the responsibility for our two children. Up until this time I had never considered myself anything but "straight" sexually. I suspected many of my friends of being secretly "gay" and the first insult to explode from my lips when I was angry or upset or frightened in street altercations was "cocksucker" or "faggot." I was learning to control that, to see the error of my straight, macho ways. I was also being encouraged to let go of my straight, male defenses.

With the example of macho women and tough, unafraid gay men, I slowly began to accept the idea that being queer was not necessarily being a victim, or a pushover, or a wimp. In fact, this "revolutionary faggot collective" was so "right on" politically and even stylistically—wearing the most confrontational and outrageous mix of male/female garb—I had to admire them and hoped they admired me as well. Especially their leader, who seemed fearless.

He was small, with long blond hair and a long blond beard. His face was sweet looking, and his body was almost like a teenager's, so slim and lithe. But he could be incredibly gutsy, standing up at mass meetings or jumping up on the stage after a show or a movie and shouting out his defiance to the "straight" leftists or general audience, challenging them to drastically alter their conception of gay people and of themselves. I was so impressed the first time I saw him do it, I thought he was speaking directly to me.

My best friend in the commune was always revealing the secrets of his life to me, including the sexual details of his encounters with various men. But in fact, I could never quite grasp the idea of sex between men. I had fantasized sex between two women, often. I had had sex with a long string of women before my wife and a few since. And in my marriage I had been compelled, after several years, to resort to what seemed like kinky fantasies to keep my sexual interest up. But the sexuality was relatively normal, and the fantasies were hardly more deviant than the image of some sexy female stranger joining us in our lovemaking.

But as the various gay men and women continued to influence our commune and focus on the problems with straight

30

men that needed to be corrected, and as I gradually gave in to the criticisms and tried being more open, tried discovering the softer side of my nature, I began to rely on these people for a sense of what was right and what was wrong. The leader of the "revolutionary faggots" especially impressed me, so his opinion became crucial. I could no longer rely on the opinions of my straighter friends, because they were resisting everything the feminist movement seemed to stand for, and the correspondent "gay liberation" movement. They were tolerant of some aspects of it, but wary of most of what it was about.

As I became isolated from my straighter friends and more dependent on the women and gay men surrounding our commune and gradually developing within it, I began to experiment with aspects of my personality I had thought were permanent. I began sitting, standing, reclining as comfortably as I could in a very deliberate way. In the process I discovered that usually I stood or sat in a defensive, almost rigidly masculine way, as though ready for a fight at a moment's notice. As I relaxed and became more comfortable, I also realized I felt more sexy.

I began trying different clothes, more colorful, softer, even more "feminine." That too added to my sense of heightened sensuality. And as I thought before I spoke, became also more soft spoken, not wanting to be the intimidating macho man any more, I seemed to attract compliments and affection in ways I never had before. Soon, women and men alike were telling me how "beautiful" I was, or were hugging me hello and goodbye with such obviously honest affection I couldn't help but feel great about myself.

This was the situation when one day I was invited to join the heavy gay revolutionary and some of his friends on an excursion to a nearby university. He was to give a talk on what it meant to be "gay," on the oppression of gay men and women and how sexism was to blame. I had nothing to do that day, I was teaching at the time but there were no classes of mine that afternoon, so I agreed to join them. The talk was almost standard to me by then, but it still moved me. I remembered all the times I had expected my wife to do dirty jobs around the house while I sat and read the newspaper. Or the times I had insulted gay men because I felt so superior in my macho defenses. I was glad I no longer clung to my old views and beliefs. I was happy to be the person I thought I had become, more open, more accepting, more loving and kind.

Afterwards we all went to the student cafeteria where we

were joined by some of the students in the class. I sat back and watched the discussion of what was wrong and right about the way the sexes related, or how we are all basically alike, and so on. At one point a very attractive student, a dark-haired over-earnest girl, gestured to include all of us when she referred to "you gay men." It was as though someone had slapped me. Me! "Gay!"

I looked hard at her, but she wasn't noticing me. I had been noticing her, because she was pretty, sexy, the kind of female I liked to flirt with, possibly get into bed with. Now she seemed to be dismissing me with the wave of a hand. On the other hand, she seemed to be including me in some pretty positive things she was saying about "gay men." I calmed down. So what if she thought I was "gay," better that than the things she was now saying about "straight men," how insensitive, how selfish, how mean and intimidating they could be. At least I wasn't that anymore. I wasn't one of "them." But if not, what was I?

After we left the university, saying warm farewells to the students, including a hug from the girl who had startled me with her conclusion that I was also "gay," we stopped at one of the guy's apartments. He didn't live in a "commune" like the rest of us. We had some coffee and smoked some dope. I was feeling confused, vulnerable, but pretty special. I felt like I had come a long way. But when one of the others started going over the day and teased me about being one of "the boys in the band," I began to get defensive. My old instincts came back and I suddenly felt very distant from these wisecracking so self-assured "gay liberationists."

As soon as I reached the point where I knew I wanted to get away, the leader of the revolutionary gay commune, the man who had given the talk that day, the little blond in other words, put his arm around me. He did it in a friendly, almost buddy-buddy way. But there was a special gentleness in it too. I could feel his concern for me, for my feelings, coming through my jacket and shirt and making my body feel warmer. He said, "you wanna go back to your place?" And I said yes, just wanting to get away.

The swing era

In late March of '72 I touched
another man's body for the first time
with the intention of touching
another man's body to see if
another man's body could be
as exciting as mine
had become since early March of '72
when I discovered my lost sensuality
by reviving a personal interest
in my tits and armpits
hips and sides the soles of my soft
feet the insides of my upper arms
plus of course my eyelids nostrils
cock chin finger joints elbows
head hair ass and lips

women led me there
their conversations of sensuality
in the absence of some men of male
orgasms their own waves of
hand holding eye kissing or
limitless body orgasms one
after another into the future
where I sat before a mirror
responding to my own hard look
at how soft and open and vulnerable
my eyes could become from just
thinking indeed you do look
less than "straight" my dear
Joy at my own fine weight and texture
defined internally for 30 years as
too this or too that skinny girlish
faggoty soft pale lost lonely
Now it was just right for the space
I occupied until it seemed natural
to rub the edges of that occupation
against the fragile boundaries

of another and then
another and another and
another until the spring of '73
it became impossible to tell
the difference beyond shadow and touch
except the tone of voice reviewing
the eventual history of our developing
sensuality and what it might mean
to think about that not alone
but with how many and then of course
too often the answer being well
do what you have to but for me
it seems you want too much because
now you seem to be able to have it

fantasies of a natural division
of flesh that is the flower
between each woman's legs that
part of the wholeness
above it as equally natural
the division outward that makes
testicles and their extension
so real in our lives as men
ANDROGYNE becomes the confusion
of heads to unfold with the fantasies
saying yes it is here that
the world divides and the potential
for true unity begins
the plant with full plumbing
the crudeness of socialized instructions
for the dance that opens our walls
of flesh and lets the rest of
the universe in: grin grin grin

until March '72 I believed
with the faith of a devout Irish-
American-Catholic-Roosevelt-
Democrat aspiring "communist"
that it was the eyes of only women
that led me to the page
and kept me walking to the place
where I might change or die

but it was also their *example*
and in the year that followed
it was their strength that
held me up or let me fall softly
as one way of laying down the load
O brothers I see you now
the little children you were
that maybe the woman who minds your
store has seen to make her put up
with our self importance
and I find myself
within the women's ring of light
wanting to stay forever
playing out for each the response
they never demanded while the circle
of fire my faggot brothers created
their surface and awareness—
sparks stars—appeals to me too
even the shade of your coldness
sometimes sad straight men I was
for 30 years draws me in with
the promise of some recognition
some sharing if only of emptiness

I sing it's spring and my heart
the stair of my body the chords
of my 31 years have entered
my own swing era where we all
pretend to be happy
because sometimes we are

so the stars aren't really the stars
and the people who know see through
the collage we constructed to show
them we weren't what they said we would
always be but were pieces
of all the things we had loved
to see others make lives from
and now in May '73 I touch
another's body to see
if mine is still here

                                        5.26.73

L*ife*

Someone comes up to me on the street
starts talking about their "love life"—
how "fucked up it is"—pushing their need.
All the cars going by flash in the sun
like kisses blown from lost loves
disappearing over the horizon of "maturity"
and I want to say "Are you kidding me?!"
But I know I can't judge anyone else's pain
even though my father's 75 this year and complained
so much longer and louder than my mother
who "passed" ten years ago, on Mother's Day,
looking startled, as though she hadn't expected
death, or god, or whatever she saw approaching
to be so heartless about it after all.
That was pain. Or the news that
my oldest sister is "going blind" just like that
and my father dumb enough to say
"When we found out you had diabetes at seven
we never expected you to live even this long ..."
and losing the pigment in her skin so that
when statistics or simplifiers list her as "white"
they'll finally be right. Or the way that man today
waited so patiently for someone, this time me,
to come and guide his blind steps across the avenue
where cars flashed for him in ways I'll never know
and me still high on the look in the eyes
of a woman he'll never see like me. Or the news
of some money coming my way I got over the phone today
my two deaf cousins would have to wait for the mails
to hear. But maybe they should be grateful
for knowing where it hurts or doesn't hurt
or doesn't do what it's supposed to do
and feel sorry for you, or me, when we don't know
what it is that keeps us from smiling and expanding
on the grace of all that's intact and working for us
in ways that keeps us looking for "love"
as though we knew where it was all along.

M*y life*

I ate everything they put in front of me
read everything they put before my eyes
shook my ass, cried over movie musicals
was a sissy and a thug, a punk and an
intellectual, a cocksucker and a mother
fucker, helped create two new people,
paid taxes, voted and served four years
and a few weeks in the United States Air
Force, was court martialed and tried
civilly, in jail and in college, kicked
out of college, boy scouts, altar boys
and one of the two gangs I belonged to,
I was suspended from grammar and high
schools, arrested at eleven the year I
had my first "real sex" with a woman
and with a boy, I waited nineteen years
to try it again with a male and was sorry
I waited so long, I waited two weeks to
try it again with a woman and was sorry
I waited so long, wrote, poetry and
fiction, political essays, leaflets and
reviews, I was a "jazz musician" and a
dope dealer, taught junior high for two
weeks, high school Upward Bound for two
years, college for four years, I got up
at 5 AM to unload trucks at Procter and
Gamble to put myself through classes
at the University of Iowa, I washed
dishes and bussed tables, swept floors
and cleaned leaders and gutters, washed
windows and panhandled, handled a forty
foot ladder alone at thirteen, wrote
several novels not very good and none
published, published poems and stories
and articles and books of poems, was
reviewed, called "major," compared to
"The Teen Queens," mistaken for black,

for gay, for straight, for older, for
younger for bigger for better for richer
for poorer for stupider for smarter for
somebody else, fell in love with a black
woman at 18, kicked out of the family
for wanting to marry her at 20, I sucked
cock and got fucked and fucked and got
sucked, I was known for being a big
jerk off, a wise ass, for always getting
my ass kicked so bad neighborhood kids
would ask to see the marks, for running
for sheriff of Johnson County Iowa in '68
on the "Peace and Freedom" ticket and
pulling in several thousand votes, for
winning people to the cause with emotional
spontaneous speeches at rallies and on TV,
for being a regular guy, a romantic
idealist, a suicidal Weatherman, a bomb
throwing anarchist, an SDS leader, a
communist, a class chauvinist, an
asexual politico, a boring socialist,
the proletarian man, a horny androgyne,
a junkie, a boozer, a loser, a nigger
lover, a black woman's white man, a
race traitor, a greaser, a fast man
with my hands, a hood, a chickenshit,
a crazy head, an unmarked thoroughbred,
a courageous human being, a Catholic,
a fallen away Catholic, An Irish American
Democrat, a working class Irish American
writer from a family of cops, a skinny
jive time street philosopher, a power
head, an underground movie star, a
quiet shy guy, a genius, an innovator,
a duplicator, a faker, a good friend,
a fickle lover, an ass lover, a muff
diver, another pretty face, a lousy
athlete, a generous cat, an ambitious
young man, a very tough paddy, a macho
hippie, a faggot gangster, a faggot,
a big crazy queen, a straight man, a
strong man, a sissy, a shithead, a

home wrecker, a reckless experimenter
with other peoples lives, a demagogue,
a fanatic, a cheap propagandizer, a
fantastic organizer, a natural born
leader, a naive upstart, an arrogant
jitterbug, a white nigger, an easy lay,
a pushover, a hard working husband,
a henpecked husband, the black sheep,
a crazy mixed up kid, a juvenile delinquent,
a misfit, a surrealist, an actualist,
an Iowa poet, a political poet, an open
field poet, a street poet, a bad poet,
a big mouth, a voice of the sixties,
a pretty poet, a gay poet, a clit kissing
tit sucking ass licking body objectifying
poet, a gigolo, a jerk, a poor boy, an
old man, an assman, unsteady, immature,
charismatic, over confident, over 30,
impetuous, a rock, a pawn, a tool, a
potato lover, a great teacher, loyal
friend, concerned citizen, a humanist,
the bosses son, Bambi's old man, Lee's
husband, Matthew's ex-lover, Terry's
partner, Slater's main man, the bishop's
favorite altar boy, the landlady's pet,
the class clown, the baby of the family,
the neighborhood stranger, the hardest
working kid, with the rosiest cheeks, who
was an instigator, a trouble maker,
too smart for my own good, too soft,
too distant, too honest, too cold, too
tactless, uncommunicative, anal retentive,
self-sufficient, shameless, unsophisticated,
too butch, too skinny, too white, too
defensive, too hungry, apologetic, in-
decisive, unpredictable, I never hit a
woman or woke up gloomy, I'm a light
sleeper, an affectionate father, a bad
drinker, a city boy, paranoid, compulsive,
and a terrific body surfer, I love the
hipness in me I thought was black back
in the '50s, the vulnerability I took for

feminine in the '70s, I hate the poor kid
act I've pulled on strangers and friends
to start them out owing me, I learned to
cook and to sew, stopped chewing gum and
biting my nails, I was a weather observer,
a map maker, a printer's devil, a
carpenter's helper, a glazier, a locksmith,
editor, publisher, promoter and critic,
I stopped dancing at 15 and started again
at 30, math was my best subject, languages
my worst, I've been knocked out several
times but only one black eye and one
fractured thumb, I've totaled several
cars but I'm an ace driver especially
in cities, I haven't had an accident since
I stopped drinking, knock on wood, I'm
extremely superstitious, don't speak too
soon, I gave up cigarettes and coffee and
using the words chick, spade and asshole,
I've read Confucius, Buddha, Lao Tzu,
the *Upanishads*, the *Bhagavad Gita*, the
Koran, the Bible, *The Prophet*, *Thus Spake
Zarathustra*, Marx, Trotsky, Stalin, Lenin,
Mao, Che, Hesse, Proust, Firestone, Fanon,
Castaneda and Davis, I read all of Joyce
and all of Dostoevsky in translation
at least two times through on night shifts
in weather towers through 1961 and '62,
I love all of William Saroyan, Van
Morrison, Jane Bowles, Samuel Beckett,
Joe Brainard, and Bertold Brecht, I'm
finally getting to know and like some
"classical music," I went to my first
ballet, opera, and concert this year and
loved all of it, took my first trip out
of the country and was glad to get back
although it was great, I love the USA and
many of the people in it, I'm afraid of
my own anger, and any kind of violence,
I've been the same weight since 1957 though
I have an enormous appetite, my hair's
turning gray, I've had it cut three times

since 1966, I spit a lot and pick my nose
too much, I could buy new shoes, eat ice
cream, chicken or chocolate pudding anytime,
I'm afraid of dogs and hate zoos, I'm
known for my second winds especially
when dancing or eating, I used to think
of myself as a dreamer, I had a vision
at 9 that I'd die between 42 and 46,
the image was me doubling over clutching
my stomach, whenever I'm embarrassed I
see that in my head, some of my nicknames
have been Faggy, Rocky, Spider, Brutus,
Paddy Cat, Newark, Irish, and The Lal,
I'm a father, son, brother, cousin,
brother-in-law, uncle, record breaker,
war child, veteran, and nut about Lauren
Bacall, James Cagney, Robert Mitchum,
Bogie and Brando, *Last Tango* and *The
Conformist* are the favorite movies of
my adult life, I've fallen in love with
eyes, asses, thighs, wrists, lips, skin,
color, hair, style, movement, bodies,
auras, potential, accents, atmospheres,
clothes, imaginations, sophistication,
histories, families, couples, friends,
rooms full of people, parks, cities,
entire states, talked to trees since
1956 and the wind since '52, between '56
and '59 I had few friends and a "bad
reputation" which made it difficult
to get dates with "nice girls," in 1960
and '61 I had more friends and several
lovers, I was at the SDS split in Chicago
in 1969 and didn't like either side's
position or tactics, I almost cried
when I heard John Coltrane had died,
and Ho Chi Minh, Babe Ruth, Jack
Kerouac, Eric Dolphy, Roberto Clemente,
Moose Conlon, Frankie Lyman, Fred
Hampton, Allende, Clifford Brown,
Richie Valens and Buddy Holly in that
plane crash, the four little girls

in that Alabama church, the students
at Orangeburg, the "Weather people"
in the town house explosion which I
always figured was a set up, my uncle
Frank and my uncle John, my grandparents,
lots of people, I did cry when I thought
about the deaths of the Kent State and
Jackson State students, when I heard
Ralph Dickey had "taken his life" or
the first time I heard Jackson Browne
do his "Song for Adam" or when Marlon
Brando as Terry finds his brother Charley
(Rod Steiger) hanging dead on the fence
in *On the Waterfront* and before going
to get the murderers says something to
Eva Marie Saint like "And for God's sake
don't leave him here alone" or when he
talks to his dead wife in *Last Tango*
or finds Red Buttons and his wife
have committed suicide in *Sayonara*
I've cried a lot over movies especially
old ones on TV, I've never cried at a
play but I still haven't seen many, the
only Broadway plays I've seen were *My
Fair Lady* and *Bye Bye Birdie*, I
watched my mother die, I've paid my dues,
been through the mill, come up from the
streets, done it my way, had that once
in a lifetime thing, had trouble with
my bowels ever since I can remember
then in '72 my body became more relaxed,
I've had the clap, crabs, scabies,
syphilis, venereal warts, and unidentified
infections in my cock, my ass, my throat,
all over my body, I've been terribly
sunburned and covered with scabs from
fights and accidents, I only had stitches
once at 4 when I had my appendix out,
I've been earning money since I was 10,
supporting myself since 13, others since
22, I got "unemployment" once, been
fired several times, never paid to

get laid, I lost money gambling but
quit after I had to give up my high
school ring in a poker game at the Dixie
Hotel in Greenville South Carolina in
1962 waiting for my friend Willy Dorton
to come out from the room where he was
proposing marriage to his favorite
whore who always turned him down after
they fucked and she got most of his
paycheck from him, some of my best
friends were hookers and strippers,
postal clerks and shills, supermarket
managers and factory workers, heavy
revvies and punks, actresses and junkies,
who were and are the most difficult
of friends, art dealers and artists,
musicians and hustlers, dykes and critics,
shit workers and liberals, gringos and fags,
and honkies and bastards, queer and old
and divorced and straight and Italian
and big deals and dipshits, I know at least
six people who think they turned me on
to dope for the first time in 1960 in
New York City, in 1962 in Rantoul Illinois,
in 1964 in Spokane Washington, in 1966 and
'67 in Iowa City, in 1969 in Washington
DC, I once was high on opium and didn't
want to come back, I was a recreational
therapist at Overbrook Hospital in Essex
County New Jersey in 1966 where James Moody
wrote *Last Train from Overbrook* before
he was discharged, in 1960 I had a tremendous
crush on Nina Simone, I always wanted to
name a child Thelonious, I was sure
I was an orphan at 10, I wished I was
an orphan at 18, my father's alive so
I'm still not an orphan at 32, I know
a lot of orphans, I once had an
orphan for a lover, I suppose my kids
could be orphans some day, I was never
good at planning the future for more
than a couple of days, friends have

told me I always do things the hard way,
my family's response to tough times or
catastrophes was usually humor, I'm
grateful to them for giving me that,
I find cynics boring although there's
a lot of the cynic in me, I find
depression dull, mine or anyone else's,
I'm no good at small talk, I feel
an undercurrent of violent tension
in most "straight" bars and on late
night city streets that intimidates
me, I find jealousy useless and
depressing, I know people who find
jealousy exciting and even rewarding,
something to live for, I'd love to
make love all the ways I haven't yet
or haven't thought of yet, with all
the people I haven't yet or haven't met
yet, although sometimes I could care
less about sex, I write everyday
and listen to music everyday and can't
imagine living without either,
libraries and hospitals intimidate me,
being around people who seem to feel
comfortable anywhere used to make me
feel insecure, I'm getting over that,
I used to feel obliged to apologize
for or defend people whose goals I
shared even though I might not like
them or their tactics, I'm getting
over that too, I've learned to love
or at least appreciate a lot of things
I used to despise or ignore, I've had
trouble getting it up and trouble
keeping it down, I'm tired of a lot
of things but curious about more, I'm
tired of this but that's history now.

(March 1974, DC)

MENTALLY, HE'S A SICK MAN

I'm a writer. Ever since I left home in 1960 to become a famous writer everything else has just been temporary. Even the four years I did in the Air Force, actually a little more than four to make up for what they call "bad time," even that job from 1962 to 1966 was just temporary, and I knew it the whole time, that's how I got through it.

You might ask what I joined for in the first place and that'd be a good question. But the answer would take too long. It'd involve my falling in love with a girl from Atlantic City named Joan, who was called Bambi because her eyes were so big and brown and deep and innocent and like that. She was what was then called "Negro" and I wasn't. And it'd involve the possible options of those days for a 19 year old lower middle class Irish American kid who knew he could write but *The Saturday Evening Post* kept returning his stories, maybe without even reading them. The few people who broke away from the common pattern of lives in my neighborhood back then had mostly done it by joining some branch of the service. And it'd involve a fast talking Air Force recruiter who knew he had hooked one when he saw me coming, who convinced me that the only place in the world a mixed couple could survive in 1962 was the Air Force which he pictured as one big interracial family unlike what I knew the Army and Navy and civilian world to be like. Nobody I knew had ever been in the Air Force unless you count my oldest brother's stint in the Army Air Corps during the Second World War but that wasn't the same thing. And a whole lot of other stuff.

Mostly I just knew I was a writer. I played music, even made a little money at it, and held various jobs from window washer to Master of Ceremonies, but I never really thought of myself as anything other than a writer. Even when I told girls I was a "poet." What I meant by that was my spirit, the reason I had to write, the craziness in my head that had me dreaming most of the time when I was supposed to be writing or playing or doing something other than dreaming, that was what I called "the poet" in me. But I rarely wrote what I thought of as "poetry" and even more rarely let anyone else see it. But I sent my other writing, my "work" to all the big magazines, sometimes as much as several times a week all during the early sixties. While I was at the college I got kicked out of, while I was in between that and the service, while I was in the service, and then finally in 1966 a few things were accepted and published and I even made twenty-five dollars for three poems and a story. By then I had told a lot of other people about my being a writer and I was sure glad to have something to show for it. But that didn't last long.

But those years of waiting for that first publication were so full of expectation. I didn't need anything. I just sat down and wrote. I had a typewriter that the chief of police and his wife, boyhood friends of my father's, had given me when I graduated from high school. I learned to type fast with two fingers, I only wish I had learned to type by touch, but even so, as my great teacher Saroyan always said, William Saroyan, but even so, I could type pretty fast and that was great. And just before I got that present, just when I had decided to become a writer because my English teacher had given me so much trouble and so many challenges that I knew I had to do this thing (my best subjects were always math and even history, my worst, English and languages) I had gone to the public library in South Orange, New Jersey, where I grew up, and which library I didn't like, I didn't like libraries, because they intimidated me, I didn't know how to use them and didn't like the people who tried to tell me and always made me feel they thought people like me shouldn't be in libraries, but anyway this time I overcame my aversion and went in and got out their copy of *Writer's Market* and copied out the editors' names and addresses for such places as *The Saturday Evening Post* and *Esquire Magazine* and *McCall's* and a few others I had seen the works of William Saroyan and the like in.

So all I needed and all I had was my typewriter and these few addresses and this burning sensation in my chest every time I looked at something that had come out of that typewriter as if by divine intervention. I never changed a word back then. That didn't come till I reached the Iowa Writers Workshop in 1966. I was afraid to touch anything because I didn't know really who had written these things. Or if I thought that I had written them then I didn't know where they came from, whether somewhere inside me I never heard from in any other way, or somewhere outside me that just found my two fingered typing convenient. All I knew was when I sat down to the typewriter and started out I never knew what might happen. And I never worried about it, that came with the workshop. Back then I just let it happen and then was as pleasantly

46

surprised as anyone could be to read something that they found interesting and new. I wrote a lot of pretentious amateurish stuff, but then I still do, and most writers I've read have and do the same. I wrote some profound and some meaningful stuff. That still amazes me. I wrote some nice but unextraordinary stuff that sometimes I mistook for profound or great and sometimes for childish and meaningless. Meaning was an important thing to me then. I didn't know what I was going to write when I started writing something, but I always felt it was going to *say something*, at least to me, which is why I guess I liked Saroyan so much. I was already writing that way when I started reading him and he just confirmed my already firmly held beliefs about meaning, and about creativeness and about not using deodorants and a whole lot of other stuff. When I read him I said "Hello Willy!" like I knew him because he was so familiar. I fell in love with other writers, some which surprised people when they asked me who I read, or who I liked, like Beckett and Dostoevsky, or James and Empson. People, meaning usually people with some education or an interest in writing and literature, would be very surprised to hear I read someone like William Empson, if they even knew who he was. But it was just fun for me. I thought James was funny, making subtle jokes about how human and ridiculous the upper classes were back then, and him among them. I thought Dostoevsky was funny, realizing how hopelessly heavy all the tragic Russian landscape was and how his characters always knew they were carrying on for an audience, they even treated God like an audience, that was funny to me. And Beckett, I had feared reading him because of reviews I had read making me think a man without a proper education would find himself helplessly lost in all that craft and avant gardism, but of course when I read him I found all the Irish relatives I had grown up with who talked so deliberately, so slowly making their point, yet talked sparingly, their language simple and their statements often incomplete because the conclusions were obvious. He had a great sense of humor in his work, and I loved him for it and felt proud to be a writer too. And Empson? He was the funniest of all, mostly because I never had to really bother about what he was saying, it was usually relatively obvious right away and the rest was fluff, ornamentation, embellishments for their own sake and that was so much fun to watch that I could almost write my own things while reading his. And the highest respect as well as deepest affection went to writers who made me want to write when I read them. And I tried to read them all.

But mostly I wrote. That was the secret to my success as a potential famous writer, not the belief which was important, or the burning sensation in my chest, no, it was the writing. Every time I got over a bad hangover or found some spare time between playing the piano at some bar and trying hard to do the jobs I was paid to as well as they could be done but without taking my mind away from my dreaming and writing, and all the novels I wrote in my head! How many of us did that! Think of all the movies and songs and books passing you by on the street in the crowds, in the heads of strangers who will never figure a way, or work out a way, or have time or whatever to get them out to where somebody else can enjoy them. But then think of how many do figure a way to do it. I just sat down and let my two forefingers go. When they stopped I was through. Sometimes they went on for hours, even days. Those were the days!

The more I wrote, the more I read, the more I saw how much fun it could be. It didn't disturb me to read someone like Saroyan and see how much alike we were, and realize that people would probably mistake that for some sort of imitation, or worse. I knew where it came from. Besides, everyone I read who I liked I saw I had things in common with. Like Gertrude Stein. Finding her in 1962 and feeling she had written for me. Most of my friends then were musicians and enlisted servicemen with ambitions similar to my neighborhood friends, good jobs with the Post Office or fixing IBM computers or something. They didn't know who Beckett or Saroyan or anybody was. They just took my word for it I'd be a rich writer someday because I said I would and I read a lot and I had lots of writing it seemed already done, and everybody knew Hemingway and Ian Fleming and John Steinbeck and all those famous writers were rich and famous.

They even gave me advice. Told me what kinds of stories and novels to write. They'd tell me I should write a novel about the Air Force, or the Park Services when I worked there, or about window washing, or whatever it was we were doing together. They'd tell me that if they could write they would write a novel that would really show people what doing such and such was like, not an easy thing, not an unextraordinary thing, but a job or life full of drama, and of course they were right, only they couldn't write, and I couldn't write it for them, though I tried all the time, spending much of my energy identifying with all kinds of people I wasn't, but could become when I felt the need to sometimes, to some extent, to the extent that a Southern hillbilly transplanted to

Chicago figured I had to be a poor white from the South to have written something he read and liked, and several editors and one judge of a poetry contest I once almost won took me for Black, and a lot of other things like that.

The thing is, and I did use the word "thing" and "things" a lot back then, I was imprecise and blurred a lot of "reality" with a city-bred romanticism that made Saroyan so unpopular with critics after his first few successes, but anyway, now I'm back or almost, going on thirty-three, writing for myself again, trying to get the workshop technician to stop looking over my shoulder and interrupting me every few words to tell me how self indulgent I am or how vague I am or how "run on" I am or how unprofessional, rough, etc. etc. I am, but I'm back anyway, almost, using "thing" again to tell you that *the thing is*, and just letting it come out as it comes, sitting down and writing a title that came to mind, like *Mentally, He's a Sick Man* because it seemed to be somehow accurate about something, even if not about me, because also like Saroyan and other self made romantics we don't put too much faith in all those judgments and definitions about what goes on in someone else's head, and when the writing started coming and it happened to be about writing it seemed even appropriate because who else but a sick man, mentally that is, would continue to call himself a writer after so few successes, if you can even call them that, and after so many years of temporary jobs and digressions into the world of people who talk about writing, or advise about writing, or warn about writing, or etc. and after so much burning in the chest that even the writing doesn't help that much anymore, who else but a sick man mentally would call himself a writer and go on writing and living like that's all he's supposed to do, even though in order to survive, and in order to pay for the events of surviving, like the little boy and the little girl who might resent him for spending so much time writing and dreaming when he might have been earning big money to give them the life he never had but sometimes dreamt about and thought was dead certain to be his when fame came, *but even so the thing is* I am here at my typewriter doing it again and feeling the need to hurry it up because I'm anxious to see what it says, and to see if I can figure out where it came from and only after that, and sometimes never, will I worry about where it might go.

7-31-74

49

SHE WHIPPED ME WITH HER TITS

There's a lot of ways of describing (anything) say Jane Fonda's eyes that I fell in love with first when I went to see *Tall Story* with her and Anthony Perkins, I was in 8th grade at Our Lady of Sorrows grammar school. I went with my friend Jimmy McKenna. It was playing at the Maplewood Movie Theater which we weren't supposed to go to since they had shown *The Moon Is Blue* a few years earlier. And *Baby Doll* too I think. The priest from the pulpit at Mass on Sunday during the sermon told us not to go there.

Jane Fonda's eyes could be anything to anybody. Is that right? Not to me. Last night the woman I love climbed over me with her body and clean skin and me with mine under her as she rubbed her crotch, her clit and the lips of her cunt, which the clinical term for I can never remember what's what, against my tits if you can call what men have, at least this man, tits. She bent over so her tits were in my face and I started kissing them and sucking on the nipples and trying to grab them with my mouth as she began to swing them from side to side and then I started swinging my face back and forth so that her tits were slapping against my lips and cheeks and she started twisting her body from side to side, so that the momentum of her tits swinging increased and my face going back and forth under them got faster and the whole thing made me so hard we played with each other for hours, her getting off again and again and me getting so close to it and staying there longer than most times and finally coming inside her for a long time like painful need to piss after holding it in for hours finally going away with total pleasure as you get the chance to let go.

They're green I guess her eyes (Fonda) (I guess that's legally Hayden? because she "wants it that way" etc.?) and are still as sexy as *Tall Story* only now it's *Meet the Enemy* which my ex-wife says is me.

11.20.74

50

O OMALOOM

> "Carl Sandburg knew some of 'em—the great
> heroes of the Chicago night long ago, the ones
> who knew Willard from just watching one fight
> one night and touching him as he passed and then
> died in flops, from Denver clear on through: the
> density of the tragedy in America is confusing and
> immense in volume, oomaloom along the oil cloth
> with your little bug, the screendoors weren't made
> to slam for nothing and in no interesting night.
> Everybody is important and interesting."
>
> —Jack Kerouac
> *Visions of Cody*

1. "There are no adequate theories."—Henry Kissinger

What more could you want. She is beautiful. Everyone says so.
The famous writer even calls her "glamorous" as though she's the
star and not him. And she is with you. And you are looking good
enough. Everyone keeps saying "you're lookin good" these days
and you know they aren't all lying.

How weird to finally be around these people, the beautiful
and privileged ones. To have named them "the enemy" of "*The*
Revolution" and your revolution. To have despised them and
envied them and feared their acid tongues. Now here they are, relatively docile, not as beautiful as they keep saying she is, and you
are, and she is with you, not with any of them, and you have been
with enough of them now to know that your sex and your life can
be more joyous, more complete, more often, if not more bizarre or
more charming than much of theirs.

Hey these people are nothing to yell about. But you still want
them to yell about you. Yell what?

2. "In love all actions are love."—Tom Raworth

Talking about sonnets, R.G. Barnes "to describe emotional states
that are of more interest than the biographical accidents that

provoked them because they themselves, these emotional states, are to the lover unchanging truth; and while they are quite incommensurable with anything the ungentle heart could ever feel, there is no attempt to distinguish between one lover and the next so long as he" The South Orange Sonnets *Her?* "qualifies as noble."

From Atlantic City and later Manhattan Joan Robinson called Bambi because of the big brown beautiful soft eyes in her lovely dark face I still love. Veanme; ahora estoy enamorado con ANA, la cual fue Ms Chiquita Banana de Costa Rica. I love Caitlin and Miles of Iowa Maryland DC their mother and me.

Most often I feel well. Right now I don't. There is no one to blame. My body.

2. "In love all actions are love."—Tom Raworth

He put his arm around me, over my shoulder, his hand holding my right arm where I always wished a big hard bicep would appear, but instead always saw in the mirror the same thin soft pink arm I had carried with me since first being called Hey Skinny like a Charles Atlas ad.

We were sitting on his couch, a very tasteful expensive antique couch I found out later, when I found out about such things, at the time I only thought it was odd and casual of him to have a room full of such old and disparate furniture in a house so obviously expensive.

He was on my left staring straight ahead of him, listening, I guessed, to the music he was introducing me to, "classical." I was listening too and thinking "this is it, this is what you missed all those years as a 'straight' man, this is more than hip bi sexuality, more than sweet looking long haired hippies, more than the first time with that man who said he would kill anyone who ever gave his 'hangup' away, meaning you, after he treated you badly, this was being seduced, being treated like a sex object, having a grown man who didn't look or act like a fag put his arm around you after showing you beautiful reproductions, photographs of subtly erotic art work, pictures of Michaelangelo's slaves actually beginning to turn you on like only girly magazines had done before, now playing this music, the lights low, the great dinner warming your insides, the hash making the music precise and perfect in a way you never noticed before, hearing all classical music as dead, as

52

furniture, as movie scores, now it was this movie, your life as sex symbol, how did it come to this?"

2. "In love all actions are love."—Tom Raworth

There was another woman two years ago. My tongue was numb for several days afterwards from the foam she used to avoid pregnancy. She was on her stomach. My head beneath the pale round halves of her ass. She was telling of the men she'd experienced since I'd seen her last, three years before that. She was saying older Jewish men fucked best. I was licking her cunt and the tight little opening between the cheeks of her ass. She found it more and more difficult to talk, losing her breath, emphasizing words she hadn't intended to, the more I licked.

Finally I got up on my knees and pulled the middle of her body up to me, the point where it folds, and stuck my prick where my tongue and lips had been, beneath the pale and round halves of her ass, into the looser hole, her cunt, and I fucked and I fucked and I fucked her till she came and I came and all the time loving her pale Irish skin, her soft Irish skin, her crazy Irish American working girl's ideas of honesty and adventure and sex.

I stayed with her for four days and nights and then left. She eventually went back to her husband, an older Jewish man.

3. "—who cares. They did."—James Schuyler

Rebecca Wright, Michael McClure, Ed Dorn, Yoko Ono, David Smith, Jan Yoors, Maxim Gorky, Mickey Spillane, R. Crumb, Gail Godwin. I read these people, and many more. I read usually in the morning and almost always in the evening and when I'm not working or at the movies I almost always read in the afternoon. I also read whenever I have to take a shit, and with meals if I'm alone, and sometimes at breakfast even if I'm not alone.

I read on trains, in planes, and have even read and still do while driving my car and stopped for traffic lights or traffic jams. I read in bed and in chairs. I have read standing up in elevators and leaning against buildings waiting for various things and people to come or happen. I read in movie theaters before the movie starts. I read on buses and subways and boats and escalators. I read a lot.

Yet, and this has always been the contradiction that plagues me, I feel in the face of what I read, unread.

And, furthermore, and what is worse, I write almost as much and as often as I read, and feel even more insecure about that... (despite prizes, degrees, money, awards, praise, good reviews, publication, notoriety, etc...) Why?

I think it has something to do with making a fool of oneself. It seems to me any great anything takes a chance of being a fool when they take the chance of being great, and that it demands a certain kind of narrowminded simplicity, an intense directing of all energy toward the goal. I, on the other hand, and probably many others, maybe you, am constantly aware of the peripheral concerns, and stop to check them, consider them, analyze them, etc. til I'm convinced that indeed I am about to make a fool of myself, so I hesitate, or renig, only to turn around and go ahead later when the original force and inspiration has become tired and diluted, like the energy that had me go ahead and write "renig" after realizing I was going to write something I suddenly couldn't remember how to spell.

See how I lost control of that whole thing, and it started out so nicely. And to lose control in a small way like that, to fail less than grandly, is to be a fool. If I had only just written the story of the insights I had my first time in a dress! What excess! What a story! Why haven't I written it! I will!

4. "We've had too much of this patriarchal sentimentality."
—Ezra Pound

In 1913 Pound wrote to "Miss Monroe." In 1956 I pounded my pod, pulled my daisy, jerked off my prick and came all over my lean white teenaged thighs over a picture in the *New York Daily News* advertising a new movie by Marilyn Monroe. Waves of a new and old feminism swept various sectors and subcultures of the country between 1913 and 1956 and between 1956 and the present.

Many people drowned.

Many people were rescued.

Many people were cleansed and refreshed. Many other waves swept the country. Many other casualties of other waves succumbed to the feminist waves and vice versa. Horizontal oppression can be as evil or more so than vertical oppression. Miss Monroe, Miss Monroe, it was your eyes that attracted me, not your thighs. It was *my* thighs. What do I owe you now?

54

5. "Be, beget, begone."—William Saroyan

She's got the kids. Before we separated I wasn't working. I was collecting unemployment insurance and watching the kids. We were together most of the time, me and them.

They'd wake up sometime between 6 and 7 and come into my room, which was right across from their room which was right next to the room of their mother's lover. Their mother's room was and is downstairs from them.

They'd come in and wake me up and we'd play and horse around for a while and then either we'd all three go downstairs or they'd go down alone and make their own breakfast, usually something more interesting than an adult would think of. Sometimes I'd just be getting in from a night out as they came downstairs to make their breakfast and we'd all giggle conspiratorially and they'd tease me and I'd tell them pretty much of where I'd been and what I'd been up to, partying or dancing or staying with a friend just leaving in time to catch breakfast with them. It was always great to be the only ones awake in the house, the "collective."

Now they call almost every day. The oldest, who perhaps understands best what happened, usually does the calling. The younger, the male, more quiet and introverted, usually gets on and asks me if I'm coming over. I sometimes rush right over and we play and horse around for a few hours. Sometimes I say I'm too busy, or something. Today they called and he asked and said "no you can't come over" before I said no I can't come over and that frightened and saddened me. I want to cry. I probably won't, because I'm writing it down instead. For them I guess. I agreed to too much. My friend Terry has an expression: "emotional blackmail." Will they understand that?

6. "... the arrogant humility of the East."
—Christopher Isherwood

James Dean raised "up" in Indiana ("raised up" *in In* diana) started out in California moved back to California where his mother died before he moved to Indiana and where he died after he moved back there from New York. In 1957 Dean was dead, Phil Silvers was an "Emmy" award winner and *Andersonville* was a bestseller. In what year did Wittgenstein die? Bonnard?

Moving eternal delight (complete upheaval) via Spain to New York where one thing threatens another. In 1975 what moves. Between the cracks in the floorboards are the floorboards. On the back of contemporary society bad financial trouble for the first time in 37 years (rendered unrecognizable, the years) and still moving!

Movies perfected by Hollywood after moving from the East. Hollywood made them *move*. Moving only one letter of the alphabet away from loving. Sometimes we get so tired we think we can't move another inch. Moving more than that inch we cry for the changes in our social systems that might bring only more mediocrity under the guise of equality!

Only moving allowed here! Move more! Move up! Move out! Move over! Move on! Move away! Move motherfucker! Don't anybody move!

Gary Snyder refers to the North American continent as "Turtle Island"!

*　　*　　*

Syl --

Got letter & Be Post Card from Chicago—in & are real excited about it want to hear what happen ---- <u>in</u> <u>details</u> --

Also got letter that you address to Ana Gongora—Sylvia my name is Ana <u>ROSS</u> Gongora -- you got the last part right -- But since in the states they "the Americans" don't go by the whole name I only go by Ana Ross -- I dropped the Gongora -- But any way—I really want to have the painting -- the only thing is -- w Can we wait three more weeks to pay the money?? Can you ask & to let me know -- If not -- I will send it as soon as you tell me—Because I do (we do) want the painting -- the reason why we don't have money is because "We are <u>seriously</u> thinking about MOVING to N.Y.C. at the end of June -- How about that -- Surprise -- And we are trying to pay everything we owe. I am, of course, very excited about moving -- If you could call "Collect" I can call you back for Free & explain everything & you can tell us about your trip to Chicago -- Sorry about this mess -- Miss lots. But if we move to O N.Y.C. see you lots -- Ana

56

7. "All things are something else, aren't they?"
—Frank O'Hara

It's February 1975 and the VD epidemic is subsiding. So it's not just me who's settling down some.

The whole thing took off in the '60s. In the '50s it was only the outsiders, the beats and bohemians, the street blacks, and jazz musicians, the gay world, the drug world, the other side of society then. In the late '50s and early '60s the media was used to popularize the beat thing and give rise to thousands of teenagers looking for bohemia, cruising the village streets, or north beach, provincetown, chicago's rush street, st. louis' gaslight square, all the hip places, being turned away at the door of the beat pads, called "hippies" for weekend hipsters, people who didn't live the life fulltime, a derogatory term, the hip teenagers of the USA turned on by beat poetry, turned away by beat snobbism, turned away from jazz and esoteric sounds, turned away from beat style, the gaunt black bearded look, turned back to rock'n'roll and their own sense of outsiderness, turned into Hippies. What was the best thing about beats? "Free Love"!!! what was the best thing about hippie life? "Love, which can only be free," what would unfree love be? Maybe the women's movement killed all that. Although the statistics show the highest rate of VD is among "gay" men, who became even more active, found more places to go to find sex or more with your own kind, in the early '70s with the rise of "the gay movement." The lowest incidence of VD is found among "gay women." Is that because of what they do? Or because they are less promiscuous than faggots and male queers and straight freaks. Or are these statistics just unreliable and the whole thing bullshit? Did the women's movement kill VD and "free love" and the hippie life style? There's still a lot of long hair around but it doesn't mean what it used to mean. Is it the change in drugs, from highs to downs? Is it the new androgyny, a kind of nonsexual sex, less risk of VD?

In the '50s the US had a perpetual hardon. It just couldn't get off. The '60s was the orgasm. The late '60s was one long blast, shooting the load. Is the '70s simply the temporary impotence that often follows orgasm for many men? Is the '70s a time for women to discover dyke monogamy and/or to return to romantic notions of straight love with the right man who is just easier than his '50s counterpart and less frantic than his '60s counterpart and more of a woman than either ever was but still a man? Or is that just me? Would another war change all this?

8. "... things have to come in before they can go out."
—Robert Creeley

Now it's March 1975. In Miami 1972 I wore a dress for the first and, so far, last time. That was in August, during the Republican National Convention that nominated Nixon the third time. That was almost three years ago but what happened since makes it seem as far away as the '50s, which sometime seem like only three years ago. The '60s seem farther away.

It was hot and scary. The first Miami Beach policeman I encountered was on a motorcycle stopped for a redlight that I was about to cross at and as I stepped off the curb he flashed a very healthy smile all white teeth in his tan boyish face or what showed of it from under his helmet and mirror glass shades and said "We're gonna get you bastards."

Well, there's a lot more to it than that, than the heat and the look of the place, Miami Beach, like a Hollywood set overrun with old people in Bermuda shorts driving Cadillac convertibles and setting up lawn chairs from which to watch the cops chase hippies around their streets. I arrived after a twenty hour drive straight through from Washington DC with two other men, one a stranger who only ate fruit and looked sickly and frightening, pale with long stringy hair, and the other a mixture of American Indian, American African, and maybe some American European and American Island Possessions and maybe more, big and strong and healthy looking and as gentle as a sleepy kitten. Neither of them drove. And when we arrived it was almost dawn and I couldn't find my current lover who, with other friends, was supposed to be where we had arrived which smelled like catshit and dead conditioned air and too many sleeping movement bodies and later after I found my lover and friends and woke them up and walked down the block for breakfast I picked a crab off the hairs on my right leg just after the waitress set my ham and eggs down.

9. "Let's go deeper then."—Francis Ponge

My hands are dirty. It's warm here, finally. I remember the first time a woman stuck her phone call in my hands. That was an interruption, I was remembering the time I first felt a woman's little pink pointy tongue up inside my nostrils. It was at a Halloween party to which I just wore old clothes I had kept since the '50s and at which I became extremely horny for several sexy & chic young women one of whom put her tongue up my nose and after which a handsome man done up as a beautiful woman pulled me into his bedroom it was his party and down on top of him on the bed where we made out and eventually did something to come but I can't remember that part.

Many young "American" writers, which is the wrong word for those of us who come from the USA which is only a small part of the Americas, but you can't say USAn writers, do things first done by this short list of earlier "American" writers:

1. Gertrude Stein
2. William Saroyan
3. Jack Kerouac
4. Jane Bowles
5. Jean Toomer
6. Kate Chopin
7. William Carlos Williams
8. Frank O'Hara
9. John Ashbery
10. Kenward Elmslie

Some of these writers are still considered to be "young" by those who give introductions and write jacket blurbs. They aren't, perhaps to their satisfaction, or perhaps not.

The traffic is building up to a certain crescendo, surrealists seem trapped in a tired diction that smacks of the 19th century, and I still haven't been able to find a way to do right by my kids. How is it there?

10. "(I have always considered myself as the *rear*-guard of the advance)" —William Carlos Williams

Jeez I was a kid then. 1948 Rudy Burckhardt. Cabaret life. Big bars with big stars with big cigars. I was there I was there. Not in the bars but in the cars. The jump seats of the yellow checker cabs and back seats of Buicks before or just about the time of Dynaflow, or what *was* it called, V-8s. The advent of the automatic transmission instead of the advent of the automobile. The difference between the turn of the century and the turn of the asses (I was thinking!) in those long skirts! I meant, of course, the difference between the turn of the century and mid century. Big changes for the early ones. Changes, pretty effective but lots of doubts, for the later ones. The difference between Picasso and Pollack. The difference between Stein & Day. I'm invited to a publication party for a poet, female, attractive, tough, big, foreign born, acts and looks comfortable and confident and is the first poet to be published by Stein & Day. Says my hostess, another poetess … no, she's a *poet*, so we should probably also maybe do you think say *host* instead of hostess? Are they any good! Does it matter! What of 1975 will be memorable in "the arts" in the USofA anyway. Many fortunes will rise and fall on guesses to just that question. Not mine. I second guessed them all (you shoulda seen me in 1957 arguing with my dad about blacks and knowing it was coming and pretty soon those lily white commercials and TV precincts would be filled with those hip enough to see it coming and I was gonna be one of them on the crest of the new wave of CONTRAST and so it goes) to end up here, maybe you too. We knew, heh? All along. What we need is a forum. I can't go back, can you? What'll my kids do? Jesus Christ I was 5 years old when they looked like that in their long print dresses and crazy straw hats in Manhattan where my mother, god rest her soul, and father took us to show us Times Square and there, o where, was Rudy snapping a picture, just missing us, me, again.

11. "… and was it not as it all just is in dark days? There are bright spots." —Gertrude Stein

The motel "suite" was divided into rooms for everyone and rooms only for "gays" who in fact had rented the place as a base of operations with their straight colleagues in their radical media experiment in reporting the news from the convention on tapes later fed to independent radio stations around the USA. "We" had a screened in porch a few feet from the pool, a bedroom, a bathroom, and then shared the room set up as a studio, "they" had the other bathroom, the livingroom, another bedroom, and the kitchen which was supposedly shared too. Over twenty people were sleeping all over the place. Most of "us" in pairs, most of "them" singly, but not all.

There were cats, lots of dope, loud music, beer, some booze, some pills, much nudity, too much mess. I woke up on the porch the morning after my first night of sleep after the dress incident to a beautiful misty morning with this long tall pretty faced young man naked beside me who was my lover so we made love. Just before I came I realized someone was watching us through the screens. I turned around to see. One of "them" must have walked around from the front door to the place past the pool to the porch just to peek, I stared right at him. He stared back, then said with little emotion and no sign of embarrassment, "O, excuse me," and after a few minutes more of staring turned and walked over to the poolside and sat down on a lounge chair facing away from us. We laughed and came together. It was the height of the revolution.

The Dress Incident

Well, it was an epiphany, have I said that before? It was like some people describe their first acid trip back in the early '60s when it was usually pure. It was an awakening. It was like some people describe their first fuck, or getting fucked the first time after years of fucking, or any extraordinary sexual act you have held back on, resisted, perhaps convinced it wasn't for you but secretly curious. It was a first.

But I didn't let the rest of "us" know, because I had been one of "them" for so long I was embarrassed about it, when "we" put on various drag outfits, not with the professional calculations of true transvestites or even a casual cross dresser's intent, more like doing something with your hands when you're on the phone because the conversation isn't *that* engaging.

"We" were doing something with our hands. And to our bodies. Covering them in the Florida afternoon heat, after my twenty hour ride and no sleep and discouraging encounter with the nasty healthy looking cop, with light colorful print summer dresses. "We" traded back and forth. I stuck with one. An early '60s semiformal. Low cut with support stuff where the tits should be, giving me the look of something there. Green and white, the white almost silver. Hemmed just below my knees. My feet bare. My hair loose and hanging down below my shoulders.

"We" played with nail polish too. You put some on me. I put some on you. And so on. O, we smoked dope. And hash. Others put on heels and did their faces. I had no need for that. I did make up once in a play and found it too much trouble. I was tired.

People did this and that, drifted out, work went on in the studio the door closed, the last person went out through the porch door. I was alone and tired. I catnapped a little. Woke up the sun still bright and hot the dress still on. People in the pool splashing and playing. I could see them through the screened in porch

61

which I could see through the open door that led from our bedroom to the porch. The door on the other side of our bedroom
was open and led to our bathroom. The door on the other side of
our bathroom was open and led to the studio room which meant
the work was done. The door on the other side of the studio was
closed and led to the living room where noise was coming from.
Sounded like lots of people. A party.

I got up and tried to reach the zipper someone else had
pulled up for me. I couldn't. The dress was tight around me, gave
me a hardon in fact when I first slipped it over my naked body, the
silky material against my bare cock. My cock was half hard still
against the dress that I couldn't get off. I thought I would walk to
the livingroom where everyone seemed to be and ask for help. I
walked to the door on the other side of our bedroom and through
the bathroom to the door on the other side and through the studio
to the door that was closed and opened it.

The music blasted my nap head awake and there were all
kinds of "them" dancing and drinking and smoking and none of
"us" in sight and those closest seemed to be staring at me framed
in the doorway barefooted and in my semiformal dress. The
women looked right through me or smiled as though at a puppy
dog or plaything. My stomach hurt a lot. My eyes ached. My mus-
cles were stiff and tired from driving and holding myself steady in
the doorway. I wanted to turn around and go back.

After what seemed like at least fifteen minutes of standing
there saying nothing while the faces and sounds grew more and
more surreal and frightening I turned slowly and step by step
retreated through the studio and bathroom to the bedroom where
I sat down on a bed and felt very much like crying and screaming
and revenging myself on "them" in there partying like I hadn't just
gone through hell because of them and they didn't even know it as
I wouldn't have when I was one of them and maybe even the they
I was part of now wouldn't understand and who the fuck were any
of them to have so much control over me it would take me fifteen
minutes just to turn around and leave me too weak and scared to
simply ask someone to unzip me and I thought of one woman who
rode a motorcycle and wore heavy work shoes and thick faded
jeans and men's flannel work shirts even in this heat. She was
good looking. She was attractive. Even in her movement disguise I
could see the sensuousness of her ass. She looked Irish with pale
eyes and fading freckles and long dark hair like mine. I wanted to

bury my head between her thighs so bad and make her laugh and cry with the joy of it and here I was stuck in a dress afraid to go out there and be whatever was me when it was me.

12. "I was great."—John Lennon

I was 30. In May of 1972. So by August, the time of the Republican convention in Miami I had just barely crossed over into enemy territory. Even though we all knew it was a media myth that "over 30" stuff. In fact it was a relief. I could relax. I didn't have to try so hard anymore. I relaxed so much I got fucked for the first time and touched a naked man's body and o my had revelation after revelation until I was pouring zeal.

I had horrible fits of depression and suicidal thoughts for the first time too, part of expanding my consciousness to understanding what it is like, or might be, to not be "straight," and maybe even an inkling of what it might be like to not be "male." I was a project, *and* I was one of the project directors. One of the others on the board, not my lover, but my first male lover only a few long months before, the man who first touched the buttons right to make them work, sent in another project to me, another married man, another movement heavy overburdened with guilt and arrogance and confusing the two constantly.

Here he came, in movement uniform, jeans, work shirt, beard, messed hair, a man but willing to learn, through the studio and bathroom to the bedroom to sit down beside me on the bed with no inkling of what I was doing there or what I had just been through. He started talking.

The Epiphany
(the rest of the dress incident)

While he talked there was a need to do something with our hands so he filled a hash pipe and we passed it back and forth, smoking. We smoked and we smoked. He talked and we smoked. I tried occasionally to offer my perspective, turning to look into his bearded camouflage but unable to get to the one inside. He ignored what I said or dismissed it or waved it away or refuted it or corrected it or ridiculed it and went on with his importance. I got more and more loaded on the dope.

Before long he was so much into his talking he wasn't smoking and I was getting higher alone. The sun went down. The moon came out over Miami Beach and shone through the windows of the bedroom creating a metallic kind of illumination that somehow corresponded in my head with my high. I felt bathed in it. I felt clean and pure and I looked down from what seemed like some great and invulnerable height at the lovely crossed knees of a pale and fragile woman and the long thin fingers of her hand resting on her knee. The hem of her silky dress met the silky skin of her wrist and the nails of her fingers sparkled in the moonlight.

I was captivated with this vision and the sound of his voice was a low mumble in the distance. It was lovely and secure and then suddenly it was me. Jesus Christ my god in heaven almighty mother of us all *this is me I see!*

This guy's voice came rushing in as though the door in my ear had opened and I turned to him and looked at him with the eyes of the woman whose knees and delicate hands I had fallen in love with that were mine and he stopped talking, he looked frightened, he got up and walked out through the door to the bathroom closing that door behind him.

I looked back down from my height at the hands and knees and laughed low, but out loud. I picked up my head and laughed louder. It felt so good. Goddamnit but it felt so good. I picked up the pipe and finished what was left of the hash.

The smoke took my head even further from my body til I felt as though I were seeing the room through the moon's eyes or the tiny eyes in the dots of light that hung together in the rays that made the bright metallic spots in the room. I was totally spaced out on hash, Miami Beach, three months of discoveries, twenty hour ride, thirty years of defenses, the moon, the night, myself.

I got up to go into the living room to find the woman who rode the motorcycle and tell her how beautiful I thought she was. The back of the door that led to the bathroom had a full length mirror attached to it. As I worked my way across the room from the bed to that door I became conscious of this creature, hair so dark, skin like the moonlight, dress silvery and green and shapely over the thin long body on the bare quiet feet and it was me and I loved it and went to meet it and when I reached it and came close enough to look into its eyes ... The Epiphany.

What a weak word for whatever it was. The whole fucking universe, the secret, the alchemists' knowledge, the history of poor humans and lucky humans, the point where it says who we will be, the place we were before the gases expanded, the darkness and beyond, the whole fucking thing radiating from the point where our eyes met like a vortex for everything that had ever gone down or would or could have or might. God damn it I knew it all for that second. I had it all and was of it all. I didn't hold it, it held me until I dissolved into it only so fast it was me. No way to say it. I could see it all and did *then*. The music of the spheres and what lies between them. In the contact of our eyes I knew what it was all about. The whole fucking show. Including the nightmares. I had it and it had me. It was beautiful. It was perfect. It was it.

13. "Responsibility is to keep / the ability to respond."
—Robert Duncan

And that was it. I walked through that door, like so many others, and moved with more grace than I ever could share before, or since. But it was over. Not all over. I remember it right? I write about it right? I got back to DC and looked up alchemist works and discovered their symbol was often the hermaphrodite which I knew for that eternal moment, as they say. I had it right there in my hands only not in my hands more like me in its hands, like being rocked to sleep by the cosmos which is where we come in, right?

I walked through the studio too and into the other room but just as I stepped through the doorway to the big confrontation that didn't matter any more the woman with the motorcycle came up and through going the other way. She was looking for me. She wanted to tell me she had seen me and I looked beautiful. I told her I was on my way to tell her the same. We laughed. We talked. We touched, not much, but enough. She could see it glowing in me and felt somehow proud, knew instinctively we shared it. Not that she knew, I didn't either any more already but I knew I had had it and she knew it was there. I know it sounds silly but how else would it sound speaking of it in a language created for the most part to explain technical things. Is that right? Should we know? I knew that too then.

Every time we looked at each other we burst into uncontrollable smiles like blissed out religion freaks or spaced out acid freaks or just lovers the first time they know it. We talked about how much of a drag it was being strong. She complained about being a strong woman understanding some of what it had been and was for me the father and husband and support and know how and handy man and breadwinner and potential savior and hoped for son and how good it was to get dressed up and just be our beautiful selves with all the eyes smiling except those that only did whatever it is they do that makes us feel so uncomfortable with being so beautiful we know it. And being weak, and crying and hysteria. I wasn't sure about all of it. But by the time over a thousand people had been arrested and the helicopters had thrown their artificial stronger than moonlight light on all of us in the parks and streets and beaches and gassed us from the air and chased us with clubs and done all they do o piss o shit I was trembling in my pants and shirt and boots and strong hippie street man's pose just shaking all over like never before unable to trash to stand up and fight to run to argue to preach to rebel to revolutionize just shaking a crying scared shitless blob of flesh hysterical. Vulnerable. Enough to finally recognize my own fear without the defenses built so carefully and painfully since childhood to short circuit the thought. What me worry? What me scared shitless? What me chickenshit? Chickenshit blues.

14. "If you want to have clean ideas, change them as often as you change your shirts."   —Francis Picabia

Well, I couldn't go on shaking and trembling and fearing the world because it is as careless about me as it is could I?

I tried to develop the defensive skills of a street queen which are considerable. But I couldn't pull it off.

I tried hanging around with tough women who now weren't intimidated or put off by my no longer blaring macho so asked me to bed. Only once we hit the sheets it was the '50s all over again. Up to me. I had to initiate, anticipate, organize, lead the attack, etc. One tough lady, who also rode a motorcycle, worked as a construction worker and had a very pretty face on a big but lovely body became so frightened when in bed she said "You almost look like a girl!" and was only satisfied when I climbed on top and between and fucked away for a while as strong as I could. She said later she couldn't handle the weirdness of my less male side. To see me look so soft and feminine freaked her out, she said.

There were many, not a scientific study or official survey, but my experience, in fatigue jackets and work shirts, no make up, and those sand colored almost orange work shoes with all the laces. They drove motorcycles, big ones, and ran projects, and looked you right in the eye when they asked me to go to bed with them. They were tough and aggressive and feminist and almost everyone of them had at least tried sex with other women if not actually labeling themselves dykes or lesbian feminists. Every one of them, maybe twenty or more, in a year's time, turned back the clock in bed and I had to perform again just like the old days. And the men were mostly the same. They wanted me one way or the other, a real man or a real lady a faggot or a father not a faggot father. There were exceptions. Few. Too few. The exceptions were usually bent on equality unable to play with roles and possibly "sexist" fun in bed. So. Constructions, restrictions, time for a transfusion.

I cut my hair, got a hold of more conservatively male clothes. Quiet colors, no prints, stopped stuttering and looked people over again.

15. "what / if / the birds don't / listen"—Larry Eigner

Ringo Starr was a favorite because he seemed easily intimidated (vulnerable), not that bright (earthy), friendly (unsophisticated), he wasn't beautiful like McCartney or cool like Harrison or a genius like Lennon. He was all right. Now he's leaving his wife and trying to act cool and it ain't right is it. O my my.

Gertrude Stein was she really like a husband to Alice and/or vice versa? O no there were feminists who understood the deception involved in those roles long before Gertrude dear.

The '50s were horrible, but there was something happening wasn't there?

The "New York School" had brains and style and taste and compulsion enough to be in New York. Those elitists.

What is Cher or Raquel Welch? Raquel Welch is dynamite, and tough too. She isn't Katharine Hepburn. Katharine Hepburn had a very secure childhood she insists, middle class and perfect.

Cagney retired before he got so old he'd look lousy up there ten feet high.

Who gives a fuck about an actor or actress('s) politics if they perform a great role? Would you really not see the movie for political reasons? Aren't these questions nostalgic?

Yoko Ono is a banker's daughter. Castro was a lawyer. Mao's folks were middle class relatively speaking. Stalin was lower class and a boor who robbed the banks to raise the revolution's money while exiled Trotsky and Lenin discussed theory and became famous. Russia is still Russia.

Mark Rothko was a Russian named Marcus Rothkowitz. He came to live in the USA when he was 10. His paintings are brilliant. He killed himself when he was middle aged already.

Vladmir Mayakovsky was a Russian named Mayakovsky. He visited the USA as a young man but didn't stay long. He killed himself in early middle age in the USSR with a pistol. His poems are brilliant.

Is "cow" really the code word for "cunt" in Gertrude Stein's writing?

16. "a common ear / for our deep gossip"—Allen Ginsberg

Listen Jack, I got my kids to worry about.
Listen up now, I worry about my kids.

Hey, my man, my lady, sister, brother, you motherfucker, a little girl and a little boy depend on me for *something. You* gonna tell me what?

17. "In the middle of the staircase I forgot how to go down"
—David Antin

My father used to say he got these things he used to say from his childhood friend Charlie Zigler:

"Snow again I didn't get your drift"
"One side or a leg off"
"He's afraid to throw a rock through the poorhouse window for fear of hitting one of his kids"
"Our class won the Bible"
"Seeing New York without a ticket" (referring to seeing up ladies' dresses)
"Get off my lip buddy, I gotta spit"

Then there were the things we thought of as "Irish" which maybe were:

"What cannot be cured must be endured"
"God bless you, and the devil miss you, the saints preserve you, the angels watch over you" etc.
"The back o' me hand to ya"
"Himself" (referring to the man of the house, or the patriarch of the clan)

I can't remember them. They're there, up here in my head somewhere I can vaguely make them out the resonances of them banging around for so many years and me not paying attention too busy jerking off or learning to play football or the piano or how to curse or smoke or dress like I'm ready to kick ass which I never have been though I'd often have liked to be.

18. "Sex is the only encyclopedia."—Robert Kelly

I dreamt I was in the high school playing field behind my house again only this time with Kenward Elmslie and we were talking through the old fence that used to be there to a young black tough lithe woman with short hair and beautiful brown eyes about forming a basketball team. The woman wouldn't bridge no shit. Kenward was where he was too. I was just lookin' as usual.

Up the street at my house which resembled the Algonquin Hotel in the lobby was the other guy responsible for doing the basketball team bit, a cross between John Ashbery and George Starbuck who said he had two people too, so we could play each other three person teams and laughed in a way that suddenly made it clear to me so lame that it wasn't gonna happen again, we fucked up, there weren't enough, o shit, and Kenward down the street and back again from the bookstore with a book that purported to translate somebody like a cross between Freud and Michael Fraenkel with little wood block prints on the cover of Elmslie giving the signs in hand and arm language for various phonetics and diphthongs and shit in the book, a brilliantly designed cover and the last thing I remember is me fucking the beautiful tough black girl in the ass and her unsure at first about it and then getting into it with me so happy about it I could've stayed in there forever.

April fool's day 1975

The day came on bright and shiny;
I didn't know what to say.
Spring finally here but
on April Fool's Day?
Does that mean more winter tomorrow?
Does it matter? Inside I feel tiny
watching my friends separate again, everywhere,
or the TV letting me know it's not over
over there,
or my special ignorance,
the dumbness only I can confront,
but still don't know how to:
not meditation,
not revolution,
not androgyny or drag in any of its forms,
not even poetry,
not even spring.
In my heart there are shelves
and on the shelves there are too many books
and too many of the books are worn out
or boring or impossible to understand.
And in my hands?
Those little hearts
the poems that
even when dumb, are sacred.

I'm glad we all aren't naked:
it's not the sixties anymore.
I want to wear nice clothes
and carry on my life behind closed doors.
I want to sit with the rich
or hustling poor and still be myself.
I want to make my kids secure.
I want to share with them
what joy a good night's sleep
with bright and shiny morning
can bring to the heart —
the chance to start
again.

1975-1982

New York City

"What doesn't come to me from me has come to
the wrong address."

> —Samuel Beckett
> *The Unnamable*

"...people who really experiment with themselves
find out that all the old things are true."

> — F. Scott Fitzgerald
> *The Crack Up*

"(Which is different from saying that he cannot *play*
magnificently and joyously—in which case not-
winning is hardly a cause for sadness)."

> —Richard Foreman

PROUD CUT

ONE

The beauties always win. "No," they say. But we don't believe
them, even when we are the beauties. When was that. Once.
(Maybe many times.) That time we lived alone. It was the start of
the seventies and no one was sure of anything anymore. I remember the first beauty. I lived alone once. Once. (Only once. All
alone. No spouse. No room mate. No kids. No brothers or sisters
or uncles or aunts or boarders or pets or live-in maids or live-in
lovers or anyone else.) For one year. A little more than one year.
Me. Looking at the floor and giggling. I could walk any way. Talk
out loud to myself. Hang up my clothes or not. (I was actually,
surprisingly very neat. Perhaps neater than I've ever been.) Sit and
"muse" for hours. Talk to myself. *Listen* to myself. It was 1974.
She was the second great beauty in my life. The first was that earlier break from "family life." 1961. This second: 1974. Me. Then.
Them. Each a different, distinct beauty. Not just that, of course.
None of us were or are ever just that, are we? Men or women.
Children or adults. Those of us who have ever recognized ourselves as true "beauties," no matter how rarely. But they never let
on they knew. Those two. Always acted as though it was something
else, something the world pretended to find more substantial,
more deference-demanding. With the first—"Bambi"—it was
nobility. One of those almost black Black women, thin, cool,
proud and *beautiful*. The second—"Karen"—the girlish delight in
life, thin, white, warm, concerned, generous, *pleasant* and *beautiful*. Neither *ever* acted like it was their *beauty* we were always
falling for. Both had enormous, dark eyes. Eyes. Yes. I loved them
both.

TWO

I was coming out of the Blimpie's on Wisconsin Avenue in Washington DC at the height of the Watergate discoveries. Not long
before, months maybe, I had been experimenting with my recently
acquired queer side, stopping at Blimpie's around three in the
morning with a tall, handsome man—another, a fellow, "beauty"

73

—"Robert"—dressed as a monk, friar's brown robes, hood, medieval air, coming from a "gay activists" dance after seeing a "gay" play—Arthur Laurent's "Enclave." Both events moved me deeply. The play with its perspective coming from the deeply felt identity and guilt of an older, conservative gay man and the frustration of a life of hypocrisy and pretense—the dance with its positive energy and hope-filled spirit, its sense of a community in the process of creating itself. Those were heady days. I was happy to be a part of them. Until Robert and I emerged from Blimpie's on to a relatively deserted Wisconsin Avenue sidewalk. The usual Georgetown preppie "Hill" crowd were long gone. The street belonged to the hardcore night life. Queens and hustlers, muggers and drunks, junkies and madmen. A small band of potential muggers—ten or so young, teenaged, blacks—one girl among them—surrounded us about two buildings north of Blimpie's. They were drawn by Robert's robes, or our white skins, or our air of gentle sensuality. Whatever attracted them, it also made them hostile and threatening. "Lookee here faggot, I know what you likes." "Whatchu think you lookin at cocksucker." Robert tried reason. "We aren't looking for trouble. My name's Robert. This is Michael." "Your name Roberta faggot." "Which one a you da wife?" I thought only of violence. I kept expecting my old, straight, street male self to hit one of them, or rap out a fast and deadly response. Instead I heard myself saying "Come on, we ain't bothering you. Why you wanna bother us." And hearing them say "You want my big black cock up your faggot white ass, don't you sissy." And seeing *smiles* on the faces of the few people passing by. *Couples. Straight.* Or acting straight. Robert again tried reason, as the band of blacks grew closer and closer in their encircling of us, looking meaner and meaner too. "We aren't your enemy you know." "Yeah, we know what you want to be, our pussy! White boy, your ass better be clean!" And then I grabbed Robert and somehow pushed through them and began walking fast. They seemed startled and at first only yelled more insults. Then they started to follow, fast, and pulling Robert by the arm I started to run. They ran after us. Shouting more insane declarations of their certainty of our lust for their stupid, mean, nasty selves. Little, dangerous fools out to hurt us, already humiliating us. We turned the corner and ran to "the block." One square block of residential sidewalk that at that hour usually sported anywhere from fifty to five hundred men, cruising for sex, or love, or some kind of perverse

74

excitement. As we got closer I felt relief and security and even the possibility of revenge. But when I turned to face our pursuers they had already stopped and were watching silently the crowd of men strolling, shouting, whistling as the cars slowly circled the same area, their single occupants sizing up the potential. The black kids shouted a few more harmless, now, insults and turned back. Robert and I found some friends, exchanged some horror stories and then walked slowly, a little fearfully, on to his room. I had never been there before. He was young, maybe 19, I was 30. But he was bigger, maybe six foot four, and slim but strong. His face was classically handsome, though a little sad. He was quiet. I rambled on about how I had wanted, had fantasized, smashing in the faces, the smirks and superior, condescending sneers of those kids with a brick from the cobblestoned, quaint touristy streets of Georgetown. Robert remained quiet. We undressed. He slept in a narrow single bed, in an attic room in a boarding house. I slept that night beside him. We held each other. We kissed each other's faces and hands and lips. We pressed the hard, maleness of our bodies, our skin, against each others' thighs and hips and stomachs and pricks. Neither of us was "the wife." We came together, but separately, as we stroked each other's cocks. It was warm and hot and hard and soft, and something like love, and something like the most intimate friendships, and the last time I saw him. I kissed his handsome face goodbye a few hours later, in the dawn and he whispered "thank you" in the pale light, his strong hand touching my cheek. A week later I heard he had committed himself to a mental institution, St. Elizabeths, where Ezra Pound had once been their most famous inmate. A few months later, much earlier in the evening, six or seven, I emerged from the same Blimpie's to run into a blond, young, eager, funny, tough hustler, occasional haircutter, and on his arm was a beauty—freckled face, big brown eyes, dark hair, perfect little nose and chin, a valentine that went straight to my heart. I was smitten. My dabbling in "how to be queer and like it" was doomed.

THREE

I remember saying over and over to myself—she's "too beautiful"—meaning dangerous, a threat, too tough to win outright and forever, or to hold so close she'd never need anyone else. Great beauties need great adventures, great spaces, great waves of appreciation. I needed little waves of adoration for my little beauty. She frightened me that way. I saw a tiny way of admiration for my love of myself and her beauty's reflection of that and I fell.

IN MY TIME

BOOK I—*What I Learned*

BOOK II—*What I did*

CHAP. 1—*A Lot*

A lot of expectations. I mean I'm a star—if *they* only knew it. Shit.

Sympathetic eyes. My eyes are too sympathetic. I attract all these nuts. And they're a drain. I mean you can't just cut them off, that's why they're nuts already, they feel cut off—eye contact gets them feeling they can get back in touch again—through me! That's why they call it eye *contact*. There's a kind of rush to it—that kind of contact. It's the mixture of fear with the feeling of power—I know it's power. That's why I'm a star. It's like JFK—*charisma*. You look at someone, into their eyes, and zap, they know it too—that you're a *star*. Only if in their eyes you suddenly see overwhelming relief, you know they were so desperate it made them crazy, till they found you—or what they see in your eyes. You're their savior. And you feel it too—that's the power. But their desperation is scary—that's the fear. Now when they're not crazy, just lonely, it means probably an easy lay, but being a star is a responsibility, so I don't like to think in terms of "easy lays." Besides, the thrill is in that first contact when you feel the power flowing and the charisma working, making magnets of your eyes, attracting people to you. Shit. I could be a really big star! If they'd only notice what I can do with my eyes. But what do I get—crazies notice, and lonely people. *They* don't make stars, they just recognize them—with or without the publicity and fame and all that.

That's what I want I guess—"all that." All that security. I mean imagine being able to get work—and work that is often like play compared to real working—just on your *name*. No other credentials necessary. That's *security*. Or all that friendliness. Sure you get some crazies and some nasties. But they're scared of you too if you're really famous—and most of the places that cater to famous people and the really rich, well, those places have ways of keeping the crazies and nasties away, or at least down to a minimum. And almost everyone else is friendly. Why, just talking to you is an honor if you're a big star. So everyone gets feeling good, feeling happy and successful to be sharing some moments with a star, and that makes them grateful, which makes them friendly—so friendly they like to buy you things, give you things, even themselves. And a lot of them are good looking. Beautiful people can see they're beautiful and want to be appreciated for it—but they're like us stars. They attract a lot of crazies. They don't need crazies and nobodies telling them they're beautiful, or staring at them like they are. They need stars to appreciate their beauty—then it seems *real*, and *important* and *effective*. The star's stamp of approval on their beauty makes it historic, and that reassures the beautiful people that though their beauty might fade, the appreciation of it won't because it's now history.

And stars always get to have easy access to other stars. Imagine making Johnny Carson nervous on his own show. *That's power!*

That kind of power probably can get you in anywhere. Shit. No more subways, no more fast food, no more nasty sales clerks and interviews with prospective employers whose questions are so dumb they ignore the miles of credentials you might have. Just *stardom*—the ultimate American dream. Damn. Don't it—Ain't it frustrating!?!

CHAP. 2

She wasn't sure if she was a star or a beautiful people. She was beautiful all right, but not that kind of cold, aloof, chiseled kind of beauty that the beautiful people women seem to have. She was more vulnerable than that—warmer. But she had a quality, an intelligence, an openness in her beautiful deep brown eyes that gave her face some star quality. But, unfortunately, and in fact, she wasn't that smart. And she had a fat ass.

CHAP. 3

But I liked it. It was round, and full, and invitingly womanly. In the 1950s it would have been referred to by hip cats as "crazy." In the 1970s, in the circles she tried to travel in and cared about, it was fat—too big. But before she was through it would be slimmed down, and her eyes would take on that distant, aloof, elitist coldness of the beautiful people, and she would be going after the real stars—the ones everyone knows about, or wants to know about.

CHAP. 4

It's pretty horrible to have grown up in the '50s feeling like an outsider because of your beliefs and insights and then in the '60s to find a community of outsiders who shared your feelings about things and the way they should be changed for the better only to arrive at the end of the '70s with that community dispersed by fear of repression and by mistrust and self-righteousness while the society-at-large, or at least the media and politicians and "spokesmen," express the very sentiments that made you an outsider in the '50s or a community of outsiders in the '60s and to know they don't know what the fuck they're talking about, and the kids think it's all true like back to the '40s again only different—you *can* grow your hair long or smoke dope and be less paranoid about it—you *can* live with someone and not worry about getting married or what the landlord, or her parents, or cops will think or do about it. Only she had grown up in the '60s in Italy and had been rich enough to come to the USA to play. She didn't have any idea what I was feeling just being alive in my time. But then, I obviously didn't know much about what it must be like to be her either. I just loved her.

CHAP. 5

Part of what I loved about her was the way she talked of course, that sexy Italian accent. And what she talked about—her rich parents and friends in Italy, her European travels, her family's servants and history, her teenage love affairs, her first marriage.

CHAP. 6

She had been married to a country gentleman—can you imagine what that must have been like in the early 1970s? He had a "place" in Spain—in the country southwest of Barcelona, and the main house in Italy, outside Florence. Like a feudal lord, his tenants made things, and grew things and he made sure smart people were hired to run things while he tended to his other "investments" and to his hunting and riding and occasional boating, and now and then spent some time at their apartments in Madrid and Rome. He looks solid, competent and dull in photographs of the two of them together. But she says he really was "fabulous in his own way," meaning he would get happy on fine liquor and the best champagne now and then, and allow her to indulge in more exotic ways of getting high, until he caught her with another man—boy really. Then all the credit, all the servants, all the access to the fine things was cut off. So she left him, and to avoid the disgrace of her presence her family sent her to "America," where she finally settled for some obscure reason in Washington DC where she met me.

Chap. 7

It was eye contact of course—but more. She was standing in the doorway in a stylishly short dress with what looked like imitation 1940s padded shoulders and this fabulously thick, black hair arranged like a luxurious and sensual frame for her deep dark eyes and puffy, incredibly seductive lips and the rest—the soft contours, slightly Latin brown skin, and surprisingly wide nose—of her fabulous face. I looked as intensely as I could and still look friendly, casual, and cool into her dark brown eyes and she smiled as sexy a smile as I've ever seen that at the same time promised absolutely nothing. But her eyes promised something—madness, insane passion, obsession, desperation, and the lonely longing of all adults and most kids for someone to trust with the tenderness of vulnerability. I mean she looked polite but interesting, and I tried to reciprocate.

She was with a tall American woman I knew, who I thought of as a girl. She was married and over 21 but her husband seemed boyish to me in ways I didn't share, and she seemed like a high school or college pin-up, just venturing out into the world of real consequences (as though that isn't the same world we're all born into and stuck with regardless ...)—

She, the blonde—named Cassie—was actually beautiful to most red-blooded American men. She had a voluptuously full, curvy figure—like what a '50s sex queen *should* have looked like (most of them—like Jayne Mansfield—poor Jane—were all tits and no ass)—and this long straight blonde hair, like a *Playboy* magazine version of the 1960s hip chick look—and the purest white skin I've ever seen. But her smile was always tentative, at least toward me. Maybe because she knew I was crazy—even if I was a star—and I was—of sorts—though not the sort that counts the money he makes because of it—though I did make some money from—but that came later—and so did Cassie—and her friend, who she introduced me to as Maria Licia—or "Lisha" to her friends— which lucky crew I was about to be counted among—

CHAP. 8

What they were doing in the doorway to my apartment was asking if I had a corkscrew they could borrow because Cassie's had just broken. Cassie lived on the second floor of the three story town-house we lived in. My apartment was on the first floor. I only knew Cassie as a neighbor since I'd only moved into the town-house a few months earlier after leaving my wife and the collective that we had shared our house with and which had seemed so ter-rific for several years previous—only now seemed oppressive and something to forget.

When I opened the door I was in my bathrobe, a white terrycloth towel-like bathrobe that my wife had bought me as a Christmas gift our first Christmas together over ten years before—just over, since it was the middle of March. I had moved into the townhouse in January, in the middle of one of the rare severe snowstorms Washington DC gets every few years. It was beautiful, turning the street into an old postcard from the turn of the century—a Hollywood set from a 1940s Technicolor musical about the turn of the century. It was a beautiful block of old townhouses that still had the magic aura of their early promise—one of several blocks like that in DC—this one East of Georgetown and just Southeast of Dupont Circle on N Street— only a special block-long stretch of N that was cut off at one end by a little triangle island that bordered on the busy traffic of Connecticut Avenue and on the other by the back of a new Holiday-Inn-style motel that shattered the illusion of another era and sense of proud style. I loved my new home. And when these two exceptionally attractive women knocked on my door I was just relaxing on my mattress after making love with the reason I finally left my wife and the collective which included our two kids. So I threw on a bathrobe to answer the knock on my door, hoping it wouldn't be the landlady—who actually wasn't the owner of the place but lived on the top floor and watched after it for the Southern Senator who owned it and for whom she worked in some mysterious capacity that I figured had to do with sex—since, though she was in her late '50s, she was still a very vivacious little Southern lady who had successfully seduced me the day I moved into the building. It wasn't her of course, it was them, vanilla and chocolate, my favorite combination in any dessert. I couldn't resist not being aggravated by their intrusion into my happy little scene.

"Hey Cassie—How are you?"

They're smiling at me in my bathrobe at only 9 PM and themselves in my doorway all dolled up and me smiling back at them and the idea of borrowing a corkscrew—

"O Kevin—I hope we're not—o excuse me—this is Maria Licia—we were just hoping you might have a corkscrew we could borrow"

She looks pleased with herself for managing everything so adult-like while her friend sticks out her hand and says simply "Hello." I say "Hold on a sec, while I check" and leave them standing in the doorway, the door open, a clear view all the way to the back of my little home where the beauty of my life at the moment is lying on my mattress on the bare floor against the wall under a sheet and embarrassed—I hope I haven't blown anything with her as I rummage around in my kitchen drawers till I find a corkscrew and hurry back to the door with it.

"Here you go"

"O thanks so much—you're a real lifesaver—I don't know where we would have found one on a Sunday night"

"Anytime."

They're still smiling as I'm standing with one bare foot on top of the other, balancing with one hand on the door jamb the other on the edge of the open door—ready to say goodnight when Cassie says

"Kevin—why don't you and your friend come join us for a drink" then as she loses confidence or gets confused or feels embarrassment coming on because of the situation—my "friend" in bed—me in my bathrobe—"we're just opening some wine—but there's plenty—and we'll be sure to save some for you—?"—so I say, of course, still grinning and unembarrassed because I've never been in the midst of so much stylish good looks that seemed so interested in me—"Sure—we'll come up in about a half hour"—they smile at each other and then me before they turn and retreat up the stairs and I close the door realizing there was something conspiratorial about their smiles as though—shit—they probably thought they interrupted our lovemaking and that I needed the half hour to "finish up"—or maybe that we hadn't started yet and that's how long they think it'll take us—or—o shit—fuck'em— here's this beautiful American mix of all the good things our European forefathers had to offer in the way of physical artistry— green eyes, a few freckles, long wavy brown hair, boyish grin but womanly hips and a happy, cocky, carefree outlook on the promise of a rosy future. She's 22, I'm 31 and still hoping.

SINGLE FATHER HOOD

1. Summer's here—it's *hot & humid*—reminiscent of DC—I miss Caitlin—can't wait to see her—Miles so cute on his way to school today in white shorts and sneakers and new hair cut (he & I got ours cut at the same place, together, he choosing the place by the look of the "barbers")—the tree outside my bedroom/workroom window moving with some breeze I can't feel yet—but o so soft and beautiful my heart is full again like the sappy teenager I'll always be, fantasizing a star filled future of success and fame, and here I am 34 years old trying to rewrite an article on "extramarital sex" in order to get an editor's job at *Sexology Magazine*!

2. Made dinner for Miles & me after picking him up at "after school" where Paul, one of the "teachers" told me they played football this afternoon and Miles was great at it!—then picked up some carrots, grapes & bananas—had the carrots raw, grapes and grilled cheese, (mine with dijon mustard & open face) pickles, banana (platano) chips and anisette toast for supper!—later, after Miles' bath I said something about his hair as I was drying it & he took it for a cut on Lee, his mother, so he came to her defence saying the hair cut she gave him (which the barber said would take months to grow out so that it could be fixed) was "perfect"—then when I said "I doubt it" he explained tearfully that he meant "almost perfect" & that she, Lee, hadn't had the chance to finish it—I said "okay, it's no big deal honey"—and he said "to you it isn't 'cause you don't love her, but I do so it's a big deal to me"—his mind is so mature for such a little kid—sometimes I feel like the child here—

3. Miles came back this evening—Cait & Lee stayed over a few hours & then took a train to DC—Cait so cute—I wish I could be with her more—I want to spoil her a little and just love her a lot—I'm still exhausted from Miles' vacation (he cried tonight, missing his sister & mother already and the dog—"Max"—at his aunt Leslie's—not even telling me they went to see his great-grandmother on the farm—or to see Niagra Falls)—I tried to comfort him by pointing out that most people have people they love in different places—and it's fun visiting them—he said "Yeah but they don't usually start at seven"—!—

84

I*n the mood*

It was in 1964 that I first read Frank O'Hara.
The book was *Lunch Poems* and it was sitting on
the kitchen table of the first intellectual I
was friends with. He was a graduate student in
a state college in Cheney, Washington, and I
was an Airman Basic (lowest rank due to court
martial) stationed at Fairchild Air Force Base
outside Spokane, Washington. The first poem
I read in the book was "The Day Lady Died"
because for years, at least 1959 to that year,
1964, I had fancied myself a "jazz musician"
and had adopted the style of the black musicians
I played with and admired and had foregone the
white world to such an extent that this guy
whose house I was in and whose copy of *Lunch
Poems* I was reading was one of the few white
people I had bothered with in several years.
I was such an obsessed hipster in my assimilation
of black style I secretly rejected the idea of
my coming from the Irish-Americans who had
raised me and instead saw myself in glowing fantastic mythological status as "the unborn son
of Lady & Bird" feeling and believing "in my
heart" that I had truly been born when I first
discovered their music and realized what it had
in common was what seemed to define me to me.
So, I found O'Hara's poem about the death of
Billie Holiday incredibly effete, though I
didn't know that term at the time and would have
found it effete to have known it, and pretentious
because I couldn't remember any of the French
I had studied for one semester and never com-
pleted and there were French words in the text
of the poem, and elitist because some of the
references were so personal and obscure that I
was sure they were deliberately intended to
leave readers like me out, and badly written

because there was none of the obvious passion of
the Romantics and their contemporary step-kids
the Beats who were really the only "new" writers
I was familiar with although among them only
Bob Kaufman and Ray Bremser and Diane DiPrima
impressed me because Kaufman was mostly black
and had a white wife and mixed baby and I
thought that was heroic since I was trying
to do the same and realizing the odds, and
Bremser was an ex-con who wrote a poem about
the New Jersey turnpike and that certainly
never seemed effete or pretentious or elitist
to me having been born and grown up in Jersey,
and DiPrima was tough and almost cynical but
not in a way that excluded me from the work
and I was so grateful for being included in
something tough and almost cynical because it
made me feel authentic and full of potential too
and not the foolish imitation black I had sometimes been, bumbling my way through beatnik
Village parties with my spade partners or
black-girl dates most of whom didn't even give a
shit about Lady Day or Charlie Parker if they
had even heard of them, they were into something
to dance to and jazz was a very esoteric thing
to them too and all my references were obscure
and pretentious and even somewhat effete
as I tried to pass on to them what I was
discovering about being white playing it black
in the USA of the late '50s early '60s. So I
told my intellectual friend what I thought of
O'Hara and his pissy poem about Lady Day, I
think I went so far as to claim he had no right
to write about "my" Lady or maybe "our" Lady.
But something about the book, the way the poems
sat on the page, some of the language, all that
stuff and something else I never figured out
kept me interested nonetheless and so I
bought the book for myself and kept it around
and read it now and then and still felt
superior to it, not only because I too often

felt it was demanding the opposite response
from me, but also because I was into Mayakovsky
and had read most of him by then and saw
traces of him in O'Hara's work and some other
stuff I figured I was hipper to than most.
I got *Meditations in an Emergency* too and
pointed out the references to Mayakovsky's
"Cloud in Trousers" which was such an arrogant
but vulnerable poem I couldn't quite appreciate
what O'Hara was doing with it, not realizing
yet that in fact those were appealing qualities
in O'Hara's work too—arrogance with vulnerability. I was still thinking there was
something too glib about it all because it
kept reminding me of warm-up work, like the
exercises I did before doing the really
ponderous and passionately meaningful and
serious work (the Beats were almost always
serious too I remember) that got me into
the literary quarterlies and through the
Iowa Writers Workshop and helped me understand
my own dark corners and sharp angles and then
one day I realized how much of what I was
reading and often admiring going on around me
in the poetry world was a kind of picking of
scabs and flashing the open sores and wounds
as badges and credentials and how O'Hara
totally sidestepped that contemporary tendency
by tone and choice of vocabulary that cut
through the hopelessness of so much poetry
and replaced it with the joy of writing the
poem. What a simple but wonderful revelation.
The joy of writing it down—that was
what it suddenly seemed to be about in
a way that made me think of all I had heard
the painters of his time were trying to do,
get across the action of the creating
rather than the product that was so finished
it showed no signs of the activity, the energy
and spirit of the actual work that went into it.
O'Hara's poems were little excursions into

the act of writing poems with the kind of
mindset that keeps us trying sex with strangers
again and again, the hope that this time
is gonna be great, give us much pleasure
and satisfy a lot of frustration and totally
annul the boring horrible deadening, killing
in fact, effects of living. But I still
couldn't reconcile that achievement with
the personal references, though they were
becoming more and more familiar and thus
less and less elitist, though still somewhat
obscure. Then one day I was teaching contemporary poetry to a college class and
talking about a poem of O'Hara's, I think
it was "A Step Away from Them" after talking
about the poem "Steps" and how it overcame
the sadness of love's ending or going sour
amid the big city grind and in discussing how
it did this mostly through the structure of
the poem because by then I'd learned so much
about movement and rhythm and construction
I could see how well made O'Hara's poems are
despite or maybe because of their conversational flow and in the process of explaining
why the poems were good from a strategic and
structural point of view because they
accomplished this message of hope in
the face of contemporary despair and despite
well founded reasons for lamenting our
condition, or his condition in the specific
circumstances of the poem, and did it through
technical agility so refined the surface
ambiance of ease and a kind of glib grace
was hardly disturbed, suddenly I caught myself
starting to cry and I never cried back then,
in fact except for a short interlude of about
a year of weepiness I never cry period, except
over old movies and musicals and it was that
heartstring O'Hara had suddenly plucked in me
through his poetry that sang so naturally
and yet skillfully of overcoming the stupidity

and the tediousness of so much of life—
the true romantic, only without the pretentious
and really elitist self-conscious and self-
satisfied seriousness of the walking wounds
of contemporary poetry, because by mocking
the tone of the real and original Romantics
partly through the use of quotation marks
and italics (which is "sort of" what
"campy" dialogue often depends on, as "others"
have pointed *out*, it means *talking in*
"italics") and exclamation points and exclama-
tions—Oh!—he was making himself vulnerable
to a two-edged scalpel, unlike the Confessional
Poets and other of his contemporaries, even the
seemingly "honest" Beats who always exposed
themselves in ways that demanded applause or
appreciation for the courage of the exposure or
the extent of self-destruction the exposure caused
or exposed, etc. But not O'Hara, his defenses
were the shrewdest and toughest of all because
they weren't defensive at all but appeared to be
all offensive only the offensive was mounted
against his own and others' defensiveness,
thus he could be attacked for elitism when in fact
he's our most democratic poet since Whitman,
bringing that "tradition" full circle by
reversing Whitman's posing as the common-man-
brother-to-all which reduced everyone to
the level of anonymity that Whitman's poems
insured would never really be his fate
so he could afford it (I'm talking about
the pose, which perhaps became reality
much the way Ginsberg's seems to have, but
which is not the poetry because Whitman's
poetry is often wonderful and amazing and
very much more the source of much that is
associated with O'Hara and "The New York
School" than many of the French writers
constantly attributed with having "influenced"
the New York scene) (although O'Hara is also
"sort of" a Baudelaire in reverse, making

the most of the worst of Baudelaire's
pessimistic perceptions and emotionalisms
the city scene can generate) but instead O'Hara
elevates everyone to the level and
attentive familiarity of stars, throwing in
the names of personal friends alongside
those of personal heroes and famous and
world renowned producers and creators of
the culture that has come to be ours and
which he defined before most of us with
the clarity of the lyrics of a Hollywood
musical or a Madison Avenue ad, yet with
all the subtlety and imaginative exuberance
of a great wit and passionate lover.
What an incredibly seductive combination
for a poet. His poems *are* sexy. The language
is often intimate, the images voluptuous and
often exotic, the energy seemingly endless
and the point usually reassuring and flattering
and with just enough elusive connections
to make us want to put out the time and energy
to make ourselves as attractively intelligent
and perceptive and experienced and in-the-know
as the poems assume we are. He refused to
accept an audience that was not as good as
he was and in that way included us all in the
community of friends he admired and addressed
and referred to along with the proper names
and familiar rhythms of the most ordinary
people and things, all of which he incorporated
into descriptions and narratives that included
the proper names and rhythms of the most
extraordinary people and things the rest of us
are only now, years after the poems were written,
getting hip to and how well they fit the work
and complete the artistry of O'Hara's genius.
He helped me realize that the reason I wrote
poems was often simply because the rush, the
feeling that accompanied the writing of the poem,
especially when it seemed to be coming out good,
couldn't be duplicated anywhere else—it wasn't

a substitute for anything else, going to bed with
someone beautiful and tough or eating a delicious
and totally satisfying meal or outwitting a
horribly abusive competitive cretin in conversation
—and it wasn't a grueling act of anguish and pain
getting in touch with all the crabbed secrets of
the psyche and exposing them to the well organized
and systematic scrutiny of some poetic form or
strategy, no it was just writing the fucking poem
folks, just getting into the language and patterns
and rhythms and observations that all the juxta-
positions of letters and syllables and words and
symbols and phrases and images and bits of dialogue
and silly snatches of personal expressionism often
lead to and feeling it all come together like
nothing else ever seems to do with so much easy
grace and crazy variety and satisfying but
seemingly undemanding results. I keep encountering
new reasons why I finally admitted my love for
O'Hara's poetry and the man who wrote it at least
while he was writing (since I never met him and
assume in person he could be as dull or nasty or
moody or silly or whatever as any of the rest of
us) and continue to love the work and even use it
to help me get through my own big city blues now
and then, but more important than the reasons why
I came to love the work is that despite all I was
taught that was intended to keep me from appreciating
work like O'Hara's, O'Hara's work taught me more
and without making it impossible to appreciate
work outside his taste or world of approaches.
That kind of generosity and non-exclusiveness
is rare, and usually unrecognized unless self-
advertised, something O'Hara knew he couldn't do,
or at least never did, trusting in the generosity
of his audience to, a thing he wouldn't do of course
if he had been as cynical and arch as his tone
has made some readers assume he is because they
can't be generous enough to listen to what the tone
says, but only associate it with something
unpleasant and insincere in their lives, perhaps

because they were taught too well that sincerity
is supposed to be too costly (and therefore modest
though obvious) if it's real and cynicism is
supposed to lead to high minded serious conclusions
that never appear to be also silly conglomerations
of inverted cliches and conversational concessions
about the glory of life despite the futility of
"survival." Also, O'Hara is just too "American"
for a lot of folks who think watered down versions
of Spanish surrealism or Eastern European neo-
surrealist angst or extensions of English and
German romanticism or French cultural imperialism
is more American than O'Hara's "madcap pluralism"
to use the phrase of a critic so dumb he confused
"mood" with "mode" and made rigid what O'Hara
so successfully and graciously made fluid at last.

NYC 9/77

It's not nostalgia—it's always there

for Harris Schiff

they're so good to
look at, standing
in the bath tub,
towel around the
hair, powder in
hand, making all
the soft stuff
softer—
            there's only
them & us & the
others, but the others
don't count, except
when they're always
getting in the way—

once outside of
Greenville, South Carolina,
in 1962, two black guys
picked me up hitchin'
on the highway drunk
at 3AM & after some
jiving & juicehead
boasts & fantasies
they took me to some
old shack—woke up the
grumbling ancient black lady
who sold the "dog bite"
& watched me down a
big kitchen tumbler full
& then smile before I passed out

In Greenville I played
piano at "The Ghana"

—"the South's largest
colored resort" with
a troupe that did the
Southern Soul circuit
—Baby June & the
Swinging Shepherds—15
performers—musicians &
dancers—June played the
trumpet & sang & was a
tough dude but affectionate
& protective boss—I met
him when he got salty
at my white presence
& I, pretending to ignore it,
asked him what the
name of one of the foxy
dancers was 'cause I had
to meet her she was so
fine—eventually he
hired me to be the crazy
white boy piano player
running onto the stage with
the rest of them—screaming
in sequined "waiters jackets,"
cummerbunds, crazy colored
show clothes doing a crazy
colored show—with one crazy
white boy pounding
the ivories, standing up,
jumping, dancing while
I comped those chords
and felt the joy of
being my own love
affair with music as
the romance of my air—
the audiences loved it—
I would out sblib the
sblibs & stay in the
background to do it
cause in fact I couldn't
hold a musical candle to

those wonderful motherfuckers

I wish I had hung on to
that outfit—
                    Sidney
Bechet was corny to me
then—though like "Pops"
he was great anyway—
now I can fuck to the music of both,
digging how close they
came to turning it all
around with just their
sound—shit—ain't
that what the ladies
do to me & you?—
turning us around too?—

Mayday means a lot to me
—processions with a
statue of Our Lady &
the girls in white dresses
scattering flowers all
the way—speeches by
the priests against the
Commies who were
having their own parades—
and theirs all started in
Chicago & the fight for
the 8-hour-day—ours in
the forests of Europe &
the worshipping of May
as the start of the good
times of Spring & Summer
—fucking in the woods
all day—
                    dreaming—
like
you in the Southwest
where I'd be so scared

& was when the sheriff
& his boys stopped me
outside Needles in my
van looking for the
Manson family &
suspecting us!—my
hippie friends & wife
& baby—
                guns drawn—
"everybody out with
your hands up!"

—where's Alice & her
bigtime Needles father?

nobody here but us
& these hungry looking
special deputies—I'm
so cold I stick my hands
in my bell bottoms
& some nervous kid's
gun starts shaking
at me!!
                "get 'em
up!"—& I do—
holy shit—they mean
it—I'm the father—
the owner of the van—
the one who sensed the
trouble coming before
the guy driving—I
demand a fucking
explanation—
                "we're
looking for some hippie
murderers—now get
back in this thing &
get the fuck outa
here"—
                you fucker
—I'm a taxpayer &

one time I ran
for sheriff myself—
                    only I'm
also soft & sensitive
& tired of all the
rough stuff—I'm
going home—
                    only
that's been 24
places in the 18 years
since I left my first home
for good—
                    she's outa
                    the tub
                    & into
                    my life
                    again &
                    this is the
                    one I want
                    to stay in—

it's your book did it
Harris—
          so distant
          from my life
                    but—
          goddamit I
          love *the truth*

as we see it
unfolding our moments alone

to share

just out of the Air Force
in 1966 walking down
the main street of a
midwest farm & college
town a bunch of local
boys drive up to where

me & my wife are
strolling & start calling
me names I thought
I'd left behind—"What!?"
I yell, half an ice
cream popsicle in my
hand, the wrapper in
my other hand, both
out a few inches from
my sides—unthreatening
alone with my bride
of two years—I'm 24
& glad to be free of
court martials & brown
shoe reactionaries riding
herd—or trying to—on
me—& now these cow
town boys are piling
out of their old Chevy
to my amazement
not believing they really
were cursing at me—
I don't even know them!
I think—nobody would
take this kind of chance
in a *city*—I might
be *packing* a *piece*!
ready to dust these
dudes off the earth—
only they been watchin'
TV too & one big blond
boy punches me right
in the face—only I don't
go down, I just bounce
back a little on my
feet while he looks
surprised & I drop my
popsicle & paper &
go crazy—grab him
by the hair and
start banging his

head on the fender
of a nearby car—
another, older guy
jumps on my back
yelling "Leggo my
brother" & me screaming
back, not letting go,
"Whadda ya mean,
let go? He just *hit*
me!"—fraternity jocks
& their dates are out of
the local bars to see
the commotion & out
of the Chevy comes
the smallest & oldest
guy—older than me—
maybe as old as I am
now—35—& he coaxes
the boys back into the
car & I see there's four
of them—goddamn!—
I'm glad it's the main
street!—they pull
off and as they do
the one who hit me
leans out & curses me
again—just then a
cop walks up—my
wife, almost hysterical
starts screaming at him
to do something about
what just happened—
he listens then looks at
me & says "Well, with
hair like that, whadda ya
expect?"—& walks
away—Lee cursing *him*
          all the way—

—at home I check the
mirror—it looks

worse—much worse—
than it feels—it's
all swollen & cut
& a black & blue &
yellow eye for sure—
my first one—all
the fights & scuffles
& getting 86'd—proud
of my clean face even
if I'm skinny—now
I'm proud of this—
I was just letting my
hair grow 'cause I was
so happy to be free of
the A.F. regulations—
still in my pointy-toed
shoes & tight pants—
I didn't know I was
part of a movement—
but now I got my
badge—the next
meeting I went to
about Viet Nam I gave
a little rap on being
an ex-serviceman
getting beat up by
kids who hadn't even
voted or paid taxes or
been drafted yet—I
was a big hit—and
it was all true—
I meant it—my
face was fucked up
from it—my fellow
anti-war activists
were impressed—I needed
a way to remember
being fast with your
hands wasn't always
the answer—any more

I take her picture
with her hair still
wet & tangled &
it's sexy & different
& all about how we
see things—not in
the magazine ads
or latest fads—punk
or chic or SoHo elite—
it's about how dis-
tracted she is & tense
—her father's dying
like the rest of us
only he knows when
or about when & is
fighting with nothing—
the words of strangers—
promises—treatments—
operations—only to
delay or maybe
not even that useful—maybe
only to offer the appearance
of stalling the effects of
what we know will get
some of us—the epidemic
of cancer—industrial
civilization's answer to
our polluting the rest
of life & the world's
natural forces—I don't
mean anymore with
that than my own
frustration & anger—

       shit—
it's like
Mayday—
       a call for
      help—
the Haymarket riot—
all the dead workers

(Mayday 1937 in Colorado
—the film of those
cops arriving at the
strikers picnic to open
fire on unarmed men,
and women, and
children—all that
death—deliberate &
against *us—our
kind*—
          continues—
and us
against   each other—
          your book again
               Harris—
     "running for cover"
she covers her frustrations
with the rituals of covering
her body only to uncover
it soon enough to lose
it—or so I hope—
& believe—for a while
with mine—
               Ted says his
               "bye bye Jack"
               telegram
ain't the same
as Duchamp's to Picabia—
he's right of course—
it's never the same—
Winch is an orphan—
you're an orphan now—
me too—& this isn't
even her "real" father—
it's her "step-father"—
only the only one she
knows—& she loves
him—& he's dying—&
taking some time to do it
in—the changes making
him mad, depressed, dis-
tracted, determined, deadly—

shit—does all this "art"
really do anything to help
me outwit my fate?—I
wanna think I'm great—
& sometimes do—& some-
times you & others—
like her & not only for
me—but her father?—
what can he tell me?—
what can I do for
him? —what does it matter
to either of us?—with
her between us & death
so close—I don't
wanna die for a long
time & when I do I
want it to be gentle—
but I know there ain't
shit I can do—my
grandmother would say
"If you're born to be
shot, you'll never be hung"
I wish we knew—

                  only
he knows & it must be
driving him crazy—it's
getting to her—& that's
getting to me—&
into this & therefore to
you—who knows what
I'm talking about that's
why I'm "talking"—not
"walking" like I sometimes
do—I mean in my work—

her work—it moves me like
the books I love—including
yours—never do—her
music especially—is that
enough?—to live with &
love & be loved by a
person who creates music

103

that few get to hear but
me & it moves me beyond
my greatest expectations
for any art?—is this
the Paradise they sing
about in *Saturday Night
Fever* or Reznikoff
wrote of in his Adam
& Eve in the contemporary
city—New York in the
'30s?—poem? I read in
the late '50s & recognized
(so have in me still as
I will yours & all I ex-
perience that shocks me
with its clarity—I *love*
to *see* the edges *and* the
blurs—I'd like to be in
Frank O'Hara's mind when
he's drunk & in love & the
city is out of focus but
gorgeous & his—when he
wrote those things—some
of them—I was drunk
too & in love & wandering
the same streets—a kid—
away from Jersey & home—
immersed in my romantic
self-pity & incredibly intelligent perceptions about
life & wages of concern &
sensitivity—it was the
'50s—you were in the
Bronx maybe?—or on
the same Manhattan
streets—I slept in the
park, walked in the
rain, was afraid of
anyone as graceful &
erudite as O'Hara or
I can be sometimes now—

& she—
she was getting to know
her new dad—jealous of
him & his son—she was
a little kid already
planning her escape—
while we were practicing
ours—

      this time three
      years ago I came
      back—to the
      city—for good—
(drove my Toyota back to
DC to my ex-wife's
house—who hasn't driven
in 15 years—& gave her
the car keys & title—letting
my license expire—through
with my "ace" driving days—
& I loved driving in the
city—that's what I'd do
now—if it was then—
drive around for a few
hours, shifting gears hard
& fast, outflanking
traffic, judging tight
spaces like a cat, feeling
the limits with my
shoulders as if I were
the car—I loved driving
—making love to the
street with my body-
machine—but I love
so much else I had to
give it up—I was
coming out the other
end anyway brother
& dig it—we are too
often the ones who die
first or use it up fast
or never get to it—

105

not me—
I want to do it all
once as fast and intense as I can
& then move on—
                    but
I'm here now—back
where I started or
started starting—
& 3 moves later in 3 years
it's Mayday, the
anniversary of my
farewell to DC where
I "came out" not only
as a lover of men but
a lover of men who loves
women in all those ways
as well and did so
first and will always—
I don't know what that
means—it confuses me
too—but I know I feel
good about feeling good
about me & loving the
way she smells &
moves & feels & lets me
get close as I can—
I loved it sometimes with the men—
but not as easily—as
gracefully—as romantically
—that's it—there was too
much cynicism & con-
fusion there—& not just
dope—that's maybe
the thing I've clung to
most—turned on the
first time by a black
dude at the Figaro
Cafe—McDougal &
Bleecker—in 1959—I was
17—always in love—
romantically with

106

women—brotherly
with men—
          Charles Wicks
—"Charlie"—"Cochise"—
the football star of
my youth—Columbia
High—when I was in
grammar school—the
toughest spade in town—
maybe the toughest
period—no white guy
ever tried—he was
beautiful—from a
poor family, with a
wife like a picture &
all the women he
could do—& he did—
& told me how he did
& who & what I should
do & I was already doing
by the time we were
friends in 1957 or '58—
in 1972 I realized how
much I loved that dude—
& saw him again then—
a little paunchy &
pushing 40—me just
30 & newly into my
own beauty—so late—
but *in time* goddamnit
in time—
          Charles was so
sweet—but always noble
& generous & offhand in
his easy masculinity & pride
—I never knew a kinder
man—he helped me see
that kindness could be
more than rules & gestures —
& so did you—& I hardly
know you—& maybe it

isn't always true—but
it made me think of
all this & you in it—
it's the first Mayday in
12 years I haven't done
something to commemorate—
& now I have—thank you

NYC April 28–May 2 1978

assembly line breaks—
the critic combing our cells as though on the
table's keys, wallet (worn)
coins, comb, did not
imply empty pockets or
empty (clean) ashtray non-
smoker or extra tidy guest—
the bad tasting, worse
smelling water (only
matched by the dogs here)—
empty case for eyeglasses—someone reading or watching
TV—or writing in a note-
book the choices of a career
in self-observational anticipation—*life*—like that—

making a lamp out of a
milk can in Virginia—
out near the mountains—
kids at the swimming hole
of 1978 using the language
of the beatnik bar of 1958—
a hairbrush—a Christopher Isherwood book (early and
relatively obscure)—the
sudden burst of '60s "rock"
from outside competing with
the river ("born under a bad
sign")—dirty socks—crickets in gangs—the nastiness of
flying ants—the "pleasures" of the country life outweighed
by the inconveniences for
those addicted to the "pleasures"
of city life—open doorway
to adjoining bathroom that
serves the teenaged daughter's room as well—more
aged than teened—not old but
older—her yellow bathing-suit and big boned girlishness—
the remnant's of a doper's life—

the single wildflower in the cut
glass vase—the blues base of
most rock—tiresome "black"
derivation—unlike the real country origins of non-
blacks—sun supporting
somehow the haze that defuses its explosive
impact on everything here—
more trees than people in Manhattan—no more horizons
outside the stereo or TV and
those all inside now—the
end of a century before it
has ended—we look up once
before—

C OUNTING

The party was in a loft, not in the now chic neighborhood known as "SoHo," although he was sure real estate agents listed it as such, but closer to Chinatown, almost in Chinatown. The only people on the streets were Chinese and bums. The old factory buildings had none of the nostalgic ambiance of the prefabricated cast iron ones that allegedly attracted artists to the area in the first place, and now were all clearly marked on the tourist maps and guidebooks, they just looked like old factories and warehouses. The one the party was in was just as rundown as the others. The entrance included a door for the freight elevator, but when he finally found the buzzer and rang, another door made the electric noise that always came close to panicking him, as did fewer and fewer things the more years that piled up between him and the past no one he knew now was aware of. Loud dogs, screeching tires, backfiring trucks, any kind of siren but especially those horrible devices they made for cars that were supposed to scare away thieves but only woke up the neighborhood in which the car was parked, and some threatening gestures and intonations from people on the streets. And the buzz of an electric lock being opened for him, but only for so long, so that he had to grab fast for the doorknob on the heavy metal door, painted black, and rush through a small alcove-like entry way to grab the second, inside door that was also buzzing, even louder, as though the little brick lined foyer were some sort of audial device for magnifying it, and grab that before the buzzing stopped and he'd have to go back out and start the process all over again, embarrassed at not having made it or at running into other guests on their way in and turning around to come in with them, or just facing the streets again.

By the time he was inside the inside door and on his way up the stairs that was all there was on the other side of it, he began to settle down and look around him a little more leisurely. It was a pretty raw looking place still, but better than the outside. The brick walls were all covered with dry plaster dust and the floors were covered with plaster dust and maybe sawdust, but they were freshly sanded, and whatever factory dirt and soot may have layered them it was nowhere in sight. Even the exposed pipes in the corner of each landing on the stairs, as he climbed up the three

111

floors to the party, showed no signs of the years, decades, probably a century or more, of whatever industrial activity had defined this place to previous generations of daytime inhabitants. The only thing that had probably been around this time of night, in this building before now, was a night watchman and the rodents, whether mice or rats he wasn't sure, though the trays of poison in the shadows of the steps and hallways looked too big for mice. When he got to the loft that the party was in, there was someone there to take his coat, not the hostess, who he hardly knew anyway but a younger woman, equally as attractive, with the makeup of a model and the clothes of a college bohemian, or of what he assumed a college bohemian might be dressing like these days, tightly fitted fatigue pants with the big pockets on the thighs and some sort of sneakers, probably imported and expensive, and some sort of nondescript sweater reminiscent of the sweaters every beatnik "chick" seemed to sport back in the days when he was first becoming acquainted with this city and falling in love with its women. He could fall in love with this kid who was taking his coat, except she hardly noticed him, smiled politely, even warmly, and then was gone with his coat, the old three-quarter length black leather that once marked him as a kind of outlaw not only from the square, then straight, then and always uptown worlds, but just as much from the Beat and Hippie and Glitter and SoHo scenes. He realized at some point in the past few years that at least that vestige of his original style, or the one he first left home with, was finally hip, in a less authentic form as "punk," when the only reason he had dressed that way, spent so much time working so hard to earn the money to buy a real classy leather, was to overcome, avoid at all costs, the image of a "punk" and instead convey the quiet but solid strength of the real studs of the white street life of the fifties after whom the "punks" styled themselves, but with so much less class.

Now here he was, underneath the leather, without it, walking into one of the most elegant lofts he had ever been in, the design so spare and yet so warm, unlike the sterile imitations of Brancusi's original of the SoHo mode. He really felt like he was walking into someone's home, only the room was full of strangers he would have to confront in one way or another, and their various styles were making his head whirl, as often happened these days when he walked into a room full of strangers. It was as if the old *Twilight Zone* stories of time traveling had all been cut up and randomly collaged together to form this crazy montage of the styles of the past three decades, all of which he had felt himself to be not only an active participant and contributor to, but one of the ultimate expressions of. Only who knew that, besides himself and the few people he knew long enough and intimately enough to trust with his self-assessments. No one here, that was for sure. He was folding up the cuffs of the dress white shirt he had recently bought in an old clothes store, just like the dress white shirts he had worn to weddings and dances when he was 16 in 1958 or 20 in 1962. Now it was 1979 and he had to pay someone more than he had paid back then for a shirt he might have kept all these years and had in probably as good a condition since the call for a shirt so classy was rare for him. Banlon had been more the daily uniform back then, where was that touch of the past in the current "retro" styles, nobody at this party in banlon, he should have worn that. When the cuffs were neatly and precisely turned up a double fold, he put his hands in the pockets of his pleated baggies. In the shop that sold him the shirt there were pleated slacks from the '40s that the clerk actually referred to as "baggies," a term he had privately used for the slacks he was wearing for years, though he thought it publicly only referred to the old surfers' cutoffs the Beach Boys sang about along with the "huarache sandals." But now pleats were chic again, and he was glad, he always liked the pocket room they gave you, seeing himself and Humphry Bogart in his mind, both in pleated pants with their hands in their pockets looking relaxed but ready. He had tried to emulate that style for years, then one day in 1969 he had no choice but to assume it for real or find himself in the custody of the authorities that had always plagued him, but suddenly meant more than a reprimand or cold eye, in 1969 they meant prison and possibly death. He had some bellbottomed pants then, pants he was sure would soon be hot again as the movie *Hair* and others like it reinstated the sixties as a bland enough time to reintroduce into styles without meaning again. But the pair of slacks that most made him feel like the star he had always seen himself to be in his own imagination, and yet left him feeling comfortable and relaxed enough to outwit those who would take away his freedom to even wear, let alone buy, let alone find the store and browse around in it where he found them. They were on sale, no one seemed to want these wide legged pleated even cuffed slacks in 1969. They weren't old, reused, or from some musty warehouse of the forties, they were some designers attempt to bring back pleats too soon. He or she lost out to the times, but now here he was at this party where at least a fifth of the men were also wearing pleats, only none quite so comfortably familiar as his, for he had been wearing his to special events for ten years, and they still looked classy enough to wear a classy white shirt with and feel you were really stepping out into a party where people would be happy to look at you, to admire your good taste and sexy style. At least that's what he hoped, although it was apparent so did almost everyone else at the party.

He found the table that served as a bar and poured himself some Perrier, one of the few benefits of the seventies was Perrier at parties so that non-drinkers, or reformed ones like himself, might have something to hang on to, to fill up with, besides the overwhelming challenge of club soda or the syrupy sweetness of ginger ale. He looked around the room once he had swallowed some Perrier and tried to decipher the various signals and styles that had felt like an unexpected wave does when you only want to go in for a lazy swim. The women were outrageously sexy, for the most part, and confident enough about it to be checking out themselves and each other as aggressively as they checked out the men. The men weren't so physically attractive, but their own brand of confidence filled the room as well, in fact seemed to be the underlying foundation of the atmosphere. There's a lot of successful people here, he thought. A lot of the men were older than him, and he was feeling old lately even though he wasn't quite forty yet. But they didn't look like him, at least to him. They had the style of businessmen, even though several were in very casual dress, from blue jeans—or what they used to call them when he stopped wearing them at 14 in 1956, dungarees—to more "retro" styled straight-legged pants. The kind of skinny-legged slacks he wore for a while in the early sixties, but didn't remember too many others wearing outside of rural highschool kids and urban black ones. Gary Busey had forever altered Buddy Holly's image by wearing those kind of tight legged skinny high water pants in *The Buddy Holly Story*, when the picture in his mind of the man his friends all said he looked a little like back then, back when Holly and The Crickets were the private property of a handful of teenagers and one or two radio stations, his private picture of Holly always had him in much looser legged styles of the fifties, but no one cared about these things unless you were like him, so long a fugitive, a literal impostor, your recognition of the slightest

114

stylistic discrepancy might be the key to another several years of freedom or a lifetime of the loss of same. Maybe that was only an excuse, he was always aware of style, even long before 1969 and the events that turned him into someone else forever, he was aware when he aligned himself with the politicos, so much the definition of those particular times, he didn't like their style, it wasn't his or the people they thought they were going to lead into a better future, or even earlier in 1959, in a high school where, like all high schools, the "in" crowd mainly meant money and a style just as anathema to him as the unhip politicos, the style of boys and girls who found his style so amusing they could make jokes about what he might use such pointy-toed shoes for, like killing cockroaches in corners, while the boys lugged their heavy cordovans or later wingtips around like special forms prefabricated for their future lives as the businessmen and doctors and lawyers whose money and bad taste would determine what might last or at least represent the times they passed through together, and wouldn't you know it would be their pale, inaccurate, foundationless interpretation of the style they had found so much below them then. No matter what, money talks bullshit walks was still the rule. At least the ladies seemed to understand it here. The men so obviously understood it they could appear cocky and even tough in a way that implied there was never a need to prove it in any physical manner, despite their bald heads or aging bodies or unappealing looks and manners of speech. They didn't care, this was a party for successful people, that's why they were here, and their success made them right, and being right meant they could relax about what they looked like, as long as they were clean, everyone was certainly clean enough. The women were something else, they still cared about being sexy, in fact the way they were dressed and moved around in that way of dressing it might seem that's all they cared about. But when you talked to them it soon became clear that the sexy looks were just their way of getting a foot in the door. These were tough, aggressive, ambitious, and successful post-"liberation" women, this was 1979 even if the woman he first talked to looked like 1956. She had on an outfit that only a very successful and well-protected movie star might have worn in 1956, but nonetheless it took him back somehow to those days and his first fantasies about Marilyn Monroe and the women he might know when he broke loose from home and neighborhood. This woman had dark hair, and was thin, nothing like the voluptuous and

115

somehow cheery sexuality of Marilyn Monroe. But the outfit she wore, some kind of silky gold material that almost looked metallic, in a slit skirt that was so tight you could see contours of her less than voluptuous hips and ass and pelvis, and the slit went high enough to give you a beautiful and clear view of a stocking leg all the way up to the upper thigh, the place that could almost make him pray, at least worship, when he was 15, and now she made him feel like he still could at 37. He couldn't guess her age, that was another thing these confused styles did, made him unsure of something he was never that sure of anyway. Her dark hair was piled on top of her head, she had some sort of feathery or furry thing over her shoulders which he kept from dusting coke off the mirror they snorted it from later in the evening when he found himself on line with her to consume those other lines, of which he hadn't nearly the number of chances to consume as the rest of these party goers, or so he assumed. But now she told him no she wasn't an actress or performer, she was a writer, screen writer and novelist with a book due out later in the year from a very reputable house and she had a very reputable agent and was on her way to some sort of monetary and celebrity success she was convinced because she was so convincing. If she could look like some sort of crazy new movie star and rekindle in him the fantasies of half a lifetime ago and not even be intending to use that to become famous and rich, he was convinced she would achieve whatever it was she had in mind to achieve. He wasn't so sure he was convincing in return. He told her he was a poet and an actor. Two professions for which the monetary rewards were so rare and for which there was so much competition, he could get away with talking about it without having to flash any credentials or tell them where they could see or get ahold of his work. It allowed him a certain leeway in style too and gave him access to a world in which the authorities, if they still cared about him, would be least likely to spend their time, it was awkward still the same, without any real success to his credit her interest waned, in him, but not in herself, as she let him know the philosophy behind commercial compromising, "it's all ego," she was saying, and when he asked what was, she replied "resistance." He thought maybe she meant him, only to what she might think he was resisting he didn't know—her? commercial success? political resistance? He had noticed a few old politicos from the sixties in the room while she was talking and he couldn't figure it out. What were they doing at a party like this.

Well, they were the famous ones anyway, the ones who had seemed then and still seemed to be able to make a living out of their permanent stance as professional rebels against "the system," which so many of the others in this room were such an obviously integral part of. He just wanted to tell this lady he'd like to lick the excess coke from her sexy little nose and lips, but didn't, out of his learned hesitancy with strangers, and the often stupid consequences of involvement with a stranger who might never understand his need for anonymity and rootlessness. Although, she looked tough enough and direct enough to probably let him know if she was interested and probably be self-centered enough and self-protective enough to be glad to see him go when she was through with him. Maybe. He wouldn't find out right away anyway, as she seemed to find something more important to attend to and walked away—had she said something he failed to respond to, or had he said something insulting or just dull?

At any rate she was gone, and as he searched the room for another lone figure to approach, apprehensive about trying to insinuate himself into the little clusters of people seemingly so well acquainted with each other, he noticed one of the men was doing the same. As he caught his eye, he realized it was another fugitive, only unlike him, this one was famous, or at least notorious among some scenes, it was Abbie Hoffman for sure. The little bit of plastic surgery Hoffman had written about was obvious, the eyes and the manner were still the same, despite the slightly eccentric businessman's style he had assumed. He wondered if his own act had scared Abbie, made him see in his eyes a look that another fugitive might mistake for authority, or some sort of recognition of a world that only cops and robbers understood. Shit, even his romantic fantasy of himself on the lam and all these pretty people not understanding such a thing went out the window, here was someone not only equally underground in terms of the world, but famous enough to be still recognized and most likely known by several if not all the other people in the room. By now Abbie was talking to another beautiful woman, his style had little sexual appeal and yet the woman seemed fascinated. He was sure she knew who Hoffman really was, what if she knew who he really was, it probably wouldn't seem as fascinating, unless she were a reporter or a veteran of the really heavy shit of only a decade ago. But he doubted that, he doubted she was old enough, but then, he couldn't tell, there was a bit of the sixties about her

117

long hair, even though it was braided, and the dress she wore had an earthy peasant quality that reminded him of the dresses some of the more hippie-ish political women wore back then, but the make up, that was the new times, when a woman could paint her face for her own reasons, no longer just to please a man, now, perhaps, especially here, to please a roomful of men, a world full of men, and the other women who were trying to do the same and could appreciate a successful attempt in a competitor, because they understood there was room for more now, they were doing it their way now, they could afford to allow each other the space to do it too, the screen writers and novelists, the lawyers and photographers, even the actresses and activists, wasn't Jane Fonda the most famous leftist celebrity, and weren't Diane Keaton and Meryl Streep the screen and stage extensions of this new feminine well-roundedness, two beautiful women whose beauty somehow seemed to depend on their sense of themselves as more than beautiful or other than beautiful like smart and curious and artistically sophisticated and accomplished. But weren't they still all WASPs and just as prone to compromises for the sake of their continued success as anyone else commercially viable? He had to get out of those thoughts quick, as another lone man introduced himself to him as a recent returnee from Africa. Shit, where was the adventure in *his* life, so energetic yet conservatively constrained for the past ten years, while this guy made a killing in Zaire doing construction work that could lead to homes in the South of France and invitations to parties like this one. He was finding the old homeland inviting, especially the pretty faces and unadulterated coke and crazy speedy competitiveness of the capital of the world. That was the most interesting thing, maybe. That New York had come around again, finally, transformed and ready, no more nostalgic for the seeming peaks of post WWII or mid-'50s or the go-go years of pre-collapse Nixon sixties. New York had finally overcome the '70s, before anywhere else, not like San Francisco in the '60s and still there, or L.A. in the '50s and still there, or Paris in the '20s, or even New York in the '40s, this was different again, and this loft and these people were the proof, New York was on top again, and these people were part of the reason and part of the result. He wished he could say the same for himself, but how high can a fugitive go. Well, he knew how high a fugitive could get, he never drank booze and he only smoked limited amounts of what the first spade who had turned him onto it in 1958 called "gage."

In fact, when the hostess's boyfriend told him there was some dope in the kitchen that was so strong you couldn't smoke a whole joint, he had replied "Then I guess I'll skip it. I like to smoke, so I try to avoid stuff you *can't* smoke." Only to be directed to the bedroom where the coke was going down, or up the noses of these successful '70s people. Coke he could take without too many worries, you didn't give much away on coke besides your energy and ego. He could afford that, even a fugitive gets into dancing all night and feeling pretty good at it. He shared some lines with the lady in the gold slit skirt and kept her furry feathery thing around her neck from knocking the coke onto the floor. Then he found himself staring at an incredibly sexy blond in silver lamé pants so tight her legs could have never lived up to the image of them the pants created. He tried to stop staring, realizing that kind of intense interest in a woman was as much a throwback to the fifties as the style she was approximating in her incredibly tight pants and high stiletto heels. Did she know the kind of guys who went with girls who dressed as close to that as they dressed outside of Hollywood back then? They were like he had been and was for just a second there, obvious and unrelentingly attracted in the most obvious ways to anything with curves that enjoyed showing them. These women enjoyed it, no doubt about it, look at the way they were dressed. Even the few who seemed to be into more "new wave" or "punk" styles, short cropped hair and unevenly at that, various assortment of grubby TV versions of the decade from '55 to '65, their magazine and mass media interpretations of something much more subtle and unique than they seem able to reach, even these punkettes so cool and above these conventionally successful people put it out there for him to see and consider before they left for whatever bleak version of the future helped them make it through the night. They probably wouldn't even be impressed with the fact he was wanted in fifty states and several countries for the bombing of a building that had seemed to represent so much of what he hated and constantly confronted back then, they'd probably wonder why he bothered with a piece of real estate like that in the first place and didn't just go off and pretend the music was enough, even after it created the same competitiveness, the same commercial compromises, the same ego bumping and groupie degradation as whatever came between.

Back in the kitchen, the "help," the pretty girl who had taken his coat, was now finishing up the special chili, hotter and more exotic than any diner's cheap version, or even the kind the collective had subsisted on so often in the days when communal living seemed the answer to the problems surviving in a hostile world you were working to permanently alter but meanwhile had to pass through presented. Meanwhile the world was changing anyway, only their way. They co-opted the styles and even the slogans and let you cop out climb on and cash in or else cling to your outmoded ideals and hopes. Even now, ten years later, on the verge of an obviously about to be political decade again, the stars were all the same—here was Jerry Rubin, still living on that, and the guest speakers at the anti-nuke rally would be Jane Fonda and Tom Hayden, who had once told you in all seriousness that "the people" were "crazy" and that's why we had to do it for them, and now pretended at the Academy Awards to be one of those "people" by refusing to wear the obligatory formal stuff, whether old style black tie or new style velour jacket, just plain old real folks Tom in a plain old blue serge suit, or whatever. Nobody gets any younger, but some folks get more famous. Like the woman in the slit gold skirt, these people understood the post-Warholian axioms, art, just like everything else in this society in these times, is business, so the real art is doing business originally and well. But in a public way, not like the conservative traditionalists of the real business world, the ones who actually ran the thing, but the new celebs, the overnight killings on the stock market of salable image whether of the product or the producer, who cared, as long as it meant fame and fame could be turned into some sort of financial security no matter how fleeting.

The help was dancing in the kitchen to the disco music coming from the main space in the loft, more or less the "living room" although it was more like a ballroom, and few people were dancing, but the help was, and like a funky spade to boot, this blonde-haired, no-one-could-be-more-Aryan girl, late teenager or early twenties young woman, moving her body like a back up singer in a tough small-sized city black club's favorite group, better than he could do in his most sblibby gone nigger street days. And serving him some special successful chili while she did it. My my, how times do change and yet, the blondes he knew in 1956 were doing their best to dance like spades as well only they didn't admit it so obviously in their movements or feel so unselfconscious about it in their lower class and lower-middle class insecurities. They did party though. One thing his family had given him, his neighborhood, his background, had been the love of a party, and the partying spirit, parties were the one place where you could be as outrageous and asinine as you wanted to be, as you had to be to make your contribution to the "good time," singing, dancing, and getting high one way or another. Letting it out and letting go. None of these people though looked any higher than him, and they were drinking, and he wasn't, and some of them were doing other stuff besides the coke in the bedroom, coming out of the bathrooms in pairs and ménage-à-trois's with far away looks in their eyes, eyes that he tried smiling into but only could do it half way.

The woman he had first noticed when he scanned the room as the true beauty of the night, was all alone. He leaned against the wall beside her and offered her some chili. Would a woman so classy and successful and competitive and ambitious and looking like an ex-model, free now to put on the pounds that made her so much more inviting than any model, want to share a stranger's chili no matter how spicy and exotic and with a silver spoon out of an antique china bowl? No. He tried some other words and looks that meant to say how happy he was to be standing next to someone so lovely, but however it came out she only looked slightly panicked and in search of something other than him so that when she walked away he wasn't surprised or even hurt, just curious as to what could have drawn her so powerfully. When he finished the chili and put the dish down and turned the corner she had disappeared behind, he almost stepped on her, leaning against another wall talking to the guy he was sure was Abbie Hoffman, and as he passed them by pretending to have a great need to use the bathroom he wondered if she knew that was Abbie Hoffman and that was what had drawn her, or if Abbie was pretending to be someone just as important or more important and that was it, or if she was in fact an old friend of Abbie's and this was how they met, or if she just found guys who looked like an older, less flamboyant but equally short and unmoviestarlike Abbie attractive.

In the bathroom he checked himself out in the mirror, decided he was probably one of the best looking guys at the party, then washed his hands to have something to do and decided looks didn't mean the same thing any more or at least for him or at least at these kinds of parties or at least to women like these so attractive and aggressive and ambitious they all turned up to party with mostly older men who were obviously richer than he had ever been or hoped to be. Maybe that gave him away, maybe it was obvious he had no future, or none that they could benefit from, maybe he looked like a man just passing through and just looking. Or, maybe it really was like high school and the 1950s everyone seemed so anxious to recapture at least in looks, and this was just a rich kids' party where the other rich kids indulged their taste for exotic intoxicants but didn't seem to let it affect them in any lasting way, they still seemed in control of themselves and their spaces, and in their cocky sense of being at home in the world, especially among their own kind—the fellow and sister successful—never seemed to let down their sense of their own importance, never let their hair down, never really got down and seemed to share in some communal fun that rested only on the sense of being one of us and surviving another day, another week, another year of paying endless dues just to survive. Maybe that was it, if any of these folks had paid any dues they seemed all paid up now, while the rest of us, the rest of us owed our souls to the company store, like Tennessee Ernie Ford sang in the song that made him famous and from which he was able to fashion a life and career not unlike these folks, and never matched by anything as successful or interesting again. The woman had said "It's all ego," and he had answered "Maybe it's other things too, like your sense of what's right." What's right? Thousands of people were demonstrating the very next day in Washington DC against nuclear power in an outpouring of outrage not seen in these numbers since the time that had determined his life ever since. And he wouldn't be there. He couldn't afford to be anywhere there would so obviously be secret agents and plainclothes cops and conspirators and provocateurs and all the ugly aspects of the powers that these people so smugly thought they offered some alternative to, or perhaps admitted to themselves they were lucky to be a part of rather than on the other side looking in and only dreaming.

He finally found a woman who seemed to want to talk to him and talk about things he could understand. Like who were all these people at this party and what was fame and success all about. It turned out she was writing a book about it—all these women writers who looked more like movie sex symbols, what did that say about the times—about the effects of fame and success on those few, or many, who self-destruct. She emphasized the ones who really did it, like Marilyn Monroe or Hart Crane or James Dean or Janis Joplin as opposed to those she felt only seemed to, and in passing threw out the opinion that "If you're really going to do it you've done it by 35," and he immediately thought of those who had done it later, like the poet everyone asked him about now when he told them he was a poet—John Ashbery—hadn't he made it much later and in fact written his best work, most of his work, after 35, or was that only the illusion created by the lag that existed in publishing that made those whose works were so integral to their own times they couldn't be appreciated without them, only successful when those times were exhumed rather than the few years after the times had passed and the book finally came out, or Ford Madox Ford who he couldn't even read before he was 35 and despite his enormous output Ford didn't write the few great works he created until he was 40, at least, or how many others to set against the precociousness of a Rimbaud or Elvis. That was it, the SoHo sense of hi-tech and minimalism originally discovered by some of the early modernists of this century, and the repetitive and primitive patterns and forms of midcentury music—rock'n'roll and other versions—and popular culture in general—TV commercials and serials, movie make believe and superficial ease, all contributed to a true style of the times, you could see it in the fashion ads or even in the ways that disco extended the party music aspects of black sounds into the big business of specialized markets for maximum profits, the day of the total consumer of Burroughs' worst fantasies a fact, and yet still sexy, still figuring ways to be rebellious and make money too, still fighting the overwhelming odds and coming through for the rest of us to admire and counting on it, counting it, counting. That's what they had always done better than him, counting. All he could count were the years, two more now than the 35 he could have made it clear by. Although he had, perhaps, perhaps that building turning into flames and debris in the dawn light over a midwestern campus had been the clear and undeniable mark he had made on his times and for all history and no one would know. Maybe he should tell this lady, get her to write an article for *The Village Voice* or *The SoHo News* about him, hell, even *Newsweek* or *Time*, a cover story on what has happened to the old radicals, the real ones, the ones that took it so seriously they either died or withered away in prisons or have gone so far underground you can't tell them from the rest of the hordes coking up and dancing to the rhythm of the Sisters Sledge. Maybe he should tell her what his first 35 years had added up to. But he didn't know himself. He could never add well. That was the part of counting they had a hold on. They could put it together and get the right answer and save themselves a lot of trouble. He could only count. There goes another ten. Which adds up to—he didn't know what. Just another ten going by, even in this room, drawing his eye, by the tens, walking by, those '40s shoes on that woman with the '50s hairdo, that late '60s style long hair on the man with the woman with the early '60s punk hair going around the corner where the '70s style beauty was still probably rapping with Abbie Hoffman or someone who looked so much like him it was deliberate.

Only she wasn't there, Abbie was standing alone, knocking on the bathroom door, no one there, turning to say he thought his girlfriend was in there, she must have gone down without him, which was the door that led out? Him pointing it out to the man he was sure was Abbie now, with that voice, who else could it be, but what kind of a fugitive couldn't remember the door that led out, that he had come in through, or was that part of some silly act that wouldn't fool anybody who really cared, which maybe meant the authorities didn't really care anymore, and none of them would ever be caught unless they slipped up somewhere else, got in trouble for something new and it came out in the fingerprinting or the recognition of some super-dedicated cop. He offered Abbie "good luck" as he showed him the door but Abbie just nodded and left without returning the good wishes. He probably couldn't tell a fellow fugitive unless the gestures were encoded in some obvious and deliberate way. Or maybe he could and that was his way of making contact, sharing the misery of an anonymity that left out all chances for that kind of fame again, unless you were caught or pulled off something even bigger. Maybe Abbie meant, where was the door that led out for all of them. No, he wasn't that loaded on the coke and the little bit of smoke he'd tried after all. Abbie was disoriented, just like him, only Abbie was among friends he had to assume, otherwise he wouldn't have been there and some of them had even been recognizable from the old days, still holding out as pros on the anti-establishment lecture circuit. Abbie had needed help to find his way out, not him. He needed help to find his way in.

Fuck me in the heart acceptance!!!

Fuck me in the heart
in the acceptance
in the part
I fuck you in the heart with
when I fuck you in the fantasy
of childhood acceptance
of the cosmic connection
with our deaths
that fuck us crazy in the end.
Fuck the 1950s
till they're over and over at last
and the best of the 1970s
that refused to give in to the past
and the worst of the 1960s
that I refuse to believe was all bombast and gesture
I still live that dream
in my fucking for pleasure
fucking guilt in the ass of a brain without hindsight
or quality control
or speed monitor
or check-in-the-mirror devices.
Fuck vices
fuck vice-like grips
on the imaginations that led us here
in their failure to fuck themselves silly.
Fuck silly
and dirty
and angry
and nice.
Fuck me in my past
and my dreams
and my lights
the ones that keep blinking
in back of my brain
that ignore all the warnings
to get back on the train
that I fucked

and I fucked
to get off in the first place,
and fuck all the ladies
and men who deserve it
I'm here
at your service
if you'll only preserve it
the fucking I saw
in all your beginnings.
Big
innings
for
fucking
that's the sport
I grew up with,
I don't want to die
without fucking you all
in the ass
of your past
inhibitions.

M*y image*

So you think I'm cool?
I'm a fool you asshole.
Mean? Shit, I almost cream
at the thought of tenderness.
You think I'm some sort of
sissy? Not after I stick
this nail file in your eye
motherfucker. A faggot?
Ask your old lady, now that
she can't take your straight
stick no more. A whore?
I never took nothin more
for it than a meal, you
can steal my love and my
lovin with plain niceness.
On the other hand, I got
plans, and if you're part
of them, get a good hold
on your heart or your hard on.
I look like a nice boy to you?
A nice looking, clean living,
regular shoe? I've been the
star attraction at the freak
show and zoo. I got me
a j.d. badge "they" call a
tattoo. You think you can
see me, but I ain't lookin
at you. I'm talkin bout
m-m-m-m-m-m-m-m-my image,
and how whatever it is it
ain't true, only whatever
you think I'm not gonna do.
I'm the ugliest fucker that
ever looked good and the
baddest cocksucker that ever
stood up for the saints and
the softies like I really am,

only once in a while I gotta
kick out the jams and be
rock 'n' roll history before you
were born and get high forty
ways and never reform. I'm
so smart I'm a jerk and
so hip I'm still starving,
I telegraph your secret
fantasies when I flirt
and then jerk off to anal
retentive jargon. I'm so
blasé I'm frantic, so passé
I'm hot, so nervous I'm
calm, so mellow I'm not.

That wasn't my life;
that was my image.

LOOK THE FIFTIES WEREN'T ANYTHING LIKE THAT

"Look, the fifties weren't anything like that." It made him feel old to be talking to this woman like he was. He wasn't that fucking old. He had just spent the night with her, made her feel good, made her body light up and glow in the dark of her two bit cockroach haven, the kind he had once shared with a girl her age almost twenty years earlier. He was fucking old, maybe, to her, and maybe he should shut up about "what it was really like back then," sounding like his father describing a time when cars and radios and all the things he had taken for granted were new. Only it wasn't cars and radios, inventions they were talking about, it was "style." He couldn't stop himself.

"Nobody even knew who James Dean was. I mean, I never even heard of the guy till after he died. What the fuck did we need to see Dean for, he shoulda seen us, 'cause that's who he was trying to act like or look like...or something." She looked like she might not even be paying attention any more. They sat across from each other at a dirty kitchen table covered with stains and pieces of paper, envelopes, lists, dirty glasses, the remains of the breakfast they had just shared. "Hey," he almost whispered as he leaned across the chasm of years and the kitchen debris of her cockroach haven, "it doesn't matter anyway. You're better than James Dean" he was stroking the side of her face with his outstretched hand, she didn't seem to be into it, he was trying so hard to be more than just the guy who fucked her the morning after they fucked—the "old" guy, the guy who had despised all this "punk" stuff and pseudo-fifties bullshit styles—he was trying to be nice. "You're better than any of..." she got up from the table abruptly, with a scowl, leaving his hand sticking out in the air over her empty plate. He watched her as she stepped through her bathroom door and left it open behind her, pulling her pants down before she sat on the toilet.

She had no shirt on. Her tits were surprisingly small for the rest of her body. She was young. Maybe late teens. He was in his late thirties. She could pass for older in her clothes, her hips and ass bigger than most teenaged girls, late babyfat or early womanhood, or just the way she was. It had made him notice her, after he noticed her eyes, staring into his as he wandered down St. Mark's Place in what the real estate promoters had dreamed up as "the East Village" back in the hippie renaissance days of the late '60s. Now it was the late '70s, almost 1980 and he was back, on his own again, through with a bad marriage and a bad life, ready for something new, sure it wouldn't have anything to do with the trendiness of anything so obviously fucked up to him as "punk" seemed to be. But then he had caught this girl's eyes, or she had caught his, and he had followed her into a bar, and they had talked, and the fullness of her hips and ass had made him believe he wanted to know her, had made him believe the chopped up short hair with the green streak down the middle wasn't so much different than his own newly cut hair with the gray streak on one side. He wanted to fuck her and she looked like she wanted to be fucked. He couldn't believe the old style obviousness of it all. After the '70's "struggles" with "feminism" and "gay revolution" and "open marriages" and "communes" and all the rest of the stuff he was taking a break from, here was an obviously old style simple pick up, a guy wanting to fuck a girl and the girl wanting to be fucked by the guy. But of course they did much more than fuck, and she was much more than an old style pick up, and he wasn't sure after they were through talking and fucking and being together that it wasn't something entirely new, or as new as he had seen anything be in his day, as new as hippies who seemed to be an extension of something he had thought was dying with the beatniks before he had a chance to try it, or as new as "rock" was supposed to be when anyone old enough at the time had seen the rock 'n' roll origins when that seemed almost totally new, though rhythm and blues fans knew where it came from clear enough. Someone was always hip enough to see the sources, to understand the roots—to fucking *be* the roots, which is why blacks were once considered so hip, were once so hip, and why he had tried so hard to emulate them, without even knowing he was, just doing what seemed most alive, most on target, most with it, most *now*. And now it was this teenybopper bohemian in the "East Village" putting him straight without seeming to even give a fuck about him. Except when they had fucked, or more accurately, when he had eaten her out. Or more accurately still, when he had become obsessed with, had made love to, even worshipped the crazy stuff of her ordinariness, the stuff that made her like every other woman he had known, like every other human, the stuff that confused and delighted him with

130

its conglomeration of uses and textures and colors and smells and contradictions—wet and dry and tight and loose and protruding and receding and hairy and hairless and just plain fucking crazy. He had gone crazy, like a school boy in the 1950s with a chance to finally check it out, a chance to check it all out. And his craziness had driven her crazy, even though they both must know that going down on a woman was almost old hat, was almost old '60s style ritualization of the newly discovered importance of the female orgasm, or street extension of the pride of outlaw bikers proving something about outlaw manhood, lapping up the smells and juices and crazy funkiness of parts so fucking ordinary after all. She had dug it, he had felt good making her body so obviously happy with itself and what he did to it, and then they had fucked. And it was as old style as you could find. Straight man woman fucking—punk kid female and aging hipster/hippie male. They got it on and went to sleep. But in the morning it was back to style and garbage. And he didn't make her glow this time, he made her glower.

And the whole fucking thing about James Dean was just an outlet for his own frustrated acting career, a career he had never really given a chance, one movie in the late '60s with him playing himself playing a heavy revvie radical like he had been, in a movie that no one ever saw anyway, and, as it turned out, like in a Russian or Japanese novel he might have read when he was twenty-one and concerned about what other cultures had to teach him, this lady, this imitation extension of something he was sure he had known once better than she knew herself, except she wasn't knowable like those things had been and only confused him about what he thought he knew about her, this punkette was an actress of sorts too. At least was in the movies, which he had so longed to be and now thought what the fuck he should try it again, having read an article on how the film industry was moving back to New York and the East in general, how the opportunities were there, how if only you could get them to see what you had to offer. And here she was, Pat Punk, or whatever she called herself, green streak and sloppy habits, fat ass and small tits, beautiful fuck and lousy conversationalist, here she was, in the fucking movies, but not the kind he had been in and wanted to become a star of just once before his hair was gone and his stomach was hanging over his belt and his looks were lost to the superior self-promotion of the more famous of his times, no, she was the star of some new brand of bohemian film making, some extension of punk into super-eight sloppiness, she was her own crazy misinformed naive but totally confident version of James Dean and the Creature from the Black Lagoon, she was what was happening, she was now. It took him a while to understand he had to stop comparing it all, including her, to *then*.

2.

Her name wasn't Pat Punk, it was Pamela Parsons. A name she had hated so much she'd tried to make it synonymous with sex, with slut, with fuck, with blow job. In high school, even junior high, she'd actually been shy, but with a hot core of sensual superiority—she knew sex was the cheapest cheap thrill, and so did the boys. By the time she'd graduated, Pamela Parsons was a dirty word. Then she went away to art school to everyone's surprise but the other art students. She got into performance art, made her own sexuality the subject of her work. A videotape of herself giving a blow-job to another student with a mask of the head of the art school on got her kicked out. She moved on to the Lower East Side where she could be anybody, the person she'd always been inside, or had become, or could become—Greta Garbage. She'd come up with a better name, but for the time being she was Greta Garbage, hot new star of the Lower East Side.

As she finished peeing she wondered about the aging rock-'n'roller sitting in the other room. Sexy, but he talks too fucking much. She couldn't decide if she wanted to see him again. He was trying to decide the same thing. What the fuck was he doing in this goddamn pigsty. He'd been through this before—the whole bohemian rebel outcast bit. He was still trapped by the limitations it had created for his own ambitions and expectations and sense of the rest of the world. He sure didn't want to go back to it, all he wanted was—what? He wasn't sure. Pushing forty and still unable to answer the first big question: what do you wanna be when you grow up? A rock'n'roll star, a movie star, a sex symbol, a world famous artist, writer, actor, lover, rebel, millionaire revolutionary sex machine perpetual teenager with a hard on that never quits. Sure. Never say die.

When she stood up and began to pull her tight pants—like "bad girls" in the '50s would wear and people would ask if they "painted them on"—up over her round hips and ass, he got a hard

132

on and a realization at the same time—shit, I talk too fucking much. As she started to step out of the bathroom he stopped her, grabbing her arms. She jerked them away, almost instinctively, but he held on, pushing her backwards. Her pants were still unbuttoned. He unzipped them and yanked them down to her knees, with her making useless gestures to pull them back up as he pushed her down onto the toilet seat. He stretched her thighs apart and stuck his face between her legs and started licking and sucking. She pulled his hair hard but he kept licking the lips and clit and hair and hole of her box. His head hurt where she had his graying hair wrapped around her fingers as she continued to pull on it, only not as hard, more rhythmically, more sensually. She was digging it, and that's all he wanted. He felt almost happy, relieved. No more talking or thinking, just feeling good. He licked and sucked and nibbled and bit and rubbed and kissed and sniffed and worshipped everything between her legs with his lips and nose and face. When her wriggling became too wild to contain he got up, pulled her up, opened his fly and pulled out his stiff prick and sat down on the toilet seat. She pulled her pants all the way down and facing him lowered herself on to his lap until she was sitting on it with his cock up inside her. She danced her round little ass around while he jerked up and down inside her. He began to swear, feeling the crazy excitement of coming so close, but she suddenly got up, leaving his cock quivering and glistening in the air. He was totally surprised, what kind of punk trick—but she smiled a sexy, sultry, girlie mag pin up pornographic smile. He felt himself smiling the same way back at her, free. Then she turned and bent over the sink her ass staring at him. He leaned forward and licked—slurped—from the top of her pussy and clit around and up to the top of the crack of her ass, stopping to suck the little knob at the base of her spine. She quivered when he went back down and did it again, and again, and again, each time lingering longer and longer over the crazy little confusion of her clit and the sharp taste of her cunt hole and finally the metallic, puffy little blossom of her ass hole. She shook with a feverish pleasure and it made him crazy to feel so useful, so sexy, so privileged, until he couldn't take it anymore and stood up to rub his cock where his lips and tongue had just been. He made little frenzied wiping motions back and forth across her clit with the head of his prick and then slid it just a little way into the opening of her cunt hole then out and up to the tight heat of her asshole where he had to push it in, but just the head and then back again. She finally reached back and grabbed it and shoved it into her cunt. He went berserk inside her, used every rhythm he could discover to prolong the ecstatic sensuality of the sensation of fucking until he couldn't control it anymore and they both pumped and ground themselves into each other until she came and he came and it was like starring forever, it was like perfect, like definite, like really, like thank you, like—and then it was over again.

3.

He was on St. Mark's Place, walking west, totally distracted. He couldn't believe it. *Again.* His heart, his head, his fucking intentions, everything wrapped up in some piece of ass's reactions to his loving, and his rap, and his—himself. He was gone again. Shit. How many times can you get yourself wrapped up in trying to love & be loved & fail at it & still go back for more—another try. And this, this, *punk!* No, he was the punk—a goddamn almost 40-year-old punk. She was just a kid, trying to be hip—or whatever the new/old word for it was now. Shit, not trying, *being.* She was *new,* him & his obsession with *love* & all that stuff, was old.

WHEN HE SAW HER LYING THERE

When he saw her lying there, stiff and frightened looking, unable to respond, to "wake up," to "come to," destined, in the words of the expert doctors who hovered about, for the life of a "vegetable," he knew it didn't matter anymore, none of it mattered. And when he leaned over to whisper to her, after waiting for the others to disappear, to leave them alone for a moment, to stop treating her like she was deaf or five-years-old, talking baby-talk and slowly enunciating their well-intentioned but idiotic sentiments, when he was finally alone with her, and could look closely and be sure that he was right in his feeling that she looked scared and in pain despite the doctor's reassurances that she "wasn't feeling anything," when he leaned over to whisper in her ear and touched her arm and said at the same time, "I swear to God Lee, you got so many people who love you and care about you I'm almost jealous—I *am* jealous," and she shivered, her body stiffened even further than it already had—her head reaching up toward the top of the bed as though she might discover a way out through it—and her feet stretching down toward the bottom, almost lifted off the sheets, so intense in their stiff struggle to form the kind of ballet-like toe stance she had always regretted being too short to ever have a career executing. He was sure she had heard him and understood that this was as much a declaration of love and sympathy, but more importantly respect, as she had ever gotten out of him, despite all the pretenses to otherwise. And she must have known he was right, he wouldn't bullshit her, especially now, especially in the face of all the others who thought they knew her, who thought they knew what had gone on between him and her, who thought she was right in whatever extreme condemnation or description or exaggerated emphasis of his faults and extravagant charms she might have created for them after he was gone. Well, he was never quite all the way gone from this woman he had known intimately for more years than her family or friends or any other lovers or even their kids. She was one of his generation, they had shared a life and a way of life for a decade, after sharing their thoughts through the mail for almost half as long, and they had remained in contact, sometimes even friendly, but always carefully observant and precisely accurate in their exchanges of ideas and perspectives and solutions to each other's problems or confrontations over the kids. She had been his match, one of his own kind, hitting puberty just when Chuck Berry and Little Richard, Elvis and Jerry Lee Lewis were hitting the renegade radio stations with the music of the future, their future, together, and eventually apart. He knew her like no one else did, and now he knew what was her was fucked forever, had suffered the ultimate unfairness of their fucking miserably failed future—being brought back from death by panicky doctors who thought their equipment and extreme techniques could save the world, when all it did was create more problems, like what do you do with a 37-year-old "vegetable" who was once one of the toughest women of her times. Their times, he had always been so possessive of. All these rip-offs of the '50s, revising of the real gains made in the '60s, disillusionment with the positive aspects of a still misunderstood '70s, he was sure his perception and experience was the most accurate, the most vital, the most real, and now watching her settle down from the shakes that he was sure his confession had caused, he knew none of it mattered, who the fuck cared who was right, someone else's version would outlast his anyway, he had missed his chance for fame and lasting authority when he had decided to remain true to his experiences and perceptions. Distortion was the basis for success, or at least concessions to the experience and perceptions of others, more successful, older, more powerful, wealthier, more "average," more acceptable, more whatever he and she had never been. Goddamnit he wished he had the nerve to put a pillow over her face like he knew she would say she wanted. They had always feared being "put away" as a punishment for their craziness and independence, and with her experience once in a mental institution for being crazy after seeing her distorted face as the result of going through the windshield of a sexy foreign sports car into the back of a truck on the New York State Freeway, and his experience "recreational therapist" style, playing ball and pool with the impoverished nuts of the Essex County New Jersey mental institution, they both had sworn to each other if either one was ever committed the other would murder them before letting them be taken away. But that was a long time ago, she, or someone else, might even argue against the truth of what he thought he remembered they had pledged to each other. Who could be sure. And besides, what would happen to the kids if he did succeed in suffocating her right here and now with this ugly white hospital pillow and someone saw him, someone walked in on him. He'd never get away with it.

4.<u>4.80</u>

ex-wife in semi-coma
daughter moves in for good
joins brother and father
reluctant (she) to accept
her mother no longer able
to be her mother as she
has been, though, whatever
"brain damage" means
her father doesn't even
try to explain or use
these terms, instead
"won't get much better"
"why me?" asks son
then spends days making
"sick" jokes about death
and brain damage, though
no one mentioned either
in his presence, and
he's the younger though
raised in New York City
with father these years
where dreams keep father
going despite despair
and recognition confusion
(is he gay or what? no,
he's sensitive and at times
super-sensual to the point
of not caring what's
different or the same—
is he any good or what?
so much potential etc.)
38 going on 17, 10 going
on 50 (the son) 12 going
on 6 going on 80 going on,
whoever survives survives,
it doesn't seem to matter
how, only who, we all

make do, you'll never
understand who or how
though try, please try,
I got a why that won't
quit, though my ex-wife
didn't always like it
and now she's shit fucking
fighting for some fraction
of a life she used to have
and everything is different
even in my dreams, I
don't know shit & can't
compete even with myself
anymore, just let me do
it once the way I meant
to be remembered, she
seems to have, despite
whatever got between us
& I hardly knew, so
fucking scared & hungry.

1982-1999

Santa Monica CA

"Literature is a fragment of fragments: the least of what happened and was spoken, has been written; and of the things that have been written, very few have been preserved."

—Goethe
Literature & Art

"Perhaps it is not the narrow-minded alone that have no interest in anything but in its relation to their personality."

—Charles Ives

"Just don't get too complicated, Eddie. When a guy gets too complicated he's unhappy. And when he's unhappy—his luck runs out ..."

—Raymond Chandler
The Blue Dahlia

"Death
should be as fast
as 2 words"
—Larry Eigner

HISTORY

There was an article that month in *The SoHo News*, what seemed to be the hippest New York paper in those unhip years. It was about the owner of a restaurant on the Western fringes of SoHo, near the Holland Tunnel, where there had always been a no man's land of barren streets and looming, dark, uninhabited buildings. The restaurant had been a workingman's bar and luncheonette, an old one in an area where real estate had always been cheaper than midtown or Wall Street or the Village, so it was a large place. The space was one big open room divided only by a long row of banquettes facing the bar stools with booths behind them opening in the opposite direction. The banquettes and booths were red— an old, well worn, deep, city red. The bar was the length of one side of the room, the longest side, and was backed by an enormous round mirror, at least ten feet in diameter. The ceilings were extremely high for the city, giving the place a grandeur that became more subtle when the new owners introduced the indirect lighting that was the only modification they had to make to create the most intimate yet public atmosphere in New York that season. Opposite the booths were tables, another row of banquettes, and windows behind them looking out onto what usually, at night, was the deserted street. This night was only different in that there were several antique Japanese lanterns hanging from the ceiling and, in the corner of the room where the two walls of windows met, there was an antique patterned white screen, French and subtle and supplying the sense of almost an altar to the corner. There was a stand with fresh cut flowers in a vase in front of the screen. This was where the wedding took place on Valentine's Day, in the evening, with the street outside dark except for the traffic light blinking somewhere high and back behind the Unitarian minister who was hired because he could be counted on to do what the bride and groom wanted, read a few short excerpts from the Bible—that were romantic, poetic, well-intentioned without being righteous or limiting—and then make way for the poet friend who read a special epithalamium written for the occasion that pointed out the violent origins of this feast day and the co-optation of most basic human celebrations of life and love by priests and poets alike, but how this event had originated only with this couple "the first time their eyes met," which was true, although she was staring over the footlights into a dark theater imagining the play of waves upon a Northwest shore while he was staring into this stranger's eyes from his seat halfway back in the house that serviced the tiny off-off-Broadway theater fifteen flights up in an old hotel off Central Park West. Another poem was read as well, by an actress friend of the bride's, who was as tenacious in defending her integrity as her friend, both having made their mark in films that didn't gross enough to put them in the category of actresses who can afford such integrity. This friend read from Donne's epithalamium for a couple of Donne's friends on a Valentine's Day several hundred years earlier but no less special or subject to fewer obstacles for the course of true love and its public legitimizing. When the vows were enacted the assembled throng of television and movie personalities that the owner kept wondering aloud about—"Who's here?"—and failing to recognize the names or faces except for the obvious few who sat at the bar and waited for well-wishers to come to them as if it were a celebration of their fame and success, she'd be told "They're very hot, everybody will know them by this time next year." Which turned out to be too true, except in the case of the few, and for them it was only a matter of more than a year. There were also some very prominent poets and artists, novelists and antique dealers, hair dressers and costume designers, a contingent of Christian Scientist middle class midwesterners on her side and Irish-American Catholic cops and teachers on his. The mixture in fact was the most volatile and potentially violent either had dared invite to any of their individual parties in many years. But the cops got a kick out of the male couples romantically holding hands or dancing close as the party got lively, and the New Jersey mentality of many of the groom's supporters and friends fit in nicely with the drunken excitement of the poets and aspiring actors feeling privileged to be at an event where so many of the participants seemed better known than them. The crowd had stood on the banquettes and tables, and even the classic old oak bar, for the ceremony, exhaling in unison a sigh of appreciation when the couple exchanged avowals to love each other for life, and then burst out into a spontaneous ovation when the couple kissed to the sounds of Johnny Mathis singing "Chances Are" as though nothing had altered the simplicity of a time when the groom had been barely pubescent and still innocent in his expectations for the fulfillment of love's longings. As he put it later, he

142

felt the earth shift a little on its axis when he said "I do." And not long afterward, while dancing to their first song as husband and wife—Gladys Knight and the Pips intoning the sentiments of gratitude for love returned "If anyone should every write my life story, for whatever reason there might be, you'd be there, between each line of pain and glory, 'cause you're the best thing that ever happened to me"—his son, barely pubescent ran into a woman who was crazy with the exhilaration of having run away from Ireland and England to discover the heartbeat of the modern age in New York City, this woman threw open her arms to his son when she saw the tears in his eyes and he said to her "that was almost too much" and cried in her arms as young starlets came up to the new spouse and whispered "You'll never be as cool as your son" because by then he was dancing too and putting his father to shame in the game of male exhibitionism as it has been played since the fifties to rock'n'roll and gratifying one's soul that way. The boy's sister was also moved by the ceremony and the fact of the real change it would bring to her life, but not to tears, though to dancing. She was a little older than her brother. Their mother was lying in a hospital in another city, "comatose" as the newspapers and lawyers put it, "brain damaged" as the neurologists said, "a vegetable," "as good as dead," "struggling with her death and the life of her soul" as some of their father's friends put it. The article in *The SoHo News* didn't mention the wedding, or the braindamaged ex-wife and mother, or the bride's fantastic Komali creation, a red dress with sashes that detached and formed a dozen combinations and styles harkening back to the glory of Hollywood in the '40s when the groom was a boy and the origins of his romantic fantasies were taking shape in the darkened theaters of New Jersey, never dreaming that some day he'd be able to buy a designer dress for his stunning bride whose face had already flooded the same dark theaters with the white light of hope. It didn't mention the boy or girl, dancing, their heads bouncing, their bodies reflecting the potential the guests once saw in their own and now struggled to maintain or regain or just let go, as the most bohemian looking member of the crowd observed about himself in an indirect way when he pulled his poet wife up to dance with the bride and groom to Gladys Knight and the Pips and took up as much space on his own as all three other dancers exclaiming to his friend and ex-student and fellow Irish-American poet, the new husband, "I know all about Irish weddings … I *am* an Irish wedding" and they all laughed and basked in the glow of another dream seemingly realized for at least this moment. The paper didn't even mention the song that played when the bride entered through the kitchen and down between the booths and the tables to the little pseudo-altar in the corner behind which the traffic light glowed and the ONE WAY sign shone through the window—The Fleetwoods' original recording of "Come Softly To Me." In fact the article didn't mention the wedding at all, only that the restaurant had become the "in" place that season for anyone cool enough hip enough hot enough successfully New York enough to know what and where it was without it ever being mentioned in the article, or any other, because the owner didn't want it to be invaded by creatures from New Jersey in polyester and patent leather like it had a little that night. And months later, when the memories of the wedding were lost in the gossip of people breaking up who had been there together, or getting together and discovering they had attended the same event and not known it at the time, or among the snap shots that represented the only recorded versions of the events, it mattered, to the husband, who had thought he was making history, somehow.

Moved

I'm sitting on the bed reading a book by a friend about adolescence, in fact first loves. I finish reading the chapter about the first real enduring grief of rejection from a loved one and exactly as the last word penetrates my mind's complete perception of this scene and its relation to the ones I remember, the phone rings and it is a young girl, no older than twelve, maybe thirteen, calling from the other end of the country to talk to my twelve-year-old son she obviously is very much in love with. I can't believe the timing and am still so tuned in to my own nostalgic reveries I assume the role I guess I think my son should and talk sweetly to her as though we are old friends or lovers too, and as we talk I begin to miss her, all the ones I ever felt so sweetly nostalgic for a future I knew we'd never really had but drew my energy from fantasizing about anyway, trying to make up to her for the fact my son isn't home. Home? We've only lived here three short months. Santa Monica, California, like some hybrid American Riviera and New Jersey with Palm trees. New York City, South of Houston is where our home is. Only someone else is living there now, it somehow seemed too expensive and European chic to survive any more. Now I'm trying to survive here in Southern California, where I have never lived before.

"Is it hot there?"

"Well, it's in the seventies, sometimes still gets up in the eighties ..."

"God, you guys are lucky."

"Well, yeah, there are some things to be grateful for out here ... but I sure miss New York."

Hot? I'm thinking of this little woman in her Lower Eastside apartment and am feeling warmer than I've felt all day. What I miss is her, you, them, all the ones so seemingly accessible because always so close, so jammed together everywhere in that island fortress for the most intensely controlled insanely stylish people of our time. What am I doing here?

"God, I love California."

"Well, you'll have to come visit us."

"Sure, I go to California all the time, at least once a year."

I assure her I'll get him to call her and after we hang up

(following an odd pause where I have the sense I want to tell her I love her, and I can't even remember what she looks like exactly, never really distinguishing her from the rest of my son's friends when they were all hip little New Yorkers, sons and daughters of people somehow thought of as more authentically "artistic" or "avant-garde" or "intellectual" than me or my idea of honesty, my life a work of art so delicate whenever it is fragmented into glimpses of the private movie I have always starred in and now have flashes of wanting only to direct, it comes out weighted in ways that make me feel like such a phony I have to change everything—move, get married, try wearing suits, give up shaving everyday, cut my hair off, wear a dress, get tattooed, talk like a spade, fuck everybody I can, break the law, give up drinking forever, do too many drugs that can only intensify the feelings of phoniness and then renounce them forever too, fall in love with you.

A F12646687

In the Air Force, an enlisted man, who refused Officer Training School, out of what now seems like warped ideals concerning class obligations, not wanting to be with "them"—the stiffs and cold fish I thought the officer types must have been—busted to the lowest rank from court martials and article fifteens (court martials without courts) and tired of my own drab attempts at securing some honorable position within what was more and more obviously a dishonorable organization, I intensified my need for alcohol, for various drugs and reefer, and for physical violence and rough sexual encounters with the women of small town USA circa 1962–'63–'64. Then I got married to a woman I hardly knew. It seemed at the time like there wasn't anything else left to do. I was only 22.

I'm almost twice that age now. It's been over 16 years since I was discharged and yet I can't forget so much of what they drilled into me, as I demonstrated for my kids today. Having given my daughter the gift of a book I once cherished, and still do, the first paperback version of *Portrait of Jennie*, a book as romantic and fast as I was in 1962, and hopefully my girl, at 14, can relate to that and therefore with a me I have trouble being for her nowadays (I mean a romantic connection that's full of potential for lives together and dreams shared) and on the back of this book is the imprint of the stamp they issued to us for our personal goods with my name and serial number on it, AF12646687, and not having thought of that or looked at it for over 16 years, I had her check it while I rattled it off as I had so many times during four lost years of what I sometimes considered my prime.

Then I turned it into a joke, showing her and my 12-year-old son, what it was like to be called "on the carpet" (an actual feet-sized piece of carpet in front of every officer's desk I was ever required to stand at attention for), I knocked and then entered my daughter's room with the stiff-legged march of the enlisted man, came to a proper and perfectly executed stance of attention and gave a smart salute while rapping out name & serial number with the final clipped and extra loud "*Sir!*" and then stood there at attention with my head bent to the side in a semi-wise guy posture while I tried my hand at throwing my voice as though I were also the officer in charge: "Something wrong with your neck Lally?" "*NO SIR!*" "Then try straightening it up." "*YES SIR!*" and I alter the bend in my neck by a fraction of an inch, the total wise guy punk I seemed to have been and my son cracks up: "God you really were a punk" and my daughter agrees, and when I muse out loud that I wonder why I gave it up, she says, "Because you realized it was nothing, a waste of time to be," or something so smart and correct I really wish she had been there, and we could have shared my secret non-punk pursuits, like reading romantic novels, that in fact I now remember I did share with her mother through the letters we wrote before we really met and married on the spot so hot to culminate our little lives with the surprise of "this is what our parents had over us"—nothing, except the glory of our potential to imitate them again and again and—again.

L*ost angels*

for Peggy Feury

We are the generation of lost
angels. We rarely feel these
days like we have anything new
to do or say & yet our lives
are totally changed, even from
what they were a year ago, three
months ago, yesterday, trying
to *finally* be honest about our
feelings about each other's fame
& glory, while still trying to
get or forget our own, as Billy
Idol sings and the expression
"thrillsville" is recycled in
some teenaged woman's bed, or
"oh my god" we did that too
the way rock'n'roll connects us
with the folks we never knew,
maybe spoiling us for joy &
hope & honest bullshit as we
once said to people who were
"naturals" like ourselves before
we disillusioned on the anti-
antis … like wanting to be a
movie star forever despite the
rock'n'roll & dope & beatniks
who still can't finesse the
necessary kind of classic
heroism we all continue to
love, like the idols of the
silver screen we injected
directly into the limelight
of our brains and hearts for
smarts the schoolrooms dis-
possessed and all the rest;
we don't expect *too* much, just

freedom from the assholes we
suspect have been enthralled
by their own egos making money
off ours.
                    We don't wanna go crazy & die
          in some nuthouse with no teeth
          like Antonin Artaud, the world's
          first poet movie star and father
          of whatever wave obsesses us now
          in the New York–L.A.–Berlin–Paris–
          Tokyo–Melbourne–London scene that
          is the unbraining of Hollywood's
          being influenced by us! (the obvious
          vice versa has been *feeling* our
          brains since we mainlined Marilyn
          & Marlon) & what about the "blues"
          of John Wayne? That's how we
          survived. And now it's all one,
          the sum of our music and movie
          influences spread across the
          globe for anyone to use as in
          "the new technology" which has
          been in our cells since "action"
          was a label for painting and
          not just the order for the start
          of our hearts' flicks ...
We *love* being alive
and trying to share the craziness
of what it means to know it! I mean
did we really come too late for true greatness
or just on time? What is this new place
that defines L.A.–New York and all
the rest as just a state of mind?
Energy versus Peace? FUCK THAT SHIT!
The Peace of Energy that makes us
generate a void of minuscule delights
like we once relied on artificial
stimulants for, no more, maybe at last
we can reflect the serious sensuality
of the stars we talk to in our walk
through the sea we have become—

We are the masses who survived
the troubled times that rhymed
our lives the way old Hollywood
serials did, and understand our
laughter matters. Literally.
That's the secret of creation,
transforming *laughter* into *matter*.
We can finally *accept* and still
hope, like reality is the freedom
of knowing who we are and where
we're at and the ideal is sharing
that completely, without fear,
then letting go, not hanging on
but knowing anyway, because we're
smart at last and allow ourselves
to be. What are these humming
motors anyway but mammals of our
fantasies! Sure we talk to cars
and TVs and expect the music to
invade our brains, the motors
of our smarts that drive our
hearts to caring about it all.

Hey, what's L.A. but the
city of Lost Angels where
we all were born, even in
New Jersey 'cause what's
left of that is something
close to nothing, as the
categories fade and rede-
fining the specifics is
less thrilling. Like Elvis
isn't. I wish they'd fish
him over the rainbow of
telescopic infinitude so I
wouldn't have to bother with
the memory of his collar
turned up and hair that thick
I thought it was hereditary.
The Shirelles, now there's
some memories that never quit
changing, big women and still

151

growing. We made ourselves
in the image of images and
then got rid of it before we
came. Coming isn't the game
it once was. And neither is
going.

★   ★   ★

I only wanted to go far, be a star,
understand the way you all are.
Love, money, friends, family,
a stimulating environment, some good books,
records, art, photographs, furniture,
place to sleep and eat and work,
make love and shower, shit and entertain in,
maybe a good car,
some free time,
your name in the paper now and then,
or in a magazine,
or on TV,
your image too,
or in a movie, on a record, in a book,
or on the cover,
in the titles,
on the lips of strangers,
in the minds of a worldwide audience...

So you move to El Lay
to make money and become a star.
So you lived in New York City
to make art and smart sexy friends.
Which wasn't enough.
So you move to El Lay where
She has almost transparently blue eyes,
so intense they give the impression
that there has never been a person
they haven't seen through.
She has to be over fifty,
perhaps well over, like in her sixties.
It's so hard to tell these days;

or was it always?
Her eyes communicate such strength
when you look into her still beautiful face
you feel beyond time.
Her body gives it away a little.
Small, but not delicate,
there's something obviously
deteriorated about it
that seems in such contrast to her face,
unlike those strenuously physical
geriatric exercisers whose bodies
always seem to be made up of knots
and wires and strings and really ugly
imitations of some impossible youth.
Anyway,
I love her.
I fell in love with her the first time I
looked into her eyes. I can't resist a
woman who sees right through me and
is beautiful too. She's the real thing,
a total woman, smart, beautiful, and
old enough to be my lover, I mean mother,
maybe. Maybe not.
I'm not that young myself anymore, just
having walked through the door marked forty.
The best thing about which was
suddenly realizing why old guys can find old gals
sexy. When I was a kid I could never understand
the obvious attraction
my middleaged aunts could still retain for
my middleaged uncles and vice versa.
Now I know. There's a girlish glow
to most grown women that never disappears,
and if you went through the same or close-by years
with them, you can't help but see it,
and it makes you feel some kind of sympathy and
understanding for them, and then
on top of it they have this look
of having been through some things,
around the block as many times as you,
and that creates some crazy sexy feelings too.

It's all so new,
being old,
I mean older than I thought I'd ever live to be
and still be *me*.

These are some thoughts that moving from New York
to El Lay has provoked. There's so much space here
to panic in. The idea of "image" was crucified here
for everyone's sins and then resurrected to be
worshipped for as long as this place lasts
and influences the rest of the world.
Hollywood, one of the greatest sources of power
the world has known, and no real throne, no armies
or obvious superiority except occasionally
in technical, even artistic, ways.
But oh these fucking days of driving from
one crazy studio lot to another and feeling
as much at home as I ever did
in the apartments of my peers through all the years
of poetic ecstasy and self-destruction.
What other homes have we ever had, let's face it,
than Hollywood, the New York of bebop & jazz
& street scenes & energy highs (& its flip side:
galleries & Frank O'Hara, off & off-off and then
on Broadway again) or "on the road" or on TV
or radio or stereo or juke box.

Let's face it Charlie,
we coulda been real home lovers
instead of dream chasers which is what we are.
Only worse than the Romantics of old,
we can get real cold
and see right through that bullshit
as we watch the technology unfold
into a future of dreams & nightmares we never
forgot.

154

WITH MYSELF

Watching Charlie Parker on TV; it's 1984. He's playing riffs I remember digging in 1959, when he was already dead. And on TV it's 1952. Max Roach is on drums, looking like he's enjoying Parker's playing as much as me, as though his drumming were almost incidental, though actually driving the legend on relentlessly and doing it with ease and cool grace. I'm impressed all over again.

I remember reading an article in *The Village Voice* several years ago in which Roach pointed out that artists are usually too generous to hurt others deliberately, but then their sensitivity drives them to turn on—actually I have the quote somewhere. I'll go back and look it up in a minute. I'm still mesmerized by Parker's image. He's not moving, even his fingers seem relatively still. Yet the notes are flying out, rapid fire, spilling over, chasing one another across the years and into my ears, here, on my 1940's unrenovated couch.

The refrigerator isn't working right. I'm afraid to go to bed. No, I'm just afraid I'll have to wake up and face the waste of forty dollars worth of food my sixteen-year-old daughter paid for this morning with the last of the money she earned on a summer job she quit a week ago.

This is the way I used to write when I started out twenty-five years ago. When I was so fantastic and romantic a drunk I'd tell black friends I was the unborn child of Charlie Parker and Billie Holiday. When I called myself a "jazz musician," faking a little acoustic bass, and playing a little one-key-mostly-cocktail-bar piano. But mostly chasing every black girl I saw who didn't scare me, and writing deliberately imageless, plotless, artless (I hoped, though I didn't know the term at the time) series of sentences related to one another by the focus of my approach to the truth. Which was all I was ever interested in, I liked to think. Though it was obvious I was into a lot more. Especially trouble. Not the kind I've finally ended up with. Like the refrigerator I already sunk over three hundred dollars into since someone gave it to me several months ago, (and have no more money to put into now), because rented houses and apartments in this part of Southern California come *without* refrigerators. The thing I found strangest when I moved here two years ago from New York City and lived the first few months with cheap liquor-store ice coolers for storing the milk and few perishables we bought then.

The kids were used to weird adjustments, having gone through many with me or their mother. Who was still in the hospital in DC then. The malpractice suit not having been settled yet. Their new stepmother as surprised as I was by the new refrigerator role. Though she'd lived out here before, when she was nominated for an Oscar, but hadn't met me yet. Or my troubles. Like the phone call at six-thirty this morning startling me out of a dream so thick I didn't realize until I hung up how rude the caller was. A credit card company employee, a black woman who expressed not one ounce of charity, understanding, emotion, or shame. And I already had returned the card with a letter explaining I'd pay them when I could. I didn't get into the separation from my wife—"divorce proceedings"—which fortunately don't involve much money, or effort, except emotionally.

When she moved out, which she refers to as my leaving her, she eventually moved into a house near the beach with a refrigerator. I was a little jealous when I saw it. A nice, white, not too old or too big one. The one I got left with is a sort of green, a little dented and scraped and too big to fit into the kitchen of this apartment when me and my kids moved here because the house we were renting went up for sale and the landlord wanted us out and I couldn't afford the rent anymore anyway.

That was the nicest house I ever lived in. Got me used to California. The quiet, the space, the Spanish style curves to corners and entrances and all those flowers outside, birds of paradise and roses, all kinds of colors, (even "sterling silver" like the ones I sent to her the night after we first made love and already were thinking about marrying, me breaking my longstanding vow to never go through that again). The orange and avocado trees. When me and the kids moved into this apartment, we had to put the refrigerator in the garage, which fortunately is right off the kitchen.

God, there's Jon Hendricks singing solo, live, still in good form. After Chuck Berry, Hendricks was the lyricist and vocalist who influenced me most when I started writing. Lambert, Hendricks, and Ross. I had a crush on Annie Ross. She went back to England. Acted some. Was in *Yanks* with Richard Gere, when he was still going with my estranged wife, who I used to sing L. H. & R. tunes with, usually in the car when we first got out here. Then we moved on to long arguments, or long silences.

Cable's incredible. And disappointing. Now and then you might be lucky enough to catch Bird blowing to you from 1952, and then other nights it's reruns of TV shows you didn't want to watch the first time, or movies that never made it at the box office for reasons that become obvious as you grow restless seeing them this way. Even David Suskind would be better. But I'm tired of that forced, phony kind of "truth" now too.

Damn. The show's over. I almost want to keep watching in the hopes that those incredible excercising young women might come on with their aerobics tapes that are obviously about more than health since their movements always involve bending in ways that offer throat drying perspectives ... how do you find new terms to name what we've abused for so long with an overused language of ... but no. The girls don't appear.

My son is sleeping at a friend's so they can get up at five to go surfing. Only two years ago he was riding subways, now it's waves. "You adapt or you die" he told me when I worried out loud about his losing his city sophistication. My daughter's at the movies with friends. I'm halfway through Milan Kundera's *The Unbearable Lightness of Being*. But I'm tired. The rent is due and I don't have it. But I have a day's work as "a young J.R. type" on a new series next week. And an article coming out in a Valley newspaper. And nothing to do tomorrow, Sunday, except find enough money to buy the paper, see if I can get the refrigerator working, learn my lines, write some more on the screenplay idea, think about the play idea and the autobiography and novel, try not to think about the Pulitzer Prize going to plays and novels that use the kind of language they never give prizes to poetry for, because of, uh oh, don't go in that direction, read some more of Thomas Merton's *New Seeds of Contemplation* instead, feed the kids and enjoy a day with no bills—no mail. And try not to think of New York, or 1952 or '59 or any time but now. This transition time, getting over another failed marriage, starting another "artistic" career. Trying to accept responsibility for the troubles I seem to own, and to accept being grown, and on my own again, no longer

157

black, or high school, or the sexiest mixture of Clint Eastwood and Montgomery Clift that made me perfect in my daydreams.

But before bed alone again, wondering how long it will seem new again, that quote from Max Roach, it's in this "Record" book I started in the early '60s and maybe have fifty quotes in, mostly from books, but a few from interviews I couldn't let go, oh, here it is:

"... if you're a humanitarian, which most artists are, instead of getting in a fight or breaking something up, you take it out on yourself. In fact, I would say, that most creative people who are self destructive are trying to protect other people from their outrage. If you live long enough, though, you learn you have to be a humanitarian with yourself as well as with everybody else."

L OST ANGLES

Frank Sinatra's singing a tune about how everything always goes wrong for him, just a bad luck guy, and now he's had to go and "fall in love with you." The song is one of my all time favorites, called "Everything Happens to Me" and he's singing it with the Dorsey band, back when he was in his late teens, early 20s at most. "The Voice" they called him. A young New Jersey punk, greasy long hair and a body so thin you could cut yourself on it. But he had these eyes, and this smile, and that voice. The song brings tears to my heart for a vision of the USA I never lost. Through all the distortions, of what those of us who really cared were all about, in the gang war '50s, and the clash and trash '60s, and the climb on, cop out, cash in '70s. I can picture a time when Sly Stallone will be trying to hold his frail body up at the podium to announce an Oscar in 2024, and my kids'll be moved by his valiant effort to stave off the inevitable, despite his right wing revisionism of 1985. The bottom line is I love this country and the mix of memories that are genuinely mine and those that are second hand through films and tunes and the voice of a long ago teenager who got a big break and didn't blow it. Last night I was down at the Vine Street Bar & Grill in Hollywood, yeah, that Vine Street, only a few doors away from Hollywood Boulevard, which is supposed to be as bad and scary as Times Square at night only can never be, because it's *Hollywood*, for chrissakes. Most of the street kids are long haired heavy metal burnouts anyway, and the cruising of the cars is quintessential smalltown USA, not downtown Berlin nightlife two years before the Third Reich took over. Before that I was out by the L.A. Forum picking up an older brother at the hotel next door. It was full of meticulously dressed black men with bow ties and real short hair. And women in white, their hair covered, the younger ones wearing pillbox hats with foreign legion style flaps down the back. Somehow they communicated foxiness despite the restraints. It was obvious who these folks were. Dignified and disciplined. And then, while telling my brother I figured he was in the middle of a Muslim convention, Farrakan comes out of the elevator with several large well dressed dudes surrounding him. He's carrying a brief case and looks calm and kind of small. He's looking around as people talk to him and he and his entourage walk by me and my brother, the only whites in sight. I look at him and catch his eye and nod and say "How you doin'?" and he smiles and nods back and says "How are you?" and keeps walking. Not one mean vibe passed between us. In fact I felt some real human warmth and maybe even some humility. But my brother makes a connection between Farrakan and Hitler when I say how I feel. Outside the Forum, besides lines and lines of L.A. blacks, there's a contingent of the Guardian Angels, a handful of whites, and on one corner a group of blacks with signs that say "God loves Jews" and like that, demonstrating against Farrakan's famous blasts at Jews that embarrassed Jesse Jackson's campaign only a year ago, already lost in the mists of a history that doesn't seem to really matter. This morning on KCRW, over at Santa Monica City College, Tim Hauser, the founder of Manhattan Transfer, is doing his radio show on jazz singing, only today it's strictly the old r&b male vocal groups that bridged the music of "race records" and early rock'n'roll. Turns out Hauser went to Saint Rose's High School in Belmar, New Jersey, where I served mass every summer when I stayed down my grandmother's house in South Belmar. I went to St. Rose's summer school when the priest who taught Latin at my high school in Newark failed me, because he thought it would be good for me to spend the summer in school. I saw a small news show on Bruce Springsteen a few days ago and they showed the police station across the street from the girl Bruce dated in Belmar, the same station I got dragged to by the cops in 1956 when I first got arrested for supposedly setting up a major gang war that never took place. I remember the sting of the cop's night stick on the back of my thighs, when I tried to be bad and took half inch steps going into the station. "E Street" was where we hung out, among other places. Years later, I was stationed at Fort Mommouth, not far from Mommouth College, where I heard Springsteen later went when he was playing folk music. I hung out in Redbank with the black daughter of parents who had gone to school with Count Basie when he was just a kid from around there. I played with black r&b bands in bars in Asbury Park. That was in the early '60s. My grandmother's house—and my grandmother—were long gone. The only thing that was still the same was Ocean Grove, where Woody Allen shot "Stardust Memories" many years later. You could see Ocean Grove from the old ferris wheel on the border of Asbury Park, the one with the cages with park benches inside—the first place many

160

of us french kissed when the cages came out of the roof and rose over the city in the dark. You could see the ocean, and Asbury Park and Ocean Grove (we called it Ocean Grave because you couldn't play cards or dance or listen to music or drink, or even drive a car in or out of it on Sundays). The ferris wheel cages were named after the Jersey towns most of us, first and second generation immigrant kids, came from—like Orange and Irvington and Harrison. Back when they didn't have reruns on TV, and Ed Sullivan had the Everly Brothers on his show one summer night, and we were all disappointed when they spoke because their high polite voices sounded pretty faggy to us juvenile delinquents at the time, I was having a party because my parents wouldn't let me go out nights since my arrest for the gang fight incident and my flunking Latin. So I invited some friends over, but it was the summer, down the shore, and the word passed around and over a hundred kids showed up eventually, out on the street and in the yard and all over the house, a lot of them strangers, and my parents were up in the city working. My crippled, hard-of-hearing grandmother only left her room once, to go to the bathroom. She leaned on my arm and her cane and didn't seem to notice the noise, only looked up once to smile at some of the kids, saying something funny about how she'd dance if she could. When my parents came down that weekend, the neighbors complained to them about the noise from the party. I denied it, saying I just had a few friends over since I couldn't go out. And when they asked my grandmother, she said, Oh there were only some boys, very polite and quiet. I told my 15-year-old son this story this morning because he hadn't come home until 3 AM from a friend's house, whose parents are away. The friend had invited a few others over, down at the Santa Monica beach, and a lot of strangers showed up. This kid's father is my agent, and his mother just produced her first movie, which was a big hit for a lot of women, including the first time producing team and a first time actress—who I saw around SoHo before she was a blonde and became a famous singer with an eight million dollar contract and married an actor I had lunch with recently about a possible "deal" on a movie idea of mine, but he only liked the title—and a second time movie director who had hired me to play one of the male leads in her first feature, but when the union agreement got messed up I had to quit, because of my '60s politics and my '70s decision to move on over to the other art forms I love, beyond the poetry that kept my finances terminal. When I dropped out of her first flick, Richard Hell replaced me, who I think was once a poet named Richard Meyers, and maybe wrote one of my favorite books under the name Teresa Stern (*Do You Wanna Go Out?*) and was in a magazine with Tom Verlaine when he was Tom Miller. But that was back when my son was 5 and we were living down on Sullivan Street, before we moved away from what was becoming SoHo, down to a 250-dollar-a-month loft on Duane Street in what we used to call "SoSo" or "SoWhat" but never that horrible real estate distortion "Tribeca"! And before the neighborhood bar was bought by John Belushi and turned into a private club; and before DeNiro and Midler and other Hollywood stars bought up the neighborhood and caused the prices to go too high for our type and I said fuck it, I got to beat 'em at their own game before I turn bitter and die the death of the disillusioned poet one more time. Now here I am 10 years later in Santa Monica, still trying to get my first screen play on after three years out here. Though everyone says they admire it, it's too "controversial" ("not commercial"), because it's about my experiences in an interracial relationship in South Carolina in 1962 when it was totally segregated. Instead I get hired to rewrite somebody else's story about a similar, but not interracial love story of the same place and time. And meanwhile Rae Dawn Chong, glowing like a movie queen of the golden years, appears in *American Flyers* in an interracial relationship, that emphasizes the character's "Apache" strain over her African one. And the hottest "trailer" ("previews of coming attractions" is still a better way of saying *that*) is for *White Nights* with Baryshnikov and Gregory Hines and another interracial love story. And there's several more scheduled for future films and TV shows. Just like other subjects I told them I wanted to write about, and knew would be the next hot ones, but they said they couldn't touch because they were too dead in 1985—like "rap," and the '60s. And you know it's coming, because you live in New York or L.A. or Iowa or Athens Ga. and you feel it in what makes your eyes sparkle and your secret pleasure at being a part of something fill your heart. It's happening. Like it always has been and always will. The bomb still hasn't dropped, and although the repressive and ridiculously offensive elements that make capitalism and communism totally out to lunch in 1985 are still the dominant themes of the programs of those who think they rule our lives, we know better. It's still out there in the flicks (*Insignificance, Mishima, After Hours, Choose Me,*

162

Brother From Another Planet, etc.) and sounds (X, U2, Sting, REM, the "go go" bands, etc.) creating the cross currents that always make us hip to our ultimate trip—sharing the excitement at being alive one more time. Thank God it's too late to stop now.

TALK ABOUT IT

My daughter has been doing her own laundry for a long time. Like her younger brother. But today she had to go off somewhere with a friend and left me a note asking me to bring her clothes in from the dryer, and since I wanted to use the clothes basket, I folded them for her, sitting in her room, the warm breeze coming through her window, the sun shining like a beautiful Spring day in the New Jersey of my childhood, though this is the Santa Monica, California of my middle age, and sitting there, smelling the clean laundry while I folded it, each sweatshirt that is a daily version of her uniform neatly placed on her sheets, I realized I was incredibly happy, and that doing this task on this day was the reason, because it took me back to when she and her brother were children, babies, and through the influence of the burgeoning feminist movement and its dogma of equal responsibility in the home, as well as guilt over cheating for the first time in seven years of marriage, I first began to care for my children in what was considered a motherly way when I was a child, and so I felt connected with my mother, God rest her soul, she who has never known my children, and to their mother, now over five years in what the media usually calls "comas" though I know better now, "brain damaged" is the operative term, but the reality is "vegetable," a woman I thought I'd be happy to never have to think of again, after our divorce, but since her "accident" have thought of every day, anyway, folding those clothes brought me in touch with the most peaceful and satisfying aspects of being alive, my being a father, raising children on my own and with the help of a succession of women, but mostly my being a father, my love for the kids and the richness they have added to my life and still do, until I realized that this was always the most satisfying job, most contented task I had ever undertaken, including it all, including the two years as a corporate executive, the four years teaching college, the years of bohemian excess, where I tried almost every kind of sex and drug, the day laborer jobs, the limousine driving and night guard at the hospital and unloading trucks and washing dishes and all the menial labor and the twenty books of poems published and the awards and degrees and interviews and reviews, and the film and TV acting, and picking up the old single bed from my soon to be second ex-wife who was nominated for an Academy Award a few years ago, the friends on the covers of worldwide magazines and starring in films and the lovers now famous or wealthy or burnt out or dead and the "regular folks" who make up most of my experiences with people, like myself, despite all the crazy experimenting with all that life has to offer, and still even more I can't recall right now, add it all up and talk about it, which I will do, and right now, this afternoon, here in my daughter's bedroom, folding her clothes is the answer I'd have least expected, the most happy kind of work I realize I've ever done and probably ever will, folding her clean clothes, doing one of the small labors of love that make it possible for our replacements to try their hand at doing it all or figuring it all out or not, but at least having the choice, as we all always do, no matter what the obstacles, and as far as I can see there always seemed to be very few for me, though it never really felt that way.

T*he spirit*

Once I was queer for a year
out of fear I guess—that I'd be left behind
when the feminists took over the world.
Or maybe it was just
a way to get out of a dying marriage,
or to express all the pent up frustration
of a womanizing altar boy
with a perpetual hard on, trying to be
faithful to a wife who didn't believe
he was and pushed him to
"open up" to the so-called "gay" revo-
lutionaries of a time so different from
today, there's no way to
describe it if you weren't there. The air
fairly crackled from the energy we
generated with our bodies
and the sexual frontiers we threw them
across every day. But now there's a prison
in what used to be called
"camp" and it's cold and damp from
where I can see—and all I want to be
is a little kid falling
asleep before even the fifties got started.
Remember how sweet it was to fall out on
the couch with the sounds
of grown up voices stirring the air inside
your ears and all your fears just floating
away on that reassuring
sound of those voices that ruled the world?
I was always dreaming of you then, the
woman whose eyes would
supply me with all the answers I'd ever
need, whose body would warm even the
coldest corners of my soul.
That's why I became a poet, to talk about
my love for women and that feeling of success
when I finally got inside the

dresses they wore then—that and saving
the world when I discovered the word we
were all waiting to hear
that would finally let everyone relax and
just dig themselves and each other. The only
feeling I had for you brother,
except for that queer year, was one of hope
that the truth could keep us from killing each
other over women and money
and territory and grief—the belief that we all
really are one. That's the way I started out—
despite the fights and nasty
shouts of nigger lover and chickenshit and
you better not hit on my sister boy, despite
the fear of never being clear
to those whose English never crossed my street.
Oh man, I was this poet once, who always
wrote these poems, like for
your birthday or whatever—I mean anything,
you name it and I'd write something and it was
always poetry because I was
the poet and I said so, you know? Only, you
know, the first time I said that in L.A., I sort of
turned red, my whole head
was floating away as I heard them say, "But
what do you do—I mean how do you live?"
You mean like, make money?
"Well, yeah, sure, of course, what does a poet do
to survive?" And I said the usual stuff like
"whatever it takes," or how
I always told my kids they'd never be able to
figure out how I did it, kept us together with
enough food and usually nice
places to live in. But mostly I talked about what I
needed to these L.A. ladies who wanted to know
how a poet would go about
making the dough they seemed so interested in.
I told them I acted and needed a good role in a good
movie or TV show—or someone
brave enough to make a movie I wrote and the money
and power to pull it off—the usual stuff. So they ask

167

what's this movie about that
I wrote. And when I tell them, they tell me it'll never
get made. And instead of telling them they don't know
an audience's needs from—well,
from their own—only the audience is home, not moving
to Los Angeles to get rich quick—instead of grabbing
their asses and giving a squeeze,
which they'd probably object to, but admire me for—
instead of buying them out and firing them—instead of
surprising them with my latest
deal or seal of approval from the latest hip scene—
instead of telling them all the famous lips and hips
and tips of tongues and well-
groomed holes that have made me cream and felt it—
instead of telling them I'd rather go talk to God
in the fucking suburbs, or grow
fat in some nondescript street in a depressed Midwestern
city—instead of telling them I could tear off their faces
and eat their eyeballs before
I'd let them insult me this way—I say, you'll see, it'll
get made some day. And they say, "Hey, that's the spirit."

Only, I thought the spirit was
what moved me in the night to hold you so tight I think
you're me—or when we pass each other in the street
and our eyes meet for the first
time and even if we aren't each other's types we have to
fight from tearing each other's clothes off, not because
we're so sexually crazed, but
because our days are so lacking in the kind of tenderness
we see inside each other's eyes and the only way we let
our bodies know it is to show it
when we give them to each other in the secret life of our
beds—or maybe I mean heads. Only now I know, or think
I do, that it isn't only you and
your eyes and the home I long for between your thighs—
that's all still true but there's more—it's not all up to
you—or me—or the family we
might be if we would let it—there's a spirit greater than
all that, whose home is in your heart where all the
problems of the world can be

168

resolved without a struggle. That kind of love goes beyond
my petty little troubles—that kind of love is the god in you
that I really fell into when

I looked into your eyes with that first surprise of oh great,
you too. Only I always thought it meant some sexual mystery.
I wouldn't even know how to

say the way I feel now, without sounding like some candidate
for blissed-out-object of some Woody Allen parody. But fuck
that shit, as I used to shout

when I was without a clue as to how to say to you let's all
take our birthrights back and not let phony patriots and
rightwing fundamentalists

and all the rest rob us of what's truly blessed in our lives,
like a love of freedom and the truth and the ideal of a
democracy that truly represents

us all with room for all our differences. And a God of
our very own. That's what I wanted to talk about and
didn't know how. But now it

doesn't matter anymore. I'm through that door and back
again. And what I saw I only felt, and what I felt I
couldn't say, except that when

those ladies from L.A. tell me "that's the spirit" in that
condescending way, I do believe they're finally right,
only in ways they could never

guess. Unless they too really do mean You, oh Spirit
who loves and forgives me, even when I forget to.

D ISCARDED ICONS

I'm writing under a picture of Thelonious Monk from the cover of *Time* February 28, 1964, that I tore off the magazine that day. He's wearing one of his many hats in this artist's portrait. I don't know who was the true first, but for me, in my lifetime of noticing things, this was the first *Time* cover I remember seeing a black man on, and not just any black man, but my hero of that time and for many years previous, Thelonious Sphere Monk (the legend was that the "sphere" was added later as a testament to how un-square the man was). When my only son was born five years later, I wanted to name him Thelonious. His mother talked me out of it, and out of naming him Dolphy, so we finally agreed on Miles (his sister born four years to the day after that magazine cover of Monk, I wanted to name Sea or Trees, but her mother talked me into naming her after Dylan Thomas' wife Caitlin, and the maga-zine picture of them looking young and sexy and romantic we had stuck to one of our walls).

I grew up with as close to true icons as you can get. Statues of "The Infant of Prague"—Jesus as Shirley Temple sort of, with a little crown and beautiful robes made of real material with gold edges and stuff that my crippled grandmother would sew for it, and under which was always kept a dollar bill to ensure that we'd never be broke (seemed somehow an appropriate superstition for what I thought of at the time as a Polish icon). And all kinds of crucifixes, with palm fronds stuck behind them, renewed each year on Palm Sunday. And these big oval portraits of Jesus and Mary, separate in their polished wood oval frames, hanging over me and my sisters' or brothers' beds, depending on which year it was, the one of Jesus usually over mine, with his heart, rendered in the true anatomical shape and texture, hovering a few inches before his chest, flames coming out the top of it and a crown of thorns around it and drawing bloody drops and a slit in the side of it where the Roman soldier stuck his sword. It was pretty grotesque I guess if you weren't raised with that stuff, but for me it was home, and the main connection to the universe despite the fact that it generated years of guilt as I could swear his heavenly expression turned to hurt and sadness as he gazed down at me after I played with myself again. Those were icons I wish I had now, not some modern imitation or cheap religious store plastic version, but those beautiful reproductions of some incredible medieval conception of a human sacrifice called God.

Man, it wasn't till I was alone in the attic, my sisters grown and gone, my brothers too, and me almost 14, I put my first album cover, that little two-record 45 size set of Elvis' first, on my wall, not so much because I dug him, though I did, despite the fact guys weren't supposed to (if you were seen in line going to his first movie with the girls, you were branded a faggot for life) but because of those colors! Pink and Green! I mean, my favorite colors that year were pink and charcoal gray, I had a suit that color for graduation from Our Lady of Sorrows Grammar School, with a black shirt and pink knit tie, no wonder I felt out of place at the official school party, from which I was booted. Chuck Berry was the real hero, he wrote so fucking well and he could play a guitar just like ringin' a bell and do that crazy duck walk and still look lean and cool and like he could be mean if he had to. And Brando as Terry Malloy in *On the Waterfront* too, but I didn't get ahold of that still from *The Wild Ones* till the '60s. It's hard for anyone under forty to get I guess, but there were no "posters" and stuff like that of famous people to hang on walls till the '60s. Up till then it was only movie posters you ripped off the theaters or announcements for rock'n' roll shows, but there was no official outlet for that kinda stuff, so, no James Dean, who looked to us at that time like a geek anyway, and no Brando, though I did cut out the ads for *Seven Year Itch*, the ones with Marilyn Monroe's dress being blown up supposedly by the subway draft. I glued it into an old book I'd found my brothers left behind, along with other newspaper pictures I'd cut out, of starlets on the rails of boats with their knees exposed and tight together. In the '50s that was an icon for me, those bare knees pressed together, whoa, I can still feel that thrill, and the ads for Minsky's and all the other burlesque joints that had to move to Newark near my Catholic boys high school because they got legislated out of New York. I'd play with myself and write dirty graffiti in the margins of that book, my first connection with dada and Kurt Schwitters and all the other collagists and sex-crazed artists that led the way, although I didn't know it at the time. I worshipped at that shrine every night until in a fit of guilt after I guess an especially heavy encounter with the other icons, those pictures of Jesus and Mary around the house, I threw the book out the window into the snow below realizing only now, thirty years later, somebody probably found it and figured out pretty easily where it came from. But since the little clubhouse out back where the older kids used to keep us out was now open and we could see the little drawings of genitals and dirty words they left behind, I guess it wasn't such an obvious find, my little book filled with Tempest Storm and MM and Bardot's ass in panties and all those other sex symbols of the time with my slimy thoughts surrounding them sometimes in rhyme.

Icons, icons, wait a minute, okay I'm back on track. So, in the '60s it all changed, maybe personified most by lines in a poem I wrote back then about "So I destroy the calendar (paint it blue)/take down Marlon Brando for Che Guevera/pretend it is the wind.../and you?" Although it wasn't quite true, I didn't take down Brando, I just added Guevera, same as I had added Beckett and a beautiful unidentified Jamaican woman years before. I couldn't write, still can't, or sleep, without a personal "icon" watching over me, and so for years I played with who was up and who was down, Max Frisch in for Bob Dylan in for Miles in for Bogart in for Veronica Lake and Alan Ladd. But never for long, I was sometimes reacting to how strong their popularity was and not wanting to seem like I was on some bandwagon. (After all, I first had a picture of Bob Dylan up in '64, even though we came from the same Village scene at the time, in my mind, and I was jealous of his success, since I was a musician and poet then too, only too true to my black heroes and street friends, I thought, to play something as corny and phony as "folk" shit—who knew?) I stuck most of the ones I wanted to keep in journals, glued them there like that first book discarded in the snow of that '50s guilt-ridden night.

I always glued these things to something sometime, like those early years in the Air Force in 1962, with nothing but a locker to call my own, I found a discarded broken acoustic guitar and tore off the back, that womanly shape, and to it glued a magazine picture of the artist Marisol. Years later at a party I met her and told her about how she'd been my muse in those early service years, and she just stared at me with those same intense dark eyes, as if she'd always known. Better than Carla Bley—the jazz musician and composer I was in awe of later in the '60s and '70s, whose picture I also glued to another collage—when I ran into her at a party I told her what I'd done and how much I admired her work and she seemed totally flustered and embarrassed and on the spot. Both those pictures were reglued into one of the many journals I sporadically try to keep. But back to that busted piece of guitar, I stuck a shot of Coltrane on it too, and others, and hung it on the inside of my locker door. Guys thought it was very weird at the time, this piece of guitar with magazine photos glued to it, but they also seemed to show me more respect, like I might be crazy or somehow in touch with an unknown element in life they weren't sure how to react to. Like I might be blessed.

Yeah, pictures of Kerouac cropped up too, and of course Eric Dolphy and Billie Holiday (I got a great shot of her signing autographs outside the Apollo when she was still a "babe" as my son Miles said when he first saw it, it's up there now near Thelonious and an early MM and an early Gary Cooper and the one of James Dean climbing the steps of the Actors Studio, the same ones I climbed when I auditioned there with Karen Allen, whose uncharacteristic pose in a private photo reigns above all these, and there's an Edward Hopper reproduction and a postcard image of Montgomery Clift I got from Eileen Myles yesterday and some passport photos of my son Miles in a neck brace, all metal and machine-like, that he's finally out of wearing after a neck operation the worst part of which may have been the empty dull walls of the hospital room. No, of course that wasn't the worst, or anywhere near it, but it certainly symbolizes what was horrible about it, the emptiness of life when you're almost out of it like that, or of my life without him, or his without his, or the world without the ones we love as Frank O'Hara put it so much better in that poem "Steps" or is it "A Step Away from Them"—I'm writing on this adrenaline rush and don't want to stop and check, 'cause this to me is talking to these icons 'cause they once, and still do, talk to me, mostly with their eyes, just like Jesus in those first ones, and Ted Berrigan's in a watercolor-on-paper portrait Joe Brainard did, which stares at me with amazingly handsome compassion, Ted understood, or the news photo shot of Sophia Loren eyeballing Jayne Mansfield's nipple as it shows and probably glows in color somewhere though in this black and white is just right for recalling those pictures I cut out and stuck in that first testament to my creativity.

Ah shit, I guess this is it, the realization that there aren't any discarded icons in my life, they're all still here, stuck in some book or in some trunk or to a piece of wood or in a frame or naked on the wall and sure, I know now how the famous and accomplished really live and disappoint us, I've probably done a bit of it myself, thinking of this guy I know who went into a Detroit bookstore, the one he grew up going to, and asked if the guy had any books by me and the guy led him not only to my books but to a picture of me hanging on the wall, and when he left him there another kid came up and they got to discussing poets and my friend said he knew me, when the kid mentioned my name, and the kid said, "Yeah, he used to be so crazy and cool, but I hear he moved to Hollywood and sold out." Aw kid, I ain't even famous and appreciated enough to have sold out, although I've gotten some letters here and there and phone calls over the years that made it clear someone sometime had me up there over their bed or desk too, maybe that naked view from the Koff calendar, and you know, I love the idea, man it's gotta be a part of what makes us do it all, to be an icon, like Laurie Anderson has made herself for a few, or David Byrne or guys and girls we knew, how they grew into the role and it took over, the way Ginsberg always knew he would and Kerouac couldn't stand and those Rudi Burkhardt photographs and the rare photo of F. Scott Fitzgerald that nobody ever recognizes, always taking it for my father or uncle, because I guess he is too, oh whoever cares about all this enough to get this far, it's you who is the real icon here, these images just stand for what is possible to pass between us through this stuff I'm trying to say, hey, you, the best is this and all the rest I leave my heart to.

L EE & ME

1.

Lee, the weirdest thing happened the other day. I got a letter from "Mecca"—the woman who changed her life because of you. It was from this college in North Carolina, and there was a little packet in it made from a folded piece of rough brown paper, with some pieces of stone or driftwood or something that looked like it came from the beach or woods. I figured she was trying to turn me on to some spiritual connection to the natural universe, as so many women have tried to do, assuming, I guess, because I don't like that kind of stuff in my home, that I don't like it in its own home, which of course, you know I do.

So I put the pieces back and read the letter to discover she's in medical school at last—the direction she chose after visiting you in the hospital in DC—and that yes, your old boyfriend still "felt the same way" about me (I guess that was her way of avoiding saying he "hates" me outright), though he does have a new lover—I think she's older than him too (as you were). Anyway, she saw him at the service they held for you, where, she said, P.J. and others got up and said some things. It was both emotional and tense, she said, and she had reached in the pot with your ashes when it was offered and taken some—and that's what she had enclosed with the letter, though, she added, they're really not "ashes" but more like pieces of bones—yours.

2.

Was it the summer before or the summer after we met that you saw Kerouac on Race Point in Provincetown?

3.

Miles is here right now with a little friend of his they call "Little John" (though he's taller than your 4'11" but still not much for a 17-year-old guy), anyway, they're listening with me to a tape Tom Wilson made and sent out to his friends for Xmas. That was always the way he communicated best. Remember when he got me to buy that old reel to reel tape recorder in 1964, convincing me that it was the door to the future and would make records obsolete, but I hung on to my cheap old record player anyway 'cause I liked the album covers and the way they spin and all that so much more. Anyway, Otis Redding is singing "I been loving you too long" and these guys love it. You know I got hired to write the Otis Redding story, yeah, the movie, and they talk about not using the original versions but making new ones, hiring a singer to play him, like Robert Cray (a new guy you don't know but I think would dig) or whoever. What a shame. And they didn't want all that tough Black stuff either, the street and violence and language and especially the coming up through nasty ass segregated Southern stuff during the lynching years—a big Black man with lots of ambition. So, I been feeling ever since I compromised on the thing like I really have "sold out"—and the funny thing is I still have trouble making the rent every month. Course I'm staying in a house much more expensive than anything we ever stayed in. Only not that much better, about like the house in DC on Emory Place, only not as big. No room here for the tons of people we always had staying there with us, even before it turned into a "commune" with ten other adults along with you and me and the kids. Those were pretty crazy times, weren't they kid? Yeah. I guess they all were.

4.

Slater was here a few weeks ago. With his wife, Stacey. I didn't know she was so young. He turned 44 while he was here, just a few months older than you. And she's like 27, so she was around 20 when they met and 24 when they married. That old son of a gun. We talked about you of course. He was one of the few guys you always dug, even through the deepest feminist period, when everyone thought they had to be gay to be true to the cause. Remember how Rita Mae Brown baited you back then about "sleeping with the enemy"—which was *me*—your husband! She went on to become this big successful novelist, and had a famous affair with a famous female tennis star. I always liked Rita. She had "balls"—I mean she always did things the way she wanted to and didn't worry about whether or not it was politically or socially correct. She even wrote that way. Hell, if she had submitted the kind of stuff she writes to the Writers Workshop, she never would have got in, and if she did, they would have eaten her alive. But she bypassed all that academic training for the real world. Ended up sort of doing for lesbian love stories what Jackie Collins did for Hollywood. Nah, that's mean, she's better than that. She was always so attractive too back then, when she was just another poet trying to get attention for her work and I was the star supposedly. Yeah, but we've all been through that a few hundred times since World War II, ain't we?

5.

Jesus. "Wanted Dead or Alive" comes to mind for no reason except somehow it seems to connect to my life right now, the way I feel, when really it's a movie starring Rutger Hauer who invited me to a birthday party a couple of years ago in Hollywood and I had to take the bus 'cause I had no car and was too poor to buy one. Yeah, I'm still in debt and barely breaking even on the rest. It was so funny when I wanted to leave and asked if anyone was heading out toward the beach and someone said, Why, and when I said I needed a ride and they asked how I had gotten there and I said the bus, all these jaws dropped, and one lady said, "But aren't the people who ride them just awful?" Yeah lady, like me. Maybe I still cherish that role, the bad boy, the poor kid, the street style sharpy who knows how the other half lives and is proud to be part of that. Or maybe that's just a front for the feelings of failing that hit me when I get outside after a scene like that goes down so far beyond the point when I thought I'd be dead or way ahead of the game.

6.

The reason why Rastafari is attractive to American kids is pretty obvious. It's the first rock'n'roll religion. I just bring that up because Miles came in with a new record today by a Black group called Bad Brains, sort of punk Rasta, "hard core," which he digs because you can really play what you feel without having to worry if you're good enough (technically proficient on your instrument).

But Lee, you can't believe how happy I am with our children. Cait's in New York, working in an art gallery for a "field work term" from her first year at college—Bennington—the most expensive college in the country, where she can almost do what she wants, if what she wants is creative activity in all the fields we loved so much, and yet she's nurtured by professionals, not academics, not assistants, grad students, all that garbage of the kinds of schools we knew. Anyway, thanks to you, she can afford it, on her own. I sure couldn't send her there. But I could give her all the love I have to give, and all the knowledge and insight and experience she's been willing to pick up on, or put up with. And she has, despite her resistance to her brother's and my self-assurance when it comes to being hip and creative and all that, her wanting to duck that competition by just sidestepping it and pretending not to be interested. But in fact, she's totally turned on to things we always dug. The things we had in common that made it possible for you and me to stay together after we got married, only having spent a couple of days together before we did and knowing so little about each other it took us a few years just to get close. And then another few to get apart again.

7.

What I meant about that happiness was seeing Cait doing so well, on her own, and when we talk on the phone, starting out suspicious and cool (as she always did whenever me and her brother would get ready to leave her with you and make our way back to New York from DC those five or six years they were apart) but eventually we end up laughing and giggling and sharing our fears and joys, and lately there's been much joy on her part as she finally is digging herself and her life, a life she wouldn't have without both of us. I sometimes forgot that in the years I raised them, especially him, since it was just the two of us, Miles and me, for so many years there before Cait came to join us again. And now it's just me and him again. And just now, after he played me a cut from Bad Brains called "Re-Ignition," I sat him down to turn him on to some Charlie Haden and Charlie Mingus (because he's playing bass, in his second band already, in clubs even, just like I was, only he's much more mellow about the ego side of it and so much more disciplined about the learning part) and worked my way back through Marion Brown and Albert Ayler and Charles Lloyd, thinking of you of course, and the kids when they were little, and remembering those tough years when we began to really get on each other's nerves, but not during the Lloyd, those were pretty mellow days heh? At least at home, '68, me running for

178

sheriff on the Peace and Freedom ticket in Iowa City—Johnson County really—and working three jobs, besides working on two degrees at the same time, to support you and Cait and me, and Miles conceived probably on a night we were listening to "Tagor" with the screen door open and the '55 Chevy I had everybody paint something on not running outside or the telephone van I never repainted that I worried each time I started it in the morning if the John Bircher's death threats would come true when I turned the key—but in bed it was just you and me and the doobie we loved to smoke that summer especially. And then I kept going back, to Lambert, Hendricks and Ross, before we even met, when I first had a crush on Annie Ross when they came to that first school I went to in Olean, New York, where we met when you were a senior at that Catholic girls school and came for a "Press Day" deal, and I was Pierre Salinger's student guide and had to wear a name tag I resented because I was too cool and you tried to make a fool of me because of it when I tried to say something suave and sexy to your friend, who had the most beautiful face and eyes I'd seen till then, and I didn't even notice you, which is maybe why you taunted me, and still looking at her, I grabbed the program you had in your hand and wrote down the first poem I ever wrote and the only one I knew by heart and said, "Here, read this every night before you fall asleep and then leave it to your children when you die and tell them to do the same and maybe by the time their grandchildren get it one of them will begin to understand it" or something even more pretentious and aggressive and what I thought was cool, and still feeling like a fool and angry with you I split, not having noticed even what you looked like so that the next time I saw you, almost four years later, three days before we were married, I was surprised to see you had beautiful eyes too, only different, not those limpid deep brown eyes of your friend and the Black girl I fell for and became obsessed with in between those times, and for so many years after, throughout so much of our marriage—hell, throughout all of our marriage and for years afterwards until I finally took her out again, twenty years after she and I first were together—BUT, what I started to say is I had this crush on Annie Ross and always thought I'd interviewed her back then and now I don't know, I can't remember if that's something I just wished I'd done or meant to do or did? I drank so much, and dreamed and fantasized so much, I pretty much have to rely on what others can confirm or deny about some of those times. Hell, I'm only 44 and sometimes I feel like my grandmother, talking about the details of her childhood and married years and then complaining that she couldn't remember anything anymore. I got to get a handle on this stuff Lee, or I'm not gonna make it through the second 44, or however much more I get.

8.

Your eyes were green, and intense. I dreamt of them last night. In fact, I had this dream where I admitted to you, and to me I guess, how beautiful your eyes were and how much I did in fact love them and you, despite the feeling that I never really did, not the way I did all those others I "fell for" the way I never fell for you because we never knew each other in time for all that. We were married and back in Spokane, Washington, where I was stationed then, the summer of '64, before I noticed the thing about your lip and cheek. It was even longer before I noticed your jaw, and tried to make a joke about the old comic book character from when I was a kid—"Iron Jaw"—to find out that it wasn't something you would tolerate joking about, or even talking about. You told me you had gone through the windshield of a sports car into the back of a truck on the New York State Freeway, the same route we took after our marriage in the gym of the church where your parents lived in Tonowanda outside Buffalo to our honeymoon night in a motel outside Albany. Before we drove on the next day to the city, my city I thought, New York, where we slept on the floor of my older Black buddies and you freaked out when I started talking like them and didn't even know it. You were hip, brought Thelonious Monk records and the first Bob Dylans with you to our home in that basement in Spokane. But the whole Black thing freaked you, especially the girls, even though the reason we got together was because you seemed to understand all that when I wrote you in letters. Remember? I called you "Lee, the listener," not like you didn't answer back in just as wordy a way, florid in fact, where I was more purple, but—you seemed to understand my struggles. Until we really met in our marriage. And then, so much of what I was and had been through seemed like a threat to you. Obviously. And so many areas of who you were, were off limits to me. Like your face and what had happened to make it slightly deformed like that. It wasn't until you went into the coma that your boyfriend, who was still liking me then I guess, told me your parents told him there was no accident, that it was some kind of childhood condition that had lifelong results. I chose to believe it was a combination of the two. At any rate, it sure made people remember you.

9.

It's a good thing I didn't remember more about that dream, because I hate it when people write about their dreams in books, even if they're the made up dreams of fictional characters and are supposed to be telling us something crucial to understanding the book. They always seem so self-indulgent. But who am I to talk. This kind of writing I'm doing right now, trying to talk to you and let the world overhear it (I remember vaguely a quote from Yeats where he says that's what poetry is, a conversation overheard, or maybe he meant with yourself) (but hey, you're dead, so according to most people's idea, that means I am talking to myself) (but since when did I give a fuck what most people thought heh?)—Oh Lee, I think maybe there never was a time when I didn't. But Jesus, I could pretend I didn't sometimes with you, couldn't I? And so could you. After a while it was all we had in common. It seemed. Though I know that was never true.

10.

You realize I was always a foot taller than you? That's why I didn't notice your face when I saw you the second time because you answered the door and threw your arms around me and buried it in my chest and before I had time to even think about what I was doing there we were meeting your father in the basement where he had his lab for making the teeth and dental devices that was his business. I could use him now. The kids say he's still the same, funny and loud and really pretty sweet and sensitive inside. You had as hard a time with him I guess as I did with mine. Another thing we shared when we finally got together. You said he was always so disappointed you were a girl, he wanted a son so bad. And he had his own infirmity to deal with, that gimpy foot from breaking it when he was a kid sliding into an imaginary base in a baseball game in the street and too poor to get it fixed right. I wonder what he thought about your face. I wonder what he thought about me.

11.

I knew all about Malcolm and then King, didn't I? I saw it coming when they switched from race to class in their attention. You were there Lee, you know, I said that before anybody—and nobody knew but you. Now I'm out in "Hollywood," because I always figured that some day I'd make money off that sense, that ability to make a leap from some known facts to the unknown future ones—I mean, didn't I see every trend—oh Lee—sometimes I get so fucking—I don't know. I mean, you know, you saw me, you were there for a lot of it. I did it first, didn't I? And now those motherfuckers think *they* know, they keep making turkeys and spending millions of dollars on what? Gere? I like the guy but shit Lee. I know I know—they're afraid of a white guy and a black girl in a movie, this one producer said the Southern distributors wouldn't go for a movie about an interracial love affair set in the South in 1962—you know, me and Della Jones—but they're wrong, the fucking thing would sell like crazy in the South because it's *their* story! It'd be *their* closet being opened and aired out and they'll all want to see that—or telling me there's nothing to rap, it's a black trend that's already passing and never made it to the mainstream. Where the fuck are their brains? Didn't every black trend that ever swept through the ghetto end up being the future major influence on white music? I mean—Jesus, sometimes I feel like I live in a country of one—and that sounds weird coming from me doesn't it Lee? I mean, from a guy who always prided himself on being in touch with what most people were feeling, who believed that we're all basically alike, just trying to get enough room to move around and be ourselves in, without getting pushed around or shoved back or smashed down or—or—aw Lee, I don't know. I'm still crazy I guess, but Jesus kid, didn't we take some beautiful chances in our time?

12.

So I didn't know what to do about these pieces of your bones Lee. It all seemed so cruel and unnerving, especially since the only reason we gave permission, the kids and me, to your old lesbian feminist friends to take your ashes away was because they said they wanted to scatter them on the ocean down at Ocean Park, Maryland, where you used to go with them. And then they take

182

them back to DC instead and pass them around for anyone to have some. Who knows? Maybe that's what you would have wanted Lee. I obviously lost touch with your desires and ideals once we went our separate ways. But these days, for whatever reason, I feel in touch again. And then, I literally was, when Mecca's letter arrived with its surprise. So I asked the kids, what should I do with them? Cait on the phone didn't have a clue. But Miles knew. He said he'd take them with him in the morning when he goes surfing, and he did. I went along and watched as he paddled out beyond the breaking waves and took some time to get settled into the calm he calls something like "glassed off," or another poetic term. This surfing is his spiritual connection Lee, as he explained to me once when I asked him back when we lived 26 blocks from the beach and he had to ride that distance on his bike while carrying his surfboard and then descend another long stretch down an incline and then trek across a very wide beach and all that to ride a few waves and then return the same way and shower and change and make it to school on time, he said he liked being up so early before most people were even out, and that even if he didn't catch any great waves, just being out there in the ocean as the sun came up was something he could remember during the day when things got tough as they always do but especially for a teenager in high school. What a wise little man we have Lee. Anyway, he dropped your ashes in the ocean of Santa Monica Bay, without looking at me but instead out to sea, the horizon, where indeed the son was rising. It was very moving Lee, although he had nothing to say when he came back in after catching a few waves, except that he wasn't that good at surfing as I guess he thought others were, but to me he was perfect. And I'm sure to you too.

POETRY MEANT SO MUCH TO ME ONCE I DON'T KNOW WHAT'S GOING ON

Rain tells me of her crush on Richard Hell, who published in magazines with me back when he was Richard Meyers and then, years later, after he was "famous" for his "Blank Generation" anthem and punk personality, he replaced me in Susan Siedelman's first feature *Smithereens* when I backed out 'cause the union said to and I always wanted to experience solidarity.

Rain cut her hair all off after separating from her boyfriend because they were so "incompatible" in so many ways, but they're back together because her body ached, in fact was "racked" with pain, like in the good old days, despite it being her decision to split, and funny thing, I experienced that too when I broke up with her, so we got back together again, like her and this guy now, only then we broke up after we lost the loft due to the new land-lord's gangster tactics and we had to move in with Karen who broke up with Stephen while we were living there.

Everybody thought something was going on between Karen and me, because we were so close, still are, but anything else hap-pened long ago. Long before Rain, or Gloria, or Ana, or Penny, or Helen, who I saw Saturday for the first time in over a year, since her recent success, she says they're sending her scripts now, and casting her first and then the guy to match her for the next movie. She's doing all right, except for "the partner" thing. We had our fling, too bad I was married at the time. I hear her friends still hate me for something.

Like the lesbian feminists in DC who wrote when Lee died a few months ago that she was a "lesbian poet" once married to "a gay poet" thinking they meant me, I guess because I said so once. My way of not hiding behind the privileges of the oppressive class, I thought, or was taught by those who claimed to be more revolu-tionary than me. Once I went to bed with a man, and we did what I could never quite imagine "they" do, even though I was thirty and pretty much gave up that line of pursuit by the time I was thirty-two, still, I did enjoy it, sometimes, and used it to identify once again with those I figured *had* to understand me, because I always felt like an outsider too, I didn't know what was true.

I just got back from New York a few days ago, where I read in

a "short story series" with Susan Sontag, who seemed too preoc-
cupied to say more than hello, although I noticed she gave a lot
more attention to David Mamet, who read too, and had a few nice
things to say, though in that male "bump bump" way that used to
make me hit them, or outrage them, or take their girls away. He
left before I read, which was okay 'cause I was nervous, like I've
only been a few times, like Ian Frazier said he was, because he'd
"never done this before" and I've been doing it for at least twenty
years, but he seemed fine, as did Mamet and even Sontag when
they were up there. Not me, self-conscious in my "L. A. outfit"
that Joan bought me for my last birthday. And wondering where I
fit in with street friends from long ago standing up in the back
behind the last row, and two cousins and the only sister left, all
dressed up and in from Jersey in a "limo" they kept calling a
"lime-o" in memory of one cousin's mother who died, like my
other sister, not long ago. Or "my lawyer," a book-loving, play-
devouring, generous friend and his wife, a story-writing, answer-
seeking "new woman" friend, and her family, wealthy cultured
"Russian-American Jews" who knew and seemed to see right
through my immigrant mentality. Or O'Keefe, my actor, Irish-
American little brother mentor buddy friend with whom I don't
compete too much, honest, despite the girls whose heads he
turned when we cruised the city streets, the girls who looked at
me first not so long ago.

I don't know. It's not what I expected now, knowing so many
personally or even indirectly but somehow intimately connected
to, through bed or nearly being who they seem to be while passing
through. And then there's you, who I'm always writing to, hoping
somewhere, sometime, I'll get through and you'll be so relieved I
did. Like when I hid in the bathroom of my childhood home and
tried to be alone to read some kindred soul, as they always called
it back then. I still do, just picking up my first wife's copy of
Rimbaud, that New Directions paperback from 1961, which for
that moment didn't seem so long ago. Or chapter twenty in
Kerouac's *Desolation Angels* I thought somehow below me when it
was new, I finally found again and read in the city late at night
when I couldn't sleep for all the excitement I felt to be so close to
all I thought I knew so well, and finished on the plane back. It
kept me company in ways I hope the kind of stuff I write will do
for you. Like James Schuyler, or Robert M. Coates, or W. C.
Williams's autobiography just did again, like when I was first

185

married and for Christmas Lee bought me *Paterson* and I couldn't sleep with the excitement of that *thing*, that black and white New Directions paperback, what they later called "trade" size, bigger than the earlier Rimbaud, but just as much a miracle, even more, to glorify a Jersey I had grown up in and wrote about, thinking I was the only one because I didn't know, what could I know so long ago when even Saint Francis was Italian and Jesus was a Jew and the Irish guys wrote like the relatives who sometimes gave me quarters but more often couldn't understand what made me go. "You look like one of them Teddy boys," one old Irish lady said, and me in my new Christmas gift pants I'd wanted so bad. What the fuck was a Teddy boy anyway.

It's amazing to pick up Anselm Hollo's *Coherences* and realize how much we had in common before we even met, and yet, and yet... I ran into Alice Notley on the street and both of us got teary eyed with Ted and Lee both passed and me and she knowing each other before she married Ted, or me and Lee separated. I ran into Peter Scheldahl too, and we just looked at each other, me no longer filling in those anxious gaps, the silences I thought somehow reflected on me, as though I wasn't good enough to keep up my end of the conversation, so I always filled them up, with stuff—old stories usually about me or my family or friends. That's the Irish way I grew up with, but Penny thought was a sign of my insecurity, so she always interrupted me, or poked fun, or got up and left, until I didn't tell stories anymore, believed her, and not the guys who got on airplanes or hitchhiked or rode all night in cars from Ohio or Texas or Illinois or Denver or California or wherever to DC or New York or Iowa City just to hear me "tell the one about"...

They're all okay. The ones who didn't die, especially the ladies, even Penny is nice to me again. It's usually the friends who can't let go of whatever it was that drove us apart so long, or not so long ago. Penny runs a gallery now, Rain has a band, Karen is working with people who are legends already, as she is for many, and Penny is, and Rain, and even me for some, I suppose, though not as universally as all that movie stuff. I wonder sometimes who will read or want to figure out what this is all about. I mean, the idea has always been to tell some totally precise personal truth about a life lived with the normal feelings and aspirations and frustrations but with perhaps more insight into the possibilities and missed opportunities and crazed obsessions and experience-

186

junkie lessons. I mean just another unprofessional perspective on what it meant to be alive and in these times without the filter of success or media blessings or a single relentless thread of ideology or theology or sexuality or psychology or even idolatry.

I used to write several poems a day, every day, even Sunday, for years and years and years. A lot of them got published and read and even responded to. I've had my share of "fan mail" and 2 AM telephone calls from strangers who thought because I wrote something I'd understand. Sometimes I did. But mostly, I found the little fragments of my inner life dispersed through movies, records, and the books that always were my form of meditation. Especially the poetry that kept me alive and sane and knowing I really wasn't alone or so outside it all. Just a call in the dark night of the soul, or bright light of a new morning or lazy afternoon in June, all that clichéd bunk we always bought because we felt it.

Six years in another town

And I can't believe all that's gone down—
I'm talking to the trees again
and I haven't done that since
God knows when—because I guess
it's Him, or Her, or It I'm talking to
when I look up at a tree and say
you got any advice for me today?—
and they always respond the same way
Frank O'Hara did, when he appeared to me
in the back of a checkered cab
on my way back from cheating
on the then woman in my life
a Costa Rican beauty I still miss
as I miss you all, even if I don't
call you too often—or at all—
I was high—on boo and other stuff—
we'd met at a literary awards event
where John Ashbery, O'Hara's close friend
had just received the nation's highest
poetic honor—or close enough—
and then we all piled into this bus
that took us back to the Plaza Hotel,
where Eloise once romped when I was
just her age only now it was me
thinking about this Canadian Jewish
beauty, famous for her literary liaisons
and how it would feel to be inside her
and know her famous beau, who was a rich
kid still at fifty, wouldn't know,
but I would the next time he looked
down his nose at me and my much
tougher poetry, the way I saw it—
anyway, I was full of guilt by now—
having been inside her and her home
and done the jitterbug of life and
then got up to leave and though I
had never deceived her, had told

her of my life with Ana and my son
from a still undivorced ex-wife—
she got mad and threw books at me
calling me "you bastard you son of
a bitch" as I fled down the stairs
and out into the New York night and
the checker cab that sped downtown
with me mumbling in the back seat
about my guilt although I'd never
cheated on Ana before and wouldn't
again and she'd never know—and
when we broke up it was because she
couldn't stay away from some younger
version of myself who gave her the
baby and marriage she wanted and
followed her home to Costa Rica
and some position in her family's
mini-empire—but this night we
were still all right except for my
feelings of being a rat to everyone
concerned because I never seemed to
learn that the possibility of making
love was not an imperative—I
felt so bad I thought I was dying—
from the dope and loss of hope that
I would ever be the man I thought
I was—when all of a sudden there
beside me in the cab was Frank O'Hara
in white shirt, open at the collar,
sleeves rolled up, and khaki pants
and penny loafers—he put an arm
around my shoulder and in the voice
I'd only heard on tapes and records
told me it was all right, that if I
hadn't done what I'd done that night
I wouldn't be me—the Michael
my friends seemed to love and even
admire—and that I wasn't gonna
die—or even have to lie—because
nobody would know—and I was so
relieved I cried a little—something

I only do when watching TV or a movie
and when I got home Ana didn't seem
to notice anything, only Miles, my
little five-year-old locked eyes
with mine and asked "What's wrong?"
and when I told him nothing, he
kept looking to see if I was telling
the truth, so I added "I'm just
glad to be home" which he accepted
as true, because it was—

Wait a minute, that was so many years ago,
what does it have to do with being here
in Southern California with you, writing
about "six years in another town" for
the new friends I have now, who never
knew me when I jitterbugged through
life's opportunities, cutting a rug,
giving everyone a hug of true affection
because I knew, or thought I knew back
then that every person was a friend
because inside they wanted just what
I did, to be free to really dig what
life has given us, including each other—
Even the woman I moved here with in 1982,
even the files they keep on me and you
to see if we might get in the way of
Bush or J. Danforth Quayle or whoever
else the powers that be get to run the
show up front while they continue to
milk us all for what they need to keep
that power to themselves, and if that
sounds like another decade, well, it's
almost 1989, time for this one to end
and leave us, my friends, as Dukakis
always calls complete strangers—and
leave us with only memories of what
someone has accurately called "The Mean
Decade"—and enter the time of
saving ourselves and each other again—
it's the earth and the universe too

now—what an awesome responsibility—
and how we continue to fuck it up—but
hey, we're only human, doing our best
to muddle through until tomorrow when
somebody else gets the job we thought
we wanted—I remember after Ted Berrigan
died, who also knew Frank when he was
alive, like I didn't—two Irish-American
poets like me, haunted by Catholic guilt
and dreams of sainthood and sex—or
sexhood and saint—I always think of
O'Hara as Saint Frank—and Ted, the
last time I saw him was in heaven—
I guess it was a dream—but there he
was, newly arrived—looking better than
he ever did when he was alive, trim and
healthy and clean and sharp and totally
quiet—a big surprise for a man who
lived on speed and machine-gunned his
every thought into the faces and minds
of anyone who crossed his path and even
those who didn't—he didn't say a
word, and I walked over to him and sat
down beside him to tell him how good
he looked and how happy I was to see
him because I was, he was my friend,
who helped me out when I needed help—
he knew the same codes I did and lived
his life that way so he could say, when
he loaned me a few hundred bucks he didn't
really have and I promised to pay it back
right away—"Hey, Michael, it would be
an insult for you to give this back man,
it's a gift, it's nothing compared to
all the pleasure your poetry has given
me" and I could say, when I did the same
for him when he was down and out like me,
which we both were most of the time back
then, I could tell him "vice versa only
double"—he was my friend—and now
here he was, in heaven, and not saying a

191

word until he smiled at me, as handsome
as I ever saw him, when I asked how he
was doing (dead and in heaven) and he
said "Michael, you don't know how great
it is not to have to talk anymore" and
it hit me, that must be heaven to a
guy like him, who never shut up and only
because he was so generous and smart and
had such a huge heart did we all put up
with the din when he let us in when we
went to pay him a visit—

Wait a minute! What has all this
got to do with living in L.A.?
Well, Ted passed away after I moved
here, and it pissed me off so much
I got in touch with my own need to
pass up speed and all the rest and
try to be the best I could be for
whatever time I had left—including
letting go of sex as the answer to
my disappointments in life—but
hey, it isn't always used that way—
sometimes it's just the most exciting
and convenient and fastest way to say
we're still alive today and glad of it—
Hey, you all say, wait a minute, he
calls this stuff poetry? I can do
that—which makes me feel real good
because the code of this boy's art
is the normal heart no matter how
surreal the circumstances—what
I mean is, the scene I dug the most,
came up through, and once was host to,
made it clear that if you're smart
you don't have to keep on proving it
in the work so that the person on
the receiving end goes: wow, I could
never do that, it's so difficult
and clever and precious and like a
machine I wasn't trained to run—

but we say, fuck that look-at-me-
I'm-educated-up-the-ass bullshit—
we say the work has got to be fun
even while it's taking on the Huns
of our existence, the bad guys in
the house of lies who disguise it
all as in our best interest—
these guys hypnotize with banality
as mean as genocide—while they
hide their true intent behind the
sense of expertise and techniques
we can only compromise—forget it—
art that makes you go, hey, I can
do that too is what moves me to see
life through to the end and still
be friends with myself—forget
the "off the shelf" operations that
the experts think we're better off
not knowing about—NO WAY! we
gotta shout our way back into history
because it's ours, just like these
six years here were mine—a time
when I got clean and sober unlike
any film by that name, but not so
different I couldn't recognize the
games we all play with denial in
those phony smiles Keaton threw around
playing the clown for death instead
of life where we all live whether we
like it or not—hey, wait a minute!
I wanted to tell you about my first
Oscar party at Spago—where I
threw some tuxedoed guy against
the wall when he tried to tell me I
couldn't cut in front of him on the line
to the men's room—I thought I blew
my whole career as a star when I'd
realized what I'd done—but later
he told my then wife that it was
the most exciting thing that had
happened to him all year—

I thought, wow, I'm glad I'm here
where coked up craziness gets
rewarded—only really I was full
of fear when I moved here a few
weeks later in '82 and met a lot of you,
fear I'd never be able to expose
myself as honestly as I had to friends
that went back so much further—
fear that I wasn't good enough
because I didn't have the money—
was like the honey the health nuts
pretend is better for you than all
that sugar we consumed when we were
kids—wait, I really want to stay
on track and get back to the art
I came out here to practice—and
did—that's what's gone down
in these six years too—I did get
to see myself on TV in a way I used
to dream I would—and even when it
wasn't very good—or I wasn't—
hey—goddamnit it was fun!—after
all it isn't like the war on AIDS or
the creeps who think this government
is theirs to run is gonna be lost or
won by what I do as a bad guy on a
nighttime soap—no, what it's gonna
do is give hope to the people I came
up with who think, or thought, that
guys like us didn't get this far and
if we did we were stars then and forgot
what it was like to not take any of it
too seriously—oh six years in another
town without the renown I thought would
be mine has left me so much more humble
which is something I guess I need
to be—but it has also left me
with all of you—and the chance to
make a new dance beyond the jitterbug
I flew through the bedrooms and back
seats and closets of my past with—

I mean hey, in '86 the dirty tricks
of Nixon were dismissed and suddenly
he's an "elder statesman" and if that
doesn't make us wake up and laugh
out loud at all those who would make
us proud of our worst qualities what
will? We still got some time left—
for some of us to get tough with the
stuff of life that turns us on and hold
a light to it for the rest of us to get some—
I mean I gave a reading where I read
for the first time only work written
here in this town, and it not only
went okay, an old old friend did
say—"Now that's a real poetry
reading"—and I thought they all
were—and they were—only now—
it's not to stir your juices only
and have you remember me as the star
of poetry that sounds the way we
sometimes think and talk and share
what we're afraid others might find
trite or at least not as mighty as
the real art stuff—no—I meant
to share a vision that has driven me
since my first memory—of a world
where love is not just an advertiser's
cliché but a way of life that isn't
serious like lying, but hopeful and
funny and important and honest and
significant and something that effects
all of us, the entire community, the
community of the universe, like dying
does—okay, that's not heavy, just
take a second look, what I'm saying is
there is no book of love without death
and there is no death without love—
unless it's a death that is lying—
and I know that truth is something
so elusive we can never really reach
it, but hey, we can approach it if

we try, and there's nothing saying we
can't dance as we do, and even dance
till we die, even if our dance is only
in the eye of those who love us—
that's what's really gone down these
six years, my heart, to the depths of
despair and fear and regret and sorrow
only to rise again for the miracle of
today that was only yesterday's tomorrow.

M^{Y WORK 2}

When I was a boy, I fantasized about becoming a policeman, like my grandfather, brother, brother-in-law, cousin next door, and the boarder in our house, or a "hardware man" like my father, or even a movie star or legendary musician, but I never thought about becoming a poet, I just wrote poetry as soon as I knew how to write, and never stopped.

My father had a 7th-grade education, and books and writing were considered something others did, not us. It was even considered a little dangerous, best left to the priests. But even so, my father would write little poems to send to customers or promote his work, and the words to the songs he sang around the house, or my older brothers and sisters played on their instruments or listened to on the radio, resonated—along with the litanies and hymns from church—through my soul and contributed to my addiction to language.

I was a print junkie as early as I can remember, reading everything I could get my hands on. They had these religious books in a little rack at the back of the church, and one of them, the deepest and most difficult was *The Dark Night of the Soul* by St. John of the Cross, the 16th-century Spanish mystic. As a teenager, I thought he was saying that in order to reach the heights of ecstasy, like the greatest saints, you had to first plunge to the depths of decadence, like the greatest sinners. That's not what *The Dark Night of the Soul* said, but that's what I got out of it. And since I was obsessed with sex, and the guilt involved in that for an Irish-American Catholic at that time, I thought St. John of the Cross was giving me permission to lead the life I knew was mine anyway, and to write about it while I did.

In that way, and in many others, I always felt and still do that poetry saved my life. When I was a kid trying to understand where my place might be in the world, it gave me something to look forward to. And later, when I was a young man on the streets trying to live some version of my truth, that I thought at the time was the only authentic one, and nearly killing myself in the process, it kept me in touch with the pure intentions of the child I had started out as—the feeling of being on a mission to find the words to express the truth I felt inside but rarely saw expressed outside in the world around me.

I had this naive but beautiful idea that if I could only write or say the word that perfectly expressed what we all—humans, animals, plants, rocks, earth, the whole universe—share in common, that it would end forever the fighting and strife and oppression and repression that keeps us from being who we really are. In the meantime, poetry gave me a home where I could always find understanding and acceptance. When things were at their darkest I turned to poetry. Not just writing it, but opening a favorite poet's book to find some solace, some connection with a life force beyond the petty concerns and frustrations of the circumstances I found myself in at the time.

A lot of my earliest work I thought was unique, that no one else was writing in a language as accessible, without the usual poetic imagery and academic references—no matter how subtle, or competitive expressions of the "uniqueness" of personal imagination—but *with* the narrative structure and rhythms of the Irish storytelling and music—and African-American "toasting" and music—I grew up around. A lot of times, especially in the 1960s, when I was reading my poetry in coffee houses and bars, schools and wherever, all over the USA, and in the 1970s, when my work first started being published in book form and getting reviewed and discussed, some readers and critics would insist that what I was writing wasn't "poetry" in any traditional sense. But they just weren't hip to the traditions I was coming from and hopefully extending in new ways. Nowadays there's tons of people publishing and recording and standing up reading to packed houses the kind of work I felt I pioneered, along with a few others, back in the days, and I'm glad to see it.

Ever since Marcel Duchamp signed a snow shovel and called it "In Advance of the Broken Arm," "art" is whatever the artist says it is. It always seemed to me that likewise "poetry" is whatever the poet says it is; it doesn't have to conform to anybody else's idea of what poetry might or might not be. I've written all kinds of poems with all kinds of approaches to structure and rhythm, juxtaposition and shape, vocabulary and connotation. A lot has an emphasis on narrative drive but with lyric rhythms—and anti-poetic-imagery but with occasional rhyme—within language that the people I grew up around would use and understand, though in

198

my case to articulate approaches to truths I rarely heard them express or discuss.

A lot of people, when they hear the word "poetry," think of what they were taught in school. Then they say they "don't like poetry." They would never say they don't like music. What they mean is they don't like the poetry they had to read in school or heard at some boring lecture. But like music, all you have to do is change the station, listen with new ears, go to a different reading, pick up another book and be surprised to find out poetry isn't always what you thought it was but can be something much closer to the thoughts and feelings, experiences and fantasies, or just rhythms and creative energy, that have been repressed inside you for years and now someone has finally given voice to them. That's the kick for me, and I always want to see anyone who can do any kind of poetry get to do it, so we can have all kinds to choose from. Freedom of choice in everything, including poetry, that's my platform.

WORK, PLAY, AND PRAYER

I always say I started working for a living when I was 10—I never had the chance to play, except the musical instruments I picked up on in my spare time back then—but I think it was 11 or 12. I didn't stop until I was 30—weekends, after school, vacations—I even worked on Christmas day every year until I left home—and joined the Air Force where I got busted for being such a wise ass punk and ended up doing the same routine, not just my daily enlisted man's job but spending weekends painting latrines and all that stuff that made Richard Gere's life in *Officer and a Gentleman* look like what it was, the privileged semi-vacation of officer's training. Then when I got out, already a published poet, I got tired of people telling me what I wrote wasn't poetry, and the way I talked wasn't proper English, even though I'd always say, good, I'm not English anyway, I'm Irish-American. But when I wanted to show them I had the credentials to define poetry and the knowledge of how to use the language imposed on my ancestors by foreign invaders and on me by my being born and raised in New Jersey, I went to the University of Iowa Writers Workshop, at the time the most prestigious place you could go to for poetry, and while I worked on an undergraduate and graduate degree both at the same time, and both in poetry, I also got up every day at 5 AM to go unload trucks at Procter and Gamble outside Iowa City, in fact so far outside I had to walk a mile from where the bus dropped me off because I couldn't afford a car, and then later between classes I had a little home maintenance business like I grew up working in for free for my father after school and on Saturdays. Also, at night in Iowa, I worked in a book store, and even later at night for a private press as a printer's devil—I set the type for Ezra Pound's last book but couldn't afford to buy a copy of that edition, which sold for 100 bucks each, and my boss flew off to Italy with the first page for Pound to sign before we bound the book—and I set a book of Gary Snyder's (*Regarding Wave*) only to have him pontificate at the publication party and completely ignore me, his biggest fan at the time, until my boss told him, hey man there wouldn't be any book if this guy hadn't stayed up all night setting your fucking impossible to set poems by hand trying to duplicate precisely every extended space between words, and all that stuff.... But Snyder still didn't thank me he just told me I should take my wife and kids and go out and live in the desert or the mountains if I wanted to be a real poet and I told him I already was a real poet and I was taking my wife and kids back to the city as soon as I could because I found as much spiritual significance in the bright red of a traffic light against the deep blue of a late afternoon city sky as I guess he did in telling people how to live in this world from a place as far away from people as he could get. But the point of all this was I worked all the time until I turned 30 and got 5,000 dollars from the National Endowment for the Arts for my poetry. Then I stopped working and just happened to meet a Costa Rican woman who had been raised so wealthy and spoiled she had never been allowed to even enter the kitchen to get a drink of water on her own so she ran away to America where she learned to cook for her Irish-American husband until we met and they split and she moved next door to me and talked me into taking my newfound wealth and her to Europe for the first vacation of my life. And I did, even though until then I had always put down Europe as too snobby and trendy and upper class for a regular guy like me, from Jersey, but I realized then that was just because I couldn't afford it, like the fancy restaurants I took my friends to before we left, after cashing the check and spreading the 5 grand all over the mattress-on-the-floor I slept on—I threw these hundreds around these joints that for the first time I didn't have to check the prices on the menus to order in, and my friends worried that the money wouldn't last, and they were right, but I got another check from another poetry foundation, and despite for the first time in my life beginning to worry about money, like what would happen if it ran out, I really felt like this was going to be my fate from now on—one grant after another until I was poet laureate—a word I still can't even say, like hey, they're gonna honor me for poems called "Piece of Shit" or "She Whipped Me with Her Tits"—let alone "Fuck Me in the Heart." And in fact, ten years after that first grant, long after the Costa Rican lady left when the money ran out and I couldn't pay the rent and long after some congressman had quoted me in the Congressional Record as one of "America's major poets" some other congressmen quoted from "My Life" on the floor of the house as proof that the National Endowment had funded pornography, i.e. my poetry, only these congressmen didn't get the media attention they were looking for, because the lines of mine they quoted in Congress couldn't be quoted in the media to prove their point because they would all be bleeps—so it took them a few more years to find the visual equivalent in the photographs that stirred up their latest attempt to shut down the NEA. But hey, this is about work, and now it's about play, something I only associated with music and sports which I could fake good enough, but I thought either me or my life was too tough for any other kind, and there wasn't much time to spare anyway, so sports were pretty much given up after high school, and music after the last time a group of mine got into a hassle among themselves in a club we were playing in the South, I walked off the stand and never played with a band again—if I told you when that was, most of you would say you weren't even born yet. But my kids might say I knew how to play with them, no, I guess we didn't play, we danced and still do—when all three of us are together again we usually put on some music and before long we're dancing around the house, just like we did when they were little and I was happy or high or both and despite the troubles with their mother I loved every second with them and the only way I knew back then to express it was to dance, something I quit when I was 15 and the dance that became the twist was still just a party thing and I was the only white at some girl's house in East Orange and I knew I wouldn't get this movement right so I just decided that night to never dance again so I wouldn't have to worry about not looking cool for that reason, and then when I was 30 I was in a gay bar with a bunch of men and when they all got up together I figured we were leaving so I got up and went with them but we ended up on the dance floor and they all started moving to the music and it would have been more embarrassing and uncool to walk away like a fool so I moved too and found I could not only do it but dug it and realized that maybe it was because for all those years it was my fears about what women would think of me when I tried to do anything like sports or music or dancing or walking down the street—and there I was with no women around and suddenly I was shaking the ground with my dancing hips and shoulders and feet and it felt so good I got up the nerve to try it with women around and eventually felt so at ease I didn't even have to get high to do it anymore, and now, there's no stopping me once I hit the dance floor, so I guess that's still my way of doing whatever we're calling "play"—so what's left is prayer and that's easier to talk about because it's just me talking to the God I happen to be and see in everything and everyone else, especially, when I'm down, in a tree. It's always been that way for me, I've been talking to trees since I was a kid because they always seemed to me to be the epitome of cool, they are the essence of what it means to meditate, taking one long breath each day and letting it out each night, they can feel the earth move in their roots and what they have to say comes out in this incredibly unique way, they are like machines of art, reflecting whatever the air and light and earth are going through at any given time—okay, I'm getting carried away again, when all I really wanted to say is, any good poem is a prayer. I believe that. And any good prayer is a poem.

I'M LONELY AGAIN

I'm feeling so alone again. My kids are leaving for school—not down the street or across town, but the other side of the country—college, something I got kicked out of at their age, and went back to at my new girlfriend's age, who my daughter doesn't like my being involved with because she's so close to her age—and because she's an actress and acts sometimes like she's got something together my daughter hasn't even figured out what it might be yet. It's a confusing time for all of us. But especially me right now because I'm alone and they're all out doing their own separate things. My son seeing his girlfriend, or ex-girl for the last time before he goes, his new clothes draped on his slim figure in a way that makes everyone comment on how well he looks, so far from my self-consciousness at his age over how skinny I was—he is—only he can dig it because I never gave him the Irish curse I grew up on, namely, "You're a good looking young man, who do you think you are?" His sister more like me, trapped between a three-year-old know-it-all and ready for anything, and an eighty-year-old worry wart about a future that doesn't exist and a present that isn't as intimidating as it always seems. I used to beam at them all the time, I was so overloaded with love for these kids I raised for almost twenty years. But even though my daughter and I have tears in our eyes half the time we speak to each other, it isn't all poignant or tender, it's often frustration and confusion—how to let each other go without using anger or numbness as the—oh, you know what I mean. This scene has been played out so many times before by so many more—I just thought I'd go through it differently. After all, I used to know it all before I knew it all would matter so fucking much.

ON THE ROAD

I'm tired. I'm sad. I'm waiting to get mad at myself for letting you down, for hanging around when I should be on the road again.

I remember how it was before Kerouac wrote his famous novel—before it was published—before it had the impact we still suffer from. When I was a kid after the Second World War, these new kinds of stores appeared way outside town, like huge airplane hangars full of piles of odd surplus goods from hoses to pens—so families would drive out on the fairly empty roads to see what the smart operators who discounted these remains from the logistics nightmare of the war had to offer. This was before malls. And maybe on the way we'd stop at a truck farm stand and buy some sweet corn and fresh peaches. Everybody in the neighborhood grew their own tomatoes and grapes and watermelons. But those trips in cars with Dynaflow or straight eights—were like the light at the other end of the tunnel. For a Jersey boy, the light at the end of the tunnel was Manhattan—which promised everything Jersey couldn't come up with, but heading in the opposite direction promised everything Jersey had, only more of it and sweeter.

I remember by the '50s when I was old enough to stick out my thumb on the first good day of Spring, a day like today actually, with a feeling of such sweet anticipation and excitement at the possibilities—starting with the people who stopped—cars full of black guys passing a bottle and sometimes even a joint around—gypsies with all their possessions on the roof—shy businessmen who'd ask probing questions that reminded you of all the fag jokes you ever heard and made you nervous but sure of your heterosexual superiority—proto-beatniks who didn't know where they were going either.

I'd end up in little upstate New York towns and walk into the local radio station where there was always some guy in glasses in his 20s playing some hip sound and happy to show some enthusiastic kid around for want of anybody else to impress I guess.

Or in some midsize city with a hip little district where I could pretend to be hipper than I was and meet adventurous wallflowers waiting to be discovered—I specialized in them—I knew the way they thought—and felt—and what they were waiting for—a cute

205

stranger who treated them like the sexual time bombs they always were.

Sometimes I'd almost get killed. Sometimes I'd get some sexual thrill. For years I kept a coat that combined stains from my blood from a fight in upstate New York—and from my come from an encounter in rural Pennsylvania. Really not that different from Jersey nights, except they happened on the road where most of the neighborhood toads who treated me like a freak had never been. It made me feel I had it over them—wearing that coat when I got on the road again.

I always looked for the jazz—and after the beatnik thing made *Time* magazine, I'd look for the coffee house. It was great to be a hip teenager, because grown up chicks actually hung out in places that didn't serve booze, so you could hang out there too. I even ended up playing in some of them—a little piano, a little less bass—but enough to give me credentials. That and the way I talked black—and the fact that I took so much flack back in my part of Jersey for doing just that, and for the black girls I found so much easier to cut through the lies with—or maybe just to be myself with and not be afraid of that. It's ironic that white country girls were that way too—somehow they always knew how to cut through the usual game.

Then it got more serious. Some of these rural girls were already married at 17—with kids maybe—and an ex-husband who'd catch me in the men's room in some country bar I'd fake my way into and sucker punch me with my fly down. But I knew what to do—go down like I was through—and get off with a few kicks and warnings.

Or if they were black—talk back but with a lot of respect so that it didn't look like I didn't know I had the weight of history and white society on my side and yet I chose not to use it—or something like that.

Sometimes that didn't work and I'd really get hurt. But somehow I always protected my face—as if I knew that was my out. It always looked younger and more innocent then I ever was. So when cops picked me up—I could convince them I was only slumming or I'd been misled or misdirected or lost—and they usually bought it—enough to drive me to the city line and let me go with a warning, sending me home. But when they turned around, I'd stick out my thumb and be on the road again.

It's all different now. The last time I tried to hitch a ride, nobody stopped and I had to walk the several miles from 20th Century Fox to The Improv. And I understood why—I wouldn't stop for a guy like me anymore—you just don't want to open your door to a stranger, and vice versa in these times when strangers passing by in cars might blow your brains out just because you are on the road, or on the sidewalk or on your porch. It's like the chickens have come home to roost—only they got the wrong house—it's the white house where the trouble starts. No, I guess it's in our hearts. The home we started from is where we always come back to it seems, especially in my dreams where it stands for everything I miss, or never found in all that hitching around. I wonder if it even exists.

I_s it the blues?_

You feelin bad because you're lonely,
and you think it's 'cause you're too old?
Then you must not remember
how bad life could feel sometimes
when you were too young.

Or you think it's 'cause you're too fat?
Better check out those people over there
dying of AIDS, see if the blues can't be thin.

"Hey," you say, "you know what I mean,
if I looked as clean and white as you—"
Oh, you think us nice looking white men
never feel the way you do?

You think those business cats that
supposedly run the world are feeling
happy all the time as they die in their
prime from the pressures of a job
they probably thought would save them too
from the ways we feel when we're feelin blue?

You think a beautiful blonde must have it made?
That being a celebrity or a star means
the blues can't mar your feelings of success?

Better rewrite that thought or else explain
why Marilyn made a mess of just that kind of scene.
I mean shit, ain't it time we all quit this game
of not admitting that we're all the same inside?

Ain't it time we all dropped that reverse pride
and admit the way we feel the same about
the good stuff and the bad that overwhelms us in this life?

Whether you're the husband or the wife, the kid or the old folk,
black or white, Indian or even Shi'ite—
deep down the feelings are the same.

208

The pain of separation from a loved one,
whether by death or abandonment or mutual
consent, makes anybody sad, and the feeling
of love, for any one or any thing in the universe,
is what makes us glad.

Ain't it about time we recognized that our
common welfare must come first,
and that it ain't no easier for you or me,
or that self-obsessed celebrity, to get
through a day without some sadness and some pain?

"Wait a minute," you yell, "there you go again—
a lot of money makes things easier and—fame,
well hell, everybody knows that's today's game,
and if you're winning the game—" Yeah? What?
You end up happily ever after?
Like Tyson and Givens or Amy and Stephen?

I know I know, we can't compare the pain
of a homeless old lady, or a young man in his prime
dying of AIDS, with the loneliness of a wealthy TV star
—well, unless maybe it's Rock Hudson.

See, that's the deal—it's the end of the millennium
and time to understand, that any plan we have for ourselves
is useless without the rest of the universe in on it too.
'Cause the forces we have set in motion
don't distinguish between us, that's the fucking point—

The greenhouse effect, pollution, chemical warfare,
nuclear disaster—the ocean's dying and the sky, the sky is lying
when it looks so pure and blue on a day like today,
because it too is slipping away—

unless we stop feeling sorry for ourselves
and what makes us different, not good enough,
shortchanged and discriminated against by life and the world—
and dig that every one of us depends upon the rest
in ways that mean we have to do our best to emphasize
(which is one of the positive meanings of stress)

what we all share in common—

a common threat in the ways we're destroying the world,
and a common hope in the ways we're beginning
to recognize each other in ourselves.

And that's what we're doing here tonight you know—
This isn't about the "poetry of the stars" like the paper said,
this is about poetry as the star
when it tells the truth about who we all are,
even when we come from so much fear we need
a bunch of lawyers to help us tell who are the creators
and who are the destroyers

Nah, we know all about that, it comes with the gift of life.
We know that fear is the great divider and love
is the great provider, and that everything in the universe
has to pay some dues and has the right sometimes
to sing the blues.

I mean there were six million Jews killed by the Nazis
and then five million of other kinds of humans—
including Gypsies and Catholics and Communists and Gays.

And the list of the oppressed and the oppressors changing sides
could go on for days—so let's drop it
and just stand up and be counted as a member
of the universal race, and the next time someone says
someone's too old or too white or too sexy or too polite
just say "Hey, get out of my face—"

We all take our turns in that place we call the blues,
and if you think you know somebody who doesn't
know what it means to lose, then you're just confused,
and that's only human too—and something we all do.

The blues can be righteous, I guess,
but I don't think they can take self-righteousness—
and neither can I, even from me, so I'll let this be now,
and just say—Hey, it's never too late for me to dig myself
in you, and for you to dig yourself in me.

C^{AIT SANG}

—and now and then a sound so womanly and powerful came out, it made us gasp for breath or our eyes fill with tears or our hearts fill up so fast we felt like flying. And the crying was all joy, despite the feelings for her mother gone, and mine gone too—and my father who she knew so briefly in ways she can't remember even, but mostly in ways she and I understand without the need to verbalize it, we only get into father/daughter riffs anyway. When we're on the phone it's full of love and concern and advice and understanding, and when we're face to face it's full of impatience and concern and nitpicking and intolerance and love, and we can't stand it long alone. But in the tone of her voice when she sang opera and then comedy, we all had to cry and laugh. And then we heard the nervous vulnerability and had to recognize how much we never know about each other, no matter how far we go— 3,000 miles, just to hear her sing and let her know.

MILES PLAYED

—at The House of Blues, where they have all kinds of signs and symbols about tolerance and acceptance but won't let you in if you're dressed in shorts or sandals. But none of that mattered because Miles' played bass with his band. The disembodied deep voice of authority broke through the babble of diners and drinkers—as the upstairs bar split apart in the kind of night club artistry I used to think only happened in movies—to introduce them: "Ladies and gentleman, will you please welcome to the House of Blues..." or something equally generic but sounding profound and epic to my ears as the two pieces of the bar and the walls behind them swung back to reveal the stage and a dance floor packed to overflowing with a crowd waiting for X, and I almost lost my breath, so thrilled to see my son on the giant TV screen above the stage and then for real down there below it smiling out at the crowd that not only didn't ignore them or yell for the main act they had in fact mostly come to see, but instead began grooving and moving to the bass beat Miles laid down, along with the others, and his sister Cait and I grinned beatifically into each other's weepy eyes as we realized our son and brother had finalized some vision of all of ours—of almost anybody in this modern world—to be on a big stage in front of a huge crowd cheering you on as they dance and jump around and shout and play air guitar and air drums to the rock'n'roll music coming out of *you*.

Two of the greatest nights of my life, so far—I was thinking—this one and the night Cait gave a solo concert of classic music written for the human voice, hers, at least for that night, her college senior project which began with an almost empty house just before it started, only to fill up with all kinds of people who ended up cheering her on too, as this crowd was cheering on Miles and his crew, and my heart could hardly contain my feelings of love and gratitude.

There were other nights I thought at the time would be more memorable. But they aren't, as it turns out. This is what fulfills my life, as I shout to Cait how great it is to share this delight at the sight of her brother beaming down at us and the hundreds of others boogie-ing down into this momentous night. Don't get me wrong, we all know—my children and me—that this is not what life is really all about, satisfying the urge to entertain and make happy and move a lot of people all at once, no, we know it goes much deeper than that, in fact without going deeper into ourselves until we come out more humble and honest and at peace with so much that grieves us, this wouldn't mean much. Cait shouts back how she wishes her mother could see this too, and I respond how I think she's viewing it with us, as I often do, and it's too much to express, even now, writing it down, without clichés and sentimental scenarios that even I find too much sometimes. Let's just say it was a little bit of sublime and I felt lucky to experience it.

L OOK IT UP

He moved into the little monk's room to write the book again, the one he'd been writing all his life, the book of that life, only this time in a way that couldn't be ignored. And that first night alone for the first time in so long, he loved himself, like he did as a little boy, his skin, the bones and muscle and fat that it covered, every inch, from his balding crown to the toughened soles of his feet, and in the process got excited and relieved. And hours later, when he got up to pee, picked up the come-stained tissues from the floor where he had thrown them and felt something crawl up his hand and wrist. Turning on the light he felt frightened by the sight of ants all over the Kleenex and his hand, and on the floor their trail so dark and vibrant in the bustle of their concentration on the booty of his sweet ejaculation, and he wondered what it was that drew them from their depths to this second story room with nothing but books and records and art to uncover a connection with the world he never dreamed of.

For a second he thought it was a punishment. As he flushed the Kleenex and the ants clinging to it he thought of all the priests and nuns who'd made him feel so guilty for this act of self love and affection. But he knew better now. He'd studied the texts himself to see where they'd gone wrong, not him and the others who were condemned for nature's pleasures. No sin of Onan as the fundamentalists insist. God didn't punish Onan for "spilling his seed" but for not fulfilling his duty to his brother's widow to give her the child his brother left her without. What would the world be like if the right wing Christians got their literal interpretation of the Bible's dictates? Sinners stoned to death? People living in tents and shitting on the ground? Masturbation being condemned as some enormous sin as wars are justified and guns protected? Like in Iran or parts of Afghanistan? He watched as the ants looked elsewhere for their satisfaction, until they finally gave up. By dawn they were gone, and he felt his new home had been Christened, so to speak, in the true meaning of the original Greek.

SOME KIND OF GENIUS

1. QUEER

"Well," you say, "you could have been queer and still married with two children and just not known it yet." And later on I was attracted to some men, though never sexually—never in the ways I always was and am toward women, i.e. that sensation of sensual need and ultimate satisfaction or expectation of it, that obsession with the physical detail—the curve of an ass, the soft suggestive sensuality of lips or hips or breasts or softly rounded shoulders and skin (especially at the neck and wrist and thigh and back of knees). But I did "have sex" with men in my thirties and sometimes was delighted and quite satisfied by it and even thought I was in love with one or two young men (who happened to be among the men I had sex with, though with them it turned out to be quite unsatisfying and in fact quite disappointing and what from most points of view would be considered failures).

But at least when during those years I wrote and published poems and articles and stories about being "queer" or stood up in front of class rooms, bar rooms, living rooms, meeting halls, auditoriums, churches, arenas, stadiums, neighborhoods, cities, states, the world, and proclaimed my "flaming faggotry," in order for me to be what we began calling in those days with pride at having, we thought, invented it—"politically correct"—by identifying with the oppressed in public ways and thus not copping out to some "bi-sexual" label allowing me to bridge two worlds, whenever convenient dipping into one or the other for whatever temporary rewards or escapes (as from the repercussions of being labeled a "faggot" in situations where that might be and was a liability and I could claim to not be, given my attraction to almost all women and lack of same toward almost all men, but since I once, and then again and many more agains throughout a year or two and then occasionally for a few more had sex with men and could have pretended to still be "straight" because in my deepest understanding and belief in myself I knew I still was—and am—I would have been able to avoid the repercussions of what was and is the natural, I believe, capacity for any man—and maybe women too—to be sexually gratified by almost anything once she, or he, gives in to it.

2. BLACK

But "Black?" How could I ever have believed such an obvious untruth—I'm so obviously "white" in all appearance and reality. Although, some "black" people seem to have been too. And to some "whites" back when I was 20 in 1962, I "passed" as "black" then too! In a segregated South Carolina where I was stationed as an already once court-martialed enlisted man, I ran into the barriers of that time and place and put myself on the side I'd already chosen back in Jersey years when confronted by "my own kind" to "make a choice" between them and my new "colored" friends. The choice was easy, as it was later in the South. "I'm Black," I told the guy behind the counter in the commissary when I asked for a *Jet* magazine and he in his white supremacy looked at me funny and asked "Why" I'd "want to buy that colored magazine"—"My great-grandmother was colored" I tell him, and by their rules that made me "colored" too although he could see as anyone could, except in the fantasy of those times and maybe still, that I was white as snow, or at least pink as snow with fading blood spilled on it, but he bought it and blushed in embarrassment for being so unperceptive as he took my money for my copy of *Jet* which made me feel at home to read and check out the always pretty "colored girls" in bathing suits that spiced up every issue. Or maybe he just blushed for me, so obviously not "black" who felt compelled to lie about it in those circumstances. But how explain the man who let me into the segregated dances on that base when I gave him the same excuse after being stopped and told where I was trying to enter was "for colored only"—he was a white MP, the kind that often gave me trouble in my drunken bouts of rage and wreaking havoc on the civilians of my various postings, and yet he too blushed as though I'd caught him in some embarrassing position when I explained about my (fictional) "colored" heritage and let me in where the true "blacks" (according to our weirdly irrelevant in real existence, but made real in our self-created one, "race" standards/credentials) looked on me mostly as an intruder, or at least interloper in their much looser, sexier, darker (I mean for reasons those who have experienced legally enforced segregation well know, against all rules the "white" dances had to follow—bright lights, no liquor, no grinding on the dance floor or groping in the few shadowed corners—the "colored" dances were allowed to be conducted in almost total

216

darkness where much booze and even drugs in those repressive days and certainly sex occurred with almost no supervision, except by those "Black" NCOs who were indulging in those activities too) celebrations of what life they could enjoy outside the purview of "the man." To some I was "the man" until I proved otherwise, to others I could never prove it.

There are people you and I both took for "white"—I'm thinking of an actor I once worked with who you've seen mostly in commercials, national ones for well-known products and services, playing the typical white commercial character, the white Everyman, the representative of white taste and manner and self definition, only this man's true history is his mother's "black" in terms of our divisive predilections. Or what about Jennifer Beals, who everyone seemed shocked to discover, after her meteoric exposition in *Flashdance* made her a household face—beautifully romantically ideally "American" in every way—that she wasn't "white" but was instead what once was called "mulatto"—and maybe led to her stagnated career despite her obvious commercial success and physical appeal—until by the time of *Devil in a Blue Dress* with Denzel Washington it's almost a cliché, her playing a character we now know in real life has "passed" for "white." Or another woman I once knew who was as "white" as I am and played everything from French to Irish in some movies you might have seen who when I fell in lust with the sweet curve of her incredible behind explained that it was so fine because it was "black booty" and showed me a photo of her "mulatto" mother. What good are all these categories when we can be so easily deceived? Though "not so easy" you might say if you're "black" in a way that cannot be denied or "passed" over. And yet, I once had an honor, a prize I won for my poetry, taken back when I arrived in person and they told me, after they got over the shock, that they had thought I was "black" and the prize was reserved for "minorities." They read me wrong, they later thought, but not me. Or sometimes still, on the phone, someone will assume I'm a "brother," especially when I'm angry, or tired, or any emotionally charged moment when I revert to ways of talking I picked up when I was in my teens and my adult personality was forming, and as a "brother man" I get special care and treatment on those awful hold-forever service lines and end up conspirationally sharing a chuckle or giggle or deep throated laugh at the expense of "the man" they'd take me for if they could see me.

217

3. MOVIE STAR

My name appeared in ads and in the opening credits after that word: "starring"—and my face in TV commercials advertising the films, and in the films themselves. And now my name appears in print in some movie guide books after "starring"—even if they then go on to rate the movies "bombs"—or in some video rental stores and chains in their reference books or computer listings under "Movie Stars." And yet, nobody's heard of me or knows me as such, so how can it be? These labels that once defined me, in ways that made no sense outside my own reality. What kind of genius is that?

CAN'T STOP THINKIN' ABOUT

My brother. Whenever I wrote about him he was always "my brother the priest." But except for some hazy memories of visiting him when I was a kid and he was already grown in distant homes for young men in long brown robes with rope around their waists, rosaries hanging from them like holsters from the hips of gunslingers in all the Westerns so popular back then on TV and in the movies we both love—I never really knew him. He was the oldest, gone before I was three, to a war he never fought in but that changed him so profoundly he made the decision to become a Franciscan and ask to be sent to Japan. And he was, in 1955, and has lived there ever since. Over the years, he'd come back for visits. I'd be told by my mom to write to him, this abstract figure in my life, a virtual stranger, who I remembered as having a crazy sense of humor, like the time he was driving me to an uncle's Jersey farm to help pick apples in our father's old pick up truck and he pretended his foot got stuck to the gas pedal when I worried that he was going too fast. I almost wet my pants as he laughed and finally slowed down on the old barely-two-lane country road. I thought his foot was really stuck. I believed him. He was my big brother, the oldest, good looking and light hearted, but serious too, a soon to be priest back then when he pretended he couldn't help speeding.

Now here I am, in 1993, flying to Japan. It's Easter Sunday somewhere, though where we are I'm not sure, as we cross the international dateline and arrive a day and four hours after we left L.A. for a twelve-hour flight. The airline is Malaysian and many are going on to exotic sounding places like Kuala Lumpur. The stewardesses wear sari-like colorful wrapping and though exquisitely feminine in their appearance and the way they carry themselves, their look is direct and strong and their manner polite but solidly secure, as if they fear nothing from any man. There are many Asians on board, and I am suddenly aware of the variety. From dark-skinned fine featured Indians and Pakistanis to Polynesian featured residents of less familiar lands. But even the more familiar Western stereotypes of Asians become more distinct as I encroach upon their turf and my eyes become more discerning. And then we're there, through the customs where some of these

219

so-called Asians obviously speak nothing but English and are as flustered by the lack of understanding from some inspectors as from the surface politeness of them all, even in their surprising inefficiency. After a lot of walking with my over packed and too heavy "carry-on," and then a train ride like some new American subway car, and up and down some stairs I finally arrive in actual non-international air flight territory. I'm in the Tokyo-Narita Airport, on Japanese land, and there's my brother in his casual civilian clothes, a man of sixty-six with pink face and bald head and dark brown shoes that look too big. His smile is as bright as ever, as I remember it back in that old jalopy truck, only now I think I understand much better what's behind it.

He leads me through the maze of competing signs all in Japanese with very few concessions to the foreigner, and even he's confused by what appears to be and he confirms is new in this part of the terminal until we make our way down to a subway-like train stop to wait for an express to take us to Tokyo, an hour's ride away in the dark. I'm already surprised at how familiar things seem to be. Except that almost everyone is Japanese, and white Westerners already are beginning to seem strange looking and overweight and pale and too big and almost clumsy in their exaggerated-seeming movements, the rest could be anywhere there's newer trains and stations. It isn't the famous bullet train, I discover, as it pulls in and we get on. It's Sunday so there's no rush hour crowd that has to be stuffed in by men with white gloves, it's just a newish commuter style train. My brother speaks now and then to Japanese in what I learn later is his uniquely styled version of their language—unlike some of his contemporaries, the few American young Franciscans who came over with him and now decades later speak in the deliberate and careful style of most Japanese so they are always taken for that on the phone. My brother has imbued his use of what has become his more-often-spoken tongue with his New Jersey–Irish–American–Lally personality that makes most Japanese burst out in unexpected—to them as well as us—laughter, not at his accent, which is pretty clean, but at his way of talking, which is so upfront truthful and excited and curious and genuinely awe-struck at the little things few Japanese would feel so free to comment on so honestly.

I always describe him as the kind of guy who says, as he's riding in your car, oh wow look Mike, a gas station, as if he's never seen one before, or one so unique or interesting or useful or whatever. The Japanese practice a particular kind of restraint in the ways they speak and act and look, even kids in outrageous variations of some punk or grunge (not quite there yet) or neo-American teenage style seem to still be so repressed, I'm discovering, as I check them out on the train, but when my brother exclaims, "Wow, so cheap" in Japanese at some ticket to the movies the next day they all laugh and giggle at his honesty, his commenting on such things they never question in any public way, unless organized to do so by their jobs or clubs or political movements.

As we make our way to Tokyo I see signs along the highways we pass, neon and lit-up billboards, the same kinds we have here or most places now. But somehow, more than any other foreign land I've been to, this already seems so familiar, like the roads and stores and factories and even fields and trees out there could be New Jersey. Where's the sliding paper doors and Golden Temples of my literary memory of this strange land? Then as we enter another tunnel coming into Tokyo like entering New York on Amtrak, I feel excited at the prospect of the new and different and can't wait to get outside. Well, once out of the train station the city looks familiar too, like parts of Washington DC or Chicago or even downtown L.A. until we get into a cab and the door opens automatically and the seats are covered with the kind of white doilies my grandmother used to make for the backs of chairs and couches to prevent the grease stains of men's hair tonics back then. When we get out the cab door slams shut, again without our touching it, and we go into this small city building that could be any one in Newark near where we grew up. But it's in Tokyo, and is the Franciscan Center where my brother worked for years. He even ran the place most of that time, organizing poetry readings and art shows, giving meeting spaces to twelve-step programs, and ministering to the needs of those both Japanese and foreign who might need some help in some way these good men could give it. He also said Mass in one of the chapels here of course, and morning prayers and other rituals of faith, baptizing babies and the few converts he made, marrying them when they grew up, or their parents before they were born. It's a typical city building, a little worn when I go up to the room they give me on the same floor with the priests. There's only four there permanently, or semi-permanently: one of my brother's classmates—another pink-faced bald old guy with a light in his eye who is on his way to somewhere like China or Thailand or Rome the next morning; a good-looking gray haired guy who seems aware of his charisma in an unassuming masculine and even humble way; the new head of the place, a gray-haired younger guy who does things his way now, including letting Filipino women, who are in Japan to do the underpaid and unwanted jobs stay two floors up from where we are, and on the floor between one Filipino priest and some brothers and other men who have been given homes in this otherwise underused old dorm-like setting. The rooms are small, like some cheap Times Square hotel, or worse, motel, with a cot-size bed, a desk, a wardrobe and a sink with mirror where I splash some water on my face and then go get my brother to go out for my first walk in the Tokyo night before we go to bed.

The neighborhood is called Rippongi, and I later learn, just from observation, is where a lot of foreigners end up. The "model" clubs are here, where Western girls who come over to make money modeling can get in free and others come to see if they are there. Except for a few club entrances covered with graffiti, the rest are kind of typical of clubs anywhere. And on the wider streets you could be in New York but somewhere bland like the West 50s, or even downtown Newark. I don't see any buildings that impress at least at night, and only on the narrower side streets that are almost empty on this Sunday night do I feel like I might be somewhere I haven't been before. But not really even there, because I have, in New York's Chinatown or even little Tokyo in L.A. The streets look not that new or clean, though the debris is minimal. And yes there's homeless guys around and they look the same too, just Asian faces, but the same dirt stains and attitudes. When we get back to the Franciscan Center, there's shopping bags full of rice cakes sitting on the front steps in the dark, waiting for the priests and volunteers to pick them up in a few hours and take them to the sleeping hungry homeless men. I'm impressed with what these guys are doing, the Franciscans, with what little they obviously have. I forgot that the church I grew up in has its own kind of beatnik radical class of charitable activism and that a lot of it started with Francis, the guy these guys decided to follow. I'm impressed that this is who I'm staying with and not in some hotel with tourists like I sure don't feel like by the time I get in bed and lie there digging the view outside the window: a huge blinking neon sign, like the views out any good movie detective's window in my youth, or in my own travels through the cities of the states.

222

It's somehow soothing and disappointing all at once.

In the middle of the night I have to get up to go to the bathroom, and it's like this dormitory public one, with cold damp floors and only two stalls, though Western style toilets thank God. I think about my brother living all these years of his adult life in places where he had to use a public kind of rest room like this and share it with other men. And then return to a little room where all he could fit in would be his life's possessions. Because he took a vow of poverty and therefore can't own a thing, though he does, some books, some civilian clothes that have been bought for or passed on to him, some posters and a couple of photo albums. But all that I learn later, because now, he is a guest in this place just like me, even though he ran it once not long ago, but now lives in semi-retirement in the country, a place I can't imagine, and is the reason I've come, to see his life, the way he has lived it since I was a boy, and find out why I guess.

In the morning the view seems even less exotic. A smog gray morning in a city. Yes, the sign's in Japanese, but so are many in L.A.. I don't wear a watch or carry clocks with me, preferring in my poet's romanticized imagination, maybe, to think I'll live longer and better if I rely on some interior sense of time. The streets look quiet, so I assume it's early as I go back to the bathroom and take a shower in what looks like a too short and way deep tub. I throw on a clean shirt and go looking for my brother. I find him with the others in the basement kitchen where he introduces me to the old lady cook who has been here for years, a Buddhist, by religion, but devoted obviously to these Western men who practice Catholic rites, though sometimes with their own Buddhist interpretation. She's happy when my brother says we're going to see the biggest Buddhist temple in Tokyo, and refers to the section in Japanese as "downtown" because, as my brother explains, it literally used to be in the lowest down part of the old city. But she's even happier that I'll be going up to see where my brother lives in the country, because that's where she comes from, as she says to me in her accented English, "I'm a country girl," this lady in her eighties. I help myself to some raisin bran and low fat milk, all in containers covered with Japanese words, no English, except for "raisin bran" and watch the ABC news with Peter Jennings on the TV, the only English news they get so far, no CNN yet. It's almost 9 AM , and this news hasn't happened yet in terms of public ways of telling time, but of course it has in the real world, where it is just some other day, the one ahead or the one behind, elsewhere in the world. And then we go out, my brother to get some traveler's checks for his trip to the states, going back with me in a week. And as we travel through the Tokyo streets, I am struck again by the absence of any striking building, of any traditional Japanese looking houses or structures, except for the occasional subdued design that I recognize as inherently theirs, the rest is still too familiar for my longing-for-exotica sensibility today.

Campion explains that there was only one building left standing after the war and that's down in the Ginza where he takes me to see it on what he keeps referring to as his "$2.50 tour," and yes, it seems to have more character, like the older buildings in New York or Paris or Barcelona do. But no Gaudis here, not even the kind of severely original designs the Japanese seem to have influenced back home, except for the occasional attempt at some kind of obvious artistic statement, but always so subdued, the hues all grays and browns, it almost seems like they mean to accrue nothing to themselves, just a vast facade of maybe their idea of modern normalcy filtered through their own repressive tendencies. As I talk about my takes on what I am discovering in my first daylight hours in Japan, my brother tells me, that he once could speak for days on what he thought he knew about interpreting the ways of the Japanese, but after 38 years here, he has come to the conclusion, that despite his many Japanese friends, and the fact that this is his home and has been for much more than half his life, in fact for most of it, he can never tell what a Japanese person is really thinking or feeling, unlike the Koreans, who he has seen in their own country and not just here in Japan where they have been second class citizens for so long. He says there is good reason Koreans are called the Irish of the Orient, besides the fact they like a good fight, you can tell what they're feeling and thinking because they'll let you know right away.

We take a subway, more like a new El train, to the oldest Shinto shrine in Tokyo. I'm thinking, now we'll see some real traditional Japanese stuff. As we walk up to the entrance we pass some teenaged Japanese in stylized outfits, sort of very stylized punk and club clothes without the actual attitude, and one young girl is all decked out in a Western style white wedding gown. My brother tells me on weekends this is an especially crowded hangout for teenagers who want to dress up. They congregate usually by decades, those who dress in '50's style, '60's, etc. But he

224

explains the wedding dress by telling me about a recent Japanese craze, an obsession for Western style Christian weddings, even though there are very few Christians in Japan. There are actually very few Buddhists and Shintoists as well, he explains, knowing as he does not only from his own experience, but from professional talks with his Buddhist and Shinto counterparts, the monks and priests of those state religions. It seems the Japanese are just not very religious, except for the adoption of rituals in an almost superstitious and definitely trendy way. He tells me how they usually bring a newborn to be blessed at the Shinto temple, because they do that best, and then dress up in wedding gown and tux for a Western style Christian wedding, even though the "priest" has nothing to do usually with anything other than a chain of wedding stores. (Later I will start to notice one chain called in English words, like many stores and products here, "Prior Place." It advertises all over Japan with unattractive Western models in wedding gear and has these chain department stores that specialize in wedding clothes and trappings and gifts, usually with an imitation small-town American chapel next door with a cross on top and in English, over the door, "Saint Prior Place"!) And they go to the Buddhist temples for their funerals, and anything to do with death, because, I guess, that offers the possibility of future lives or eternal bliss.

We stop to get our picture taken with a disposable camera my brother bought, he asks some kids to do it and they do, showing the kind of gracious generosity and politeness I will encounter almost everywhere here. He's speaking all the time in Japanese of course, so I have this buffer between me and them, this translator and guide which leaves me plenty of time to ruminate about what I am seeing without worrying about getting around. My brother tells me that it is always so easy to get any Japanese to take a picture because "they all understand cameras so well," a generality that seems to be proven true. The huge old-style Japanese wooden gate they take our picture standing under, turns out to have been replaced in 1970 according to the sign I read, one of the few in English too. I wonder if they got the date wrong, but my brother says no, although it is an ancient shrine in terms of the Shinto "religion," it really dates from the 1920s, and like everything else was either destroyed in the war or by time. It turns out that the traditional Japanese buildings weren't meant for this climate, but were adapted from South Sea–style structures, and once a better way of building for the seasonally cold weather was adapted, the old places pretty much disappeared, what wasn't burned down in the incendiary American bombings that did more damage in Tokyo than the atom bombs did in Hiroshima and Nagasaki.

At the shrine, we wash our hands in the traditional way, and my brother explains to me which Shinto monks are at what level according to the colors and style of their monkish garb, and explains how the temple varies only minimally from a Japanese Buddhist temple, it's almost as simple as: Shinto temples and shrines are unpainted, otherwise they are pretty much the same. On the way out, after walking the long gravel covered road up and back to the temple, passing mostly Japanese and the occasional Western tourist, we pass some of the teenagers congregating between the roadway to the shrine and the street. Even the girls dressed in "death rock" fashion seem tame and nonthreatening—even non-sexual or non-sensual in what I am beginning to see is this Japanese way. It all seems like play acting, and almost child-ish, not in the self-centered self-indulgent way of American child-ishness, but in a more innocent and unaware way of true children, or at least those not growing up on the war torn streets of less safe cities. That is one thing that feels obviously different here, the sense of safety. Yes, there is crime, but very little and it's controlled in this typical Japanese way. Everyone leaves their bikes unlocked on the streets here in Tokyo when they go into a store or restau-rant and when they come out it is still there. Homes are burglar-ized, and there are professional criminals and pickpockets and the beginnings even of American style 7-Eleven type robberies (yes, they have 7-Eleven stores here and other ones like them). But, as my brother explains to me, it is a shame based culture. And if you are caught committing a crime, you are first shamed into confess-ing to it, and then besides being punished, your name is ruined and your entire family suffers, losing their jobs, their friends etc. until there is no recourse but to become a professional criminal and enter a world of a more ancient kind of violence and risk.

As we travel around the city, I begin to notice the peculiar uses of English words mixed in among the Japanese. The news and magazine stands in the train stations have signs in English that say: "Let's Kiosk". When we stop for my brother to get travel-ers checks in a travel agency, I pick up a brochure with Audrey Hepburn on the cover, and though most of it is in Japanese I can tell it is a tour of the places in her films, like the Spanish steps in

226

Roman Holiday. The name on the brochure for the tour is just: *I'LL*. In a department store, it's disappointingly ordinary, like Barney's in New York when I was a kid before it became chic and expensive, although everything is expensive here. I forgot to bring toothpaste and when we go to a drugstore to buy some, a tube of Colgate sells for about 17 dollars! One floor I think is electronics and might be interesting, but when we check it out it's actually a ticket place, tickets for shows and closed circuit TV events, one an American boxing match advertised as "Excite Match" or the men's clothing store called "Adult House" or all the so-called "Shot Bars" or the place we stopped for some pretty bad pizza called "Milk Boy". The name of the ticket place was WOWOW, some kind of twisted acronym for world entertainment center.

By the end of the day I'm pretty exhausted. My brother, who I already knew has these open wounds on his feet from his diabetes, and who has had a few heart attacks, the reason he is semi-retired to the countryside now, and who is wearing these big clunky brown lace up shoes, has been walking me all over the city into the night and through the rain that sometimes caught us in the open and got us pretty wet—we took a break by seeing *Distinguished Gentleman* in a movie theater that was on a par with some old cheap theater in the states, not even Dolby sound, let alone THX. I'm beginning to notice that there isn't very much technical electronic wizardry going on except for a few instances here and there, no big time video game parlors or anything like that, the game places are mostly a terrible upright uncontrollable pinball type of game called "Pachinko" in these cheesy usually pink parlors that remind me of the Jersey shore back in the '50s. My brother shows me nightclubs and bars, from the outside, where mostly Filipino women dance semi-naked for the Japanese office working men who sometimes don't even go home after putting in their too long days at work and then going out to the clubs with other men to share some sort of rigorous and often drunken socializing until it is time to find a room, sometimes no more than a sort of berth container, like a slot in a morgue, to go sleep it off before starting all over in the morning. My brother tells me, most Japanese young women these days, are not interested in marrying these kind of guys anymore, and they're having trouble finding wives. As always he seems interested in everything, even though he has seen it all before many times, but he is also in no hurry, a kind of stressless aura around him which I begin to adopt

227

myself, reminding myself several times that I am here to be of service to him, to be a witness in a way to the life he lives and what he has given through choosing to live this way. Besides, I'm happily in love with a woman back home who has delighted me by hiding little plastic Easter eggs throughout my carry-on bag that I discover and open to find love notes and pictures and drawings, like the picture of an Irish harp, and even a rosary, so appropriate for this trip. There's really nothing I want to do here, except experience as much of this culture and place in a non-touristy way as I can. And I let my brother know this as we separate to go to our rooms for the night. Where I think about what an example my brother is for me. He has yet to complain once about his ailments, especially the sores on his feet, which I only ask about when I notice the blood on his socks. He says he rarely wears shoes where he lives in the country, Kiryu, where we will go on Thursday.

O*n november second nineteen ninety-three*

I spent four hours and more
on a strip of the Pacific Coast Highway
traveling between Rambla Vista and Sunset Boulevard
which would normally take ten to fifteen minutes.
It had been the brightest, clearest day
of my eleven so far living on the Santa Monica Bay.
But it grew dark from clouds of smoke
billowing up from the ridges lining the road
and blowing over the backed up panicked
and yet patient traffic and on out over the Pacific.
We—my girlfriend and roommate Kristal and me—
had driven to Malibu when we walked out of
the laundromat on Montana Avenue and saw the
piercing blue sky encroached upon by a thick and
sinewy cloud of smoke that seemed to be coming
from Santa Monica Canyon. But once there,
where we drove, on Kristal's instigation, we saw
it was further up the coast and without any
hesitation kept driving until we reached my
daughter Caitlin's street, which winds up from
the coast and bends back down, and with
her boyfriend Nels Brown she lived until that
day on which the house, the apartment they
shared was in, burnt down to the ground
of the hillside from which she had been
admiring the clarity of that day's view in
which the ocean met the sky in the kind
of sharply drawn line we thought would
always be there when I was a boy a continent
and ocean away. I mean it was a perfectly
clear day, the kind that once was normal
and expected before smog and haze and all
kinds of pollution and distortions of God's
beauty was accepted. My daughter didn't want
to leave at first. It was still early in
the fire's growth and no warnings had
preceded ours. We talked about it for an hour.

We even discussed what she might take were
a disaster truly imminent, and joked about
her dragging a foot locker full of things
from her baby years and childhood I kept for her
until she grew and moved away. But
not that day. She didn't want to make
a fuss. Every item we'd discuss and I'd
suggest might be best to take she'd get
upset and insist it would be too difficult
to try and differentiate. "It would be like
moving," she said, and instead just finally
took a couple of things, some photo albums,
address and check books, a change of clothes
for her and her boyfriend. She, and even
Kristal, had made fun of my persistent
insistence that we should go before we got
stuck up there and PCH got closed down.
But when we finally got her cat and
few possessions that she took into her car
and mine and drove down to the highway
it was already a parking lot. And the
wind had grown so strong and hot it
seemed the fire was already in the air
if not yet visible in flame and smoke
where we were. But it soon was and
thank God by then we had been creeping
forward inch by inch, it seemed, enough
to just stay forward of the smoke and
rushing flames. At one point Kristal got
out and took a walk and Caitlin opened
her door and I did mine and she said:
"Thanks—you're a pain sometimes but
thank you." And I wanted to cry and
go back and get that foot locker and
her paintings and her boyfriend's keyboards
and music and all the rest. And I wish
I had the power to make it all right.
But I don't—and never will. The rightness
is in knowing that and going on with it
still as though I didn't know. I do.

L ACEY IN LOVE

It was 1993. Clinton was in the White House. Perot was still acting like he should be there. Somebody else was Michelle Pfeiffer's
lover. Somebody was starring in serious movies. Someone was
being recognized for their contribution to world peace. Someone
was winning a Pulitzer for their new play, book of poems, novel.
Someone was being interviewed on three morning news shows
and countless late night talk shows. Lacey was still acting like he
should be—all of the above. And where was his MacArthur genius
grant? His friends chuckled at his sense of loss. They saw it as ego.
Or "über" proprietorship. Or sour grapes. Or righteous reactions
to the unfairness of life and the businesses of show and publishing
and production and awards. Some even laughed out loud and said
"Face it man, you won't be famous until after you die." And he'd
laugh with them. Like he was a character, an eccentric, with a
twitch, a quirk, this need to be recognized for all the work he'd
done in his 51 years. All the attempts he'd made to leave a mark
on this world he was born into and still thought he knew.

It wasn't like he hadn't had the opportunities. He'd met
Michelle Pfeiffer and starred in movies and run for office and
worked for peace and written plays that were produced and books
of poems that were published and novels that weren't. He was
even interviewed on TV—news and talk shows. But. The *way* he
did it wasn't quite right, the circumstances were wrong, or he was.

Michelle was married to Peter Horton the first time he met
her, long before she starred in anything. And Lacey was married
that time too. To his second wife. A brief marriage, but nonetheless official the first time he met Michelle Pfeiffer. She was so radi-
antly beautiful that time, so young, so seemingly innocent and
un-disillusioned, so pure, that Lacey forgot for a minute he was
married and at least ten years older with two teenaged children
from his first marriage living with him and their step-mother, who
was sitting right beside him as he forgot her and forgot Michelle's
husband, who was sitting right beside *her*, and all Lacey could see
and all he was aware of was this answer to his earliest prayers, this
vision of romantic embodiment of love as he always and still
dreamed it could be, not just her beauty but the stillness at the
center of it, the acceptance of it and what it was doing to Lacey as

they talked as though he wasn't falling in love and she didn't know it.

Other men at that party, friends of Lacey's, famous actors and directors and husbands of powerful agents and publicity "gals" forgot they were with their wives and girlfriends too. But none, at that party, monopolized Michelle's attention, or even got it at all, like Lacey did. Just one evening in Hollywood, not long after Lacey arrived. But she was married, and so was he, and besides, she was she and he was he.

Oh. He had already starred in a couple of movies, gotten praised in reviews in *Variety* and *Film Comment,* but they were *bad* movies, low budget horror movies, Dracula in New Jersey and agoraphobia in upstate New York. Lacey was the hero in both, but he didn't quite pull it off. In his head he had been striking an artistic blow for a kind of realism he felt he had never seen on the screen, but it turned out to be *too* real, revealing his amateurishness, his self-consciousness, his total lack of comprehension of what the movie was going to be all about. He had just started acting professionally. And before long found himself in Hollywood, on his way to his rightful place among the stars he always thought of as his peers. Or—his true family.

The next time he talked to Michelle Pfeiffer—after seeing her here and there in their Santa Monica neighborhood, before and after his divorce and then hers—was at the funeral of their acting teacher. Michelle looked older, like she'd been through a lot since he'd first met her. *He* certainly had been. But she was still beautiful, even more so now, without the innocence but the stillness there at her core drawing him into her now tragic beauty. But she acted as though she didn't want to be disturbed in her grief. And it was genuine grief. As was his. Only maybe for different reasons. After all, their teacher had nurtured Michelle through her first big roles. Lacey remembered their teacher helping him with a big audition he still blew, telling him about the work she was doing with Michelle for the remake of *Scarface* with Pacino. But Lacey didn't see it until years later. He couldn't at the time, because his own bout with cocaine was only recently over after decades of terminally hip indulgence. But when he did see it, he was shocked at how Michelle had transformed herself into the ice goddess, the coke princess, the ethereal apparition of some lowlife's ambitions. He recognized the quiet despair, and was impressed now with her talent as well as her presence. But he

232

didn't get the chance to tell her until a funeral where she was in no mood to take compliments, so they talked of their teacher, Lacey complimenting their deceased mentor instead of Michelle. But she had to know how he felt, what man didn't in her presence. And besides, he wasn't the recent star of a couple of movies, no matter how bad anymore. He was an out-of-work actor/sometime scriptwriter, in what was referred to locally as "development hell." He really didn't have a lot to say either.

There were many stars at the funeral party. The departed had been a good teacher. One of the best. A few months after the funeral, when she accepted her Tony, Lily Tomlin would especially thank her late teacher, and so would Anjelica Houston when she accepted her Oscar. And even students who weren't stars yet, Lacey saw them regularly in movies and on TV. He felt like he must be doing something wrong. Maybe he shouldn't have quit studying when he ran out of money but kept going to classes like the teacher insisted he should do. But his pride, or something more vague, got in his way that time.

Or maybe it was just that he had come to this so late in life. Not in his teens or twenties like most of the students. Or even his thirties, like some of the already established who studied with him, like Alexander Godunov, or the woman whose name he could never remember who wasn't very good but ended up hosting a TV show nonetheless. And Godunov was in *Witness*, a decent movie and a decent role. Lacey ended up on a *Dynasty* rip-off. He had a recurring role that got bigger and bigger, until one day at the MGM commissary, the old big one with tables and booths that Tracy and Hepburn and Garland and Gable had sat in, and now Lacey, feeling important, feeling appreciated, feeling good about himself and his having arrived at his true home at last, started joking with the producers and network executives when one of the stars of the show suggested they stop at the bigwigs table to pay their respects, only Lacey couldn't help telling them—tongue in cheek he thought, but they knew he meant it, and so did he—that he should be the love interest of the star of the show, and he should be this and that so important, and the next thing he knew they wrote him out of the show and the next thing he knew the show was canceled.

People, important people, powerful people, in that business told Lacey he'd be a big star after that, he was "hot" they said, the show's editors comparing him to a younger Brando! A powerful agent at William Morris telling him her mother, who once was a show business powerhouse said that Lacey had "it"—was destined for "greatness" on the screen. But Lacey didn't work again as an actor for almost two years, and when he did it was a much smaller role. And they kept getting smaller. When he met Michelle Pfeiffer the first time he had just moved out from New York where he had spent time with, "hung around" a little with, felt he had a strong acquaintance even friendship with the most famous movie star of his generation. The last time he saw Michelle Pfeiffer was at a play her then lover was in. This other movie star, Lacey's "friend" from New York was there with his girlfriend, a director who once said all she wanted to do was direct a film Lacey had written about a time in his life when he wanted to be Black so badly he thought he was, but happened to be stationed in the segregated South. She not only wanted to direct his film, she wanted to find out if he was as "dangerous" as he seemed to be. He wasn't. She went on to direct something else, after she and Lacey stopped dating, just before she married the writer of the movie she wound up directing. The movie bombed and they got divorced. And now she was dating this other movie star, the real thing. On the news, in *People* magazine with him.

Lacey wondered if Michelle would even recognize him—and was relieved when she acted as though she did when they all ended up backstage—though it was hard for Lacey to tell if the other movie star did, he seemed so different than when Lacey had last known him in New York, he seemed happy, and comfortable, and Lacey felt out of place, like maybe these weren't his peers after all. Because, after all, Lacey was there, at that play, because it was written by a classmate of his kids, a modestly brilliant kid himself who liked Lacey, or seemed to, already more successful as a playwright than Lacey ever was. But hey, who's keeping score.

That time, backstage, Michelle had seemed fragile, sad, very much alone, but she had acted at least as though she remembered Lacey when they each said hello. And it mattered to him. Soothed him somehow, as though that might be enough. But of course it wasn't. He wanted his plays produced and—well, one, partly written by him but "compiled" by a more practically ambitious director/"creator" had not long before been produced and well received though sometimes misunderstood. After hours of penetrating lines about the devastating damage of drugs and booze on the poets in the play, leaving only the hope of "recovery" as any consolation to the desperate disillusionment and rage, Billy Idol approached the cast exclaiming, "It's about time somebody wrote something *good* about drugs. All right!" And gave them all his beaming, knowing, delighted, and delightful, smile they found difficult to resist.

But even then, in that production, though Lacey co-wrote it and was one of the acting ensemble, it felt to him like a defeat. DeNiro didn't show up and want to make it as his movie directorial debut. And even the "stars" who did come, none of them were Michelle Pfeiffer, and most could not contain their admiration for and desire to meet and glowingly praise one of Lacey's fellow actors, whose performance was partly inspired by Lacey's suggestions, though the actor did so much *more* with them than Lacey ever had.

And now it was 1993, and Lacey was tired. Tired of trying. Tired of keeping up the facade of interest in anything about the people who consistently rejected him and his work while continuing to praise him and his work as if he and his work were just too good not to reject. He was even more tired of those who didn't even bother to pretend.

He went to the movies and still got excited, felt that wave of anticipation wash over him when the lights went down. And more often than not he was satisfied. Someone acted so well he wasn't even envious. Or someone wrote a screenplay so entertaining and engaging, he could only delight in what he knew must have been their delight when they wrote it. Or it all looked so good, or appropriate or accurate, or the music touched him so he had to go and buy the soundtrack. And the old stuff on TV. It kept him misty eyed and vulnerable for hours at a time. Remembering his dreams of affecting masses of people in that same way through his unique creative endeavors. And he had. Now and then. Though not masses—but many. And remembering those moments of his own impact and glory made him even more misty-eyed and vulnerable. And then it would be time to wash the dishes, or brush his teeth, or take a pill for perennial ailments that flared up enough to remind him of the price he paid for all of his adventures. You live the life, you pay the price. Only. Only he had had something more spectacular in mind.

Michelle Pfeiffer was getting married, had adopted a half black-half white baby girl and was engaged to a nice looking successful—what? producer? director?—She seemed a little happier, a little more satisfied, a little ... How would he know? Lacey hadn't seen her since the play. It was 1993 now and Lacey wasn't writing screenplays for hire, he wasn't starring in movies, even bad ones, he didn't have a recurring role on any TV shows. He had a two-line scene in a *Baywatch* and a close-up in a fish-eye lens as a comically odd dentist in a bank commercial playing somewhere in South Carolina and Georgia. And neither paid enough to dent the rent on the tiny apartment he'd moved into to save money. Fifty-one and still no cushion, no nest egg, no savings. Whenever he had made money, he had spent it. Not on anything lasting, like property or jewelry or art—he'd never made enough for that. No, he'd spent it on friends, buying them dinner, publishing their little chapbooks of poems. And he'd spent it on some jewelry, nothing too expensive or extravagant, an antique ring, some artist's earrings—like that—for the women he went out with. Mostly he spent it on food and clothes and things for his kids. But there was never enough.

And then he gave up. His deep disappointment over the way his life had turned out had been plaguing him, making everything dim and pointless, for months. Until one morning, walking on the beach, with no trees to talk to, the few palms never having much to say, he began arguing with the universe. The way it had fucked him over he thought. Over fifty. Still broke. In fact thirty thousand in debt. His kids grown and gone. And barely conscious of the toll it had taken to raise them. For over twenty years. And mostly on his own. As he too had been barely conscious of the toll it had taken on them. To be raised by one so self-centered. And sex-driven. And angry. And childish. And in constant turmoil over the lack of tenderness in the world he thought he could actually influence into becoming something other than it had always been.

But he knew better now, as he startled strangers walking by, with the intensity of the argument he was having with God. Or the Goddess. Or God the Father, or the Creator, or the Universal Spirit, or whoever it was he held responsible for his fate. Until he finally shouted out, "What the fuck do you want from me anyway!?" And a voice answered back, "Give up the dream, Lacey." He almost punched somebody as he yelled, "Give up the dream?! Give up the dream you motherfucker?!" People were getting out of his way now. Avoiding him anyway they could. But he didn't even notice. All he heard was this quiet, peaceful, even loving voice, somewhere deep inside himself say "Yes, give up the dream." He finally began muttering, mumbling to himself as it appeared to passersby. "Give up the fucking dream, heh?! Give it up?! That's what you want?! You fucking cocksucking bastard shithead?!" Until finally he stopped, and still boiling with the rage of a lifetime of disappointments, he realized there was nothing else for him to do.

He had tried it all. Everything he had read. Or thought of. Or heard of. He had tried. The short cuts. The long way round. The over the hill and through the woods ways to some sort of satisfaction. Or the kind he thought would last. The fame and recognition of being someone more than a loser. More than a bitter old poet who nobody ever heard of or read or cared about. A failed actor. A failed husband. A failed screenwriter, chauffeur, hospital guard, maintenance man, novelist, jazz musician, rock 'n' roller, wannabe cool spade Mick revolutionary sexual artist legend in his own time. Whose life and work, in fact, defined those times. "So fuck it," he thought. "Why not? Okay motherfucker. I give up. You satisfied?"

But he couldn't stop there. "I give up the dream I've had ever since I can remember. As a little kid who couldn't even talk yet. But couldn't wait to have my say that would straighten out the mess they made of this beautiful creation. The dream of being somebody. Somebody the world would care about. Pay attention to. Look up to. I give up the dream of leaving my mark on it all. Especially out here where dreams are made and fulfilled. The dream of being one of the stars that light up the darkness of movie theaters all over the world. Of being like Alan Ladd and Gregory Peck and Gary Cooper and Jimmy Stewart and all the others that made my heart expand with the possibilities of life when I was just a little kid."

Lacey was teary eyed now, just thinking about that child he had been, sitting alone in a dark movie theater, knowing some day he'd be up there too, inspiring little kids like him to see beyond the limitation of their lonely world, no matter how many people were in it. "I give it all the fuck up motherfucker," he said quietly to himself. Passersby not even noticing him anymore. "Take it all, I quit."

Within minutes, without even noticing it right away, the gloom of several months' resentment had lifted. Lacey wasn't thinking anymore about being passed up for a job working for a famous friend who had the power to create projects and put people in them but decided he didn't want to ruin a friendship with business and so hired someone who was now probably his new best friend. He forgot all about that. He forgot how pissed off it made him to see how the MGM he grew up looking to as the promised land had been sold to the Japanese. Just like Columbia was. Or how they had slowly altered the torch-bearing female figure of Columbia in their logo until she looked Japanese instead of whatever "white" European nationality she had looked like all his life. He stopped worrying about how his kids would see him when they realized all he'd done wrong by the new standards that everyone seemed to agree were the right ones finally, and not the ones he had intuited, depending on love to tell him how to treat those centers of his universe.

He stopped thinking about agents and auditioning and prizes and awards shows. And money. He had never really cared about money until now. Wasn't that a big part of his problem? That he had never really taken care of business. Because business was for some other kind of guy. Not him. And didn't that always send the women running? When they discovered how much he didn't care about any of it, except the recognition—the recognition—the recognition that all the strife and sacrifice had been worth it because now the world understood who he really was, the genius of their most frustrated longings.

He could remember a time he could walk into any room and know instantly everyone's secret sexual fantasy. And half the time he ended up fulfilling them. No matter what they were. Because people were so startled to have their secret fantasies revealed to them by someone so seductive and smart. He stopped thinking about that too. About how he never used that to make him famous or powerful or recognized as the genius of his times. Just for the fleeting pleasure of the sensuality to be shared with strangers and friends when they were together. He wasn't worrying about all that anymore, as he walked on the beach of Venice, California, early in the morning sunlight and smog so bad he couldn't even see Santa Catalina. But he didn't dwell on that either. How when he first arrived here over a decade earlier, he could see that island most days of the year and now he couldn't. Or how despite the evidence of his personal experience, the newspaper and TV stories kept saying the air was so much better. So much better he could hardly breath or see or feel anything but oppressed no matter how little or how much he dressed in. But none of that was bothering him now.

238

Without even knowing it, he kept giving up stuff as he walked. Not just the dream of himself meaning something more than what he knew he already did to those who knew him, but being the kind of figure the whole world mourns the loss of when they're gone. He gave it all up. And before more than a few minutes had passed since Lacey gave in to the voice within, he was noticing the clouds and sky again, their particular brilliance that day, how beautiful they were, and always are, and the women passing by.

Over the days and months that followed, he found himself for the first time in many, many years, happy for friends when they were recognized for achievements Lacey used to envy or judge less remarkable than his or other friends who were less successful but more accomplished in his mind. He loved them all. And was happy for them all. And felt their disappointment and despair when that was in their air and consoled them and anyone else who needed it. And all the time he accepted that he was over the hill. He'd never play that guy in the film who he always thought secretly *was* him. No. He got it. His time had passed for that. He'd never have that bad-boy-hero role. Not even in the privacy of his own home anymore. He could no longer hide from the truth of his many failures. Or from acceptance of his true and normal self.

His joy and peace kept increasing. Until he got so comfortable being just who he was, he brought it into a character he ended up playing on TV when the producers hunted him down at home, because he had no agent anymore. And despite the famous faces up for this one small role, he got it. And excelled. Although he didn't know it at the time, pestering the producer at home to reassure himself that he was doing all right, knowing he had failed again to be the cool professional when the producer told him, "Lacey, if you weren't doing all right, we'd have told you, believe me." And he accepted the burden of his doubt too. Because after all, what did it matter? because along with everything else, he had given up the image he had had of how anything should be, especially him.

And all it did was make him happier. No matter what it looked like to his old self. Like standing alone at the newsstand on the Third Street Promenade. He wasn't feeling alone, or worrying about it anymore. When a writer he had envied for years bumped into him. Lacey didn't think of the old comparisons anymore. In fact, he was delighted to see the man, who he now not only respected, but felt was a friend. And when the man said, "You know Penguin's doing this series of the important contemporary American poets," Lacey felt no envy of the writers Penguin was publishing, or loss at not being included. Lacey didn't go to where he usually would. He didn't feel the old resentment toward Penguin for turning down a manuscript of his decades before. Even after everyone from secretaries to salesmen had championed it. Because now he knew it had been his arrogance and insultingly self-centered behavior that had soured that deal, as well as poems whose titles alone would bring out the censors and defensive board members sensitive to whatever stockholder or family member or church leader might object. He didn't feel insulted that Penguin hadn't contacted him already to ask him to be a part of this series.

"I think you should send them a manuscript," the man said. And Lacey accepted the man's suggestion as sincere, not just a conversational ploy or ego stroking device to make nice to a man who otherwise might not react so friendly—himself. No. He actually went home and that night typed up a manuscript of what he thought might be the best of what he'd written but refused to try to publish over the past disappointing decade.

And instead of worrying about the final draft as intensely as he always had before—until his perfectionism paralyzed him into missing whatever deadline there might be—he let the other writer, his new friend, edit the manuscript. And when Penguin rejected it for all those toes he'd stepped on so long ago but still seemed to ache, the man sent it on to someone else Lacey had once rejected from the impenetrable fortress of the ego he no longer catered to. This time it was accepted. And while he was waiting for it to come out, Lacey ran into Michelle Pfeiffer one more time. And she was just herself. No longer an apparition, a fantasy, a dream. Just a woman with her husband and new baby in a restaurant, ordering food, like him. And Lacey didn't feel the need to intrude on her familial solitude, the aura of aloneness that kept strangers away. He was a stranger too, after all, their tenuous connection one she'd probably only been polite in reciprocating those few times he had run into her before. What a bore he must have been, seeing her beauty and stardom as something to do with him. How much happier he was this way, knowing the truth, and accepting it.

For years he'd felt sorry for people eating alone in restaurants, like he now did. He thought they were alone because they weren't as sexy as he was, as important, as much the center of the universe as he had been sure he was meant to be. And now he could see that it was a choice, or could be. That eating alone could have its own rewards. Like getting to know the waitresses and regulars, without being envious of the dishes that were named for someone other than him. Seeing Raymond Chandler in the little scenes of solitary beings connecting in the night without having to fight over recognition or seduce anyone into paying homage to their need. No, they just were like all other creatures when they feed. Filling up and moving on. But with a human aspect that respected each other's privacy and yet connected to the need for human contact in ways that didn't have to bow to anyone's conception of who they thought they were. Lacey actually ended up preferring eating alone, comfortable at last with his place in the world whatever it was, including a seat not in a booth because he was alone and booths were reserved for two or more like he had always been before. It wasn't a bore to be on your own like that. It was oddly satisfying, in ways Lacey had never imagined. How unlike who he always thought he was he turned out to be. And how nice it felt to acknowledge it.

And then the book was finally published. And respected by those Lacey cared about. Even though it didn't sell very well. And when he went to do the readings to sell whatever could be sold, Lacey discovered old friends and acquaintances who were not who he thought they were for all the years he'd ignored them or given them only his cursory attention because they weren't the movers and shakers he thought he should be. They were just decent people who still cared about him, even when he left them in his dust to go on to bigger and better stuff, to try and get people to love him who didn't. He was glad he wasn't doing that anymore, and could restore the rightful place of those who really did in his heart. God, he thought, thank you.

And Lacey kept on thanking God whenever he thought to, which began to seem like all the time, giving thanks for his being in love again, in love with his friends and his family, his children and their mother, his lovers and his wives, himself and his life, and especially for the mystery—which surpasses all attempts at leaving something permanent, the imperative urge to outwit fate, to outlast the limitations of a life predetermined, to outmaneuver the chaos and extreme unfairness of it all and come away humbled by the miracle of continuing no matter what, no matter who, no matter how many Michelle Pfeiffers got their breaks or got broken by the same fates that chose Lacey to get on with it, after giving it all up, again.

On the marriage of miles lally and jennifer baxendale

What a day, what a way to get us all together
in the circle of love that enfolds you
as it grows from this subtle shifting of your place in the universe

And in your faces we can read our love's intentions—
to be true, to be honest and honorable,
to be light and awesome rendering of love's affections
and desires,
to inspire all of us with your delight in each other's company,
to accompany us on our journey into what out hearts might sing
if this were ways to ring our days with your example,
to never trample on the secret sharings of want and
earnest leisure,
the pleasure of your solidarity—

Whose cousins are we? to be here with you for this ceremony?
if not your love's?—

Which has drawn us here like homing doves
returning to the source of what enlivened us
and gave us courage to try our wings
and fling ourselves into the destiny of consciousness
of all the possibilities of happiness that springs from love
and its luscious array of blossoms we can spy between
your shapes
as you embrace in air and flesh
and commonness of purpose in
your hidden recommendations for our lives—

Which seem today to be revealed as these—
do not conceal your faithfulness and desire to please each other,
respect for self and others—
do not concede to any objection of fear or judgment—
give in to all your whims of fancy
and release of values less than love,
consider the wings of the homing dove
and all their beauty's purpose—
to return always to where the heart belongs—   July 22, 1995

243

ᴵT HAPPENS

for Emilio Schneeman

They meet in a bar. She's the hottest thing there. At least to him. He's there to read his poetry with his son's band. Just before he gets on the stand she approaches, saying, "I'm from Jersey too."

In the middle of his reading, he decides to dedicate a poem to her. He can't find her in the crowd but feels her smile in his eyes as he leans into the microphone, "This is for my home girl."

Then he reads a poem about being fifteen and dating a girl who dismissed his romantic vision of their future together as unrealistic, but he defended it as fuel for the passion of the moment.

The poem ends with him now in his fifties, still believing in all the "romantic possibilities." A crowd surrounds him when he steps down, His "home girl" isn't one of them.

Soon he spies her talking to the singer. As he joins them, she waves the other man away but orders him to stay, as if her sexual charisma gives her royal prerogatives. To him it does.

He's already lost inside her eyes and smile where he's stumbling around to find a way to be himself without the life he knew was his just moments before.

So all he can think to say is the old cliché, "What do you do?" But she hears "*wanna* do?" and replies "What do *you* wanna do," implying with her eyes she already knew before she asked.

"Go home with you," he says and she agrees to his surprise and overwhelming gratitude for what might come of such an easy acceptance of the obviously inevitable.

She doesn't drive, so rides with him, and on the way confesses that she's married. As he hears it, to a rich old man who spends his time away on business trips while she does what she wants.

244

He thinks she means it wouldn't be like cheating or dishonesty and he can live with that. In fact it might be an ideal arrangement for a man like him who intends never to marry again.

In his room near the beach, they talk as though they've known each other all their lives only to discover they grew up a few miles—though thirty years—apart.

And in the same kind of Irish-American working-class families of beer drinking hard guys and wise ass women. He still sounds like them. Especially when angry—or insecure.

But she speaks with a sultry elegance that leaves no trace of where she's from, like some Hollywood movie star from long ago. The kind whose past and personality the studio created.

Only, she had been her own finishing school transforming a precociously sexy, teenage rebel Jersey girl into a confidant, seductive diva of whatever social scene she's in.

They're from the same tribe, he tells her, and not just Jersey Irish. They understand their power and wield it in ways that make them both sought after and dismissed.

They know so much about each other, by the time they finally kiss, their feelings are too intense for any pose of nothing new. Then she lets slip her husband is her age.

He's a rock'n'roll musician she married less than a year before, not some old rich guy who doesn't care what she does. They panic at the thought of what *they* almost did—then don't.

But they can't stop talking. By the time he puts her in a cab for home, it's the middle of the night. She scribbles down her number, which he pockets on his way back to his room.

In the morning, he throws it in the garbage can. But she leaves it later that day again, with a message of no remorse for their intimacy, which anyway was more in words than deeds.

Despite his best intentions, he calls back, and when she answers, some child he forgot lights up inside him. They know an affair is out of the question, so they pretend they can be friends.

Now and then they run into each other at a club, like where they first met, and do their best to ignore the way each other glows when their eyes meet, in fear others might detect it too.

She calls often and they talk and talk, about how much he loves living alone so he can get his writing done, or how she's always wanted children. He tells her he once felt that way.

But that was back when he was the punk avenger of his repressed childhood, a teenage drunk roaming the lonely streets of Manhattan before she was even born.

He fantasized back then of raising a son there, and later, in his thirties, he did just that. A daughter too. He spent his adult life raising those two, now older than she is.

He lets her know he feels no need to do it again and urges her to do her best to make her marriage work, while they go on pretending to be just friends

Until one night they accidentally on purpose run into each other at another club and she invites him to join her and her friends as they move on, first to a party and then some late scene bars.

He can't say no, so stands around in overcrowded boozy rooms of mostly desperation, and hopefully some joy, and wonders why he's there until she asks if he can drive her home.

She's so drunk, she claims, her ride might take advantage of her condition, since her spouse is out of town again. He agrees, again, only this time there are no illusions.

On the way she weeps, and wonders what you do if every time you think of someone you cry, because you miss being with them so much. He knows she doesn't mean her husband.

He walks her to her door and checks inside to make sure there's no unwanted surprises waiting for her there. She puts her head on his shoulder. He wraps his arms around her.

They don't kiss this time, just her leaning into his body as he holds her and keeps whispering in her ear, "I'm sorry... I'm sorry ... I'm sorry..."

The next day when she calls, he says they shouldn't talk or see each other any more. It's too difficult to just be friends. She concurs, and they hang up as though it were the end.

In the days that follow, they enter a world of tortures they never knew existed, where war is waged between their fear-filled heads and breaking hearts.

She has a guru friend come cleanse her spirit, and it heals something inside her for a moment. He uses prayer and meditation, and it works too, for minutes at a time.

But the more he prays and asks for answers, the more he hears inside his heart, "Be yourself, be honest, and be loving—but don't be afraid."

She spends her days in bed, avoiding her life, until two girl friends come and take her to a shopping mall to clear her head, but where she just breaks down and sobs.

She tells them how unhappy she's been. They suggest it might be best to end her marriage before it's more permanently shaped. Her husband will be hurt either way.

She calls the older man, to say she's moving out, and that it would have happened whether they had met or not. Maybe now they can really be friends.

They go out to dinner and to movies, where they think no one might see them, so as not to cause her husband added pain. They don't know the gossip started on the night they met.

Friends who called her marriage a mistake from the start, can't accept that when it ends, she gives an old man first place in her heart, instead of them.

One of her husband's rock'n'roll friends leaves her a message asking, "How's it feel to date your grandfather?" She calls back to leave her own: "A lot better than being married to my son."

She's left with less than a handful of friends out of a scene she'd been queen of. His friends just drift away. No acrimony, just indifference, never calling, or too busy when he does.

But *their* friendship and their passion grow like twins. They talk and make love like those things are one, discovering uncharted territory in each other's brains and bodies.

He explores her porcelain skin, so white, he tells her, it's almost blue, like mother's milk or glacier ice in moonlight. Only warmer, softer, and more vital.

Her eyes enchant him, her mouth entrances him, her face he falls into like flowers. Her body is a garden he can wander in for hours, even days.

She falls in love with his old body too, as if it knows some secrets she has longed to have exposed and understood. They accept each other's faults and frailties as if they are their own now.

He feels fulfilled by every word they share, unjudged like he has never been before. She feels accepted for the woman she's becoming, as well as the one she's been.

She moves in with him, transforming his simple room into a sacred space, an altar for their love to worship the creator of the lives that brought them there.

When she reveals that she's expecting, he's surprised at how relieved he feels. As if he's wanted nothing else for years, but didn't know it.

248

Fatherhood had always been the center of his life, the experience he cherished most and was most proud of, but had been too frightened to try again, he realizes, until now.

They relish every aspect of her body's changes—and her world's. Women she'd have threatened before, approach her now, asking how she feels, sharing their experience.

She devours books on pregnancy and childbirth, and decides to deliver the baby at home. But first, they have to find one with more room.

All they can afford is a place near the freeway, where the owner makes rosy promises about their future there, but has them sign a short lease anyway.

He watches as she changes from night life hot seductive center of attention to practical and caring mother-to-be, as if her baby's recreating her, in the image of who he wants her to become.

One night they run into a poet doing Tarot readings for a small fee. He reads their unborn baby's cards for free, predicting that their boy will be their spiritual guide and teacher.

By now the baby's due, but their landlady unexpectedly sells the place they're renting, telling them they have to move. They prepare for legal—or covert—action.

But the baby makes it clear, he doesn't want to be born there. So they search through every rental listing, finding only places they can't afford or that are too depressing.

With no time left, she finds a notice in the paper for a townhouse by the beach—near where they conceived their son—and for no more rent then they've been paying to breath freeway fumes.

Miraculously, they're the first to see it and can move right in. They do. She unpacks everything in just one day, to build a nest for their now overdue son.

The midwife sends them to a doctor, who says labor may have to be induced and orders her to bed. But, she wants to go to the courthouse downtown instead.

He shows his incapacity for any form of bureaucracy, by cursing at the fact they have to wait in lines others appear to be accepting patiently, or avoiding in ways denied to them.

She tells him to sit down, so she can wait in peace, despite her painfully swollen legs and feet. Instead he starts talking to a lady who's moving files around.

The lady tells him the Court Clerk can send out documents if he feels like it, and if he doesn't, not. "That can't be legal," he says. "Oh yes it is," she answers, adding: "We don't make the rules."

Meanwhile, his pregnant partner gets what she's come for. The final divorce decree, which should have gone out months ago. Then she leads him to a mall to buy some rings.

He thinks she's giving in to his argument that they should marry so his health insurance can cover any hospital bills incurred by a birth that might not happen at home anymore.

But she thinks she knows why the baby is overdue. Her son has waited for them to move, and now to wed. She goes to bed, but spends her time calling local courts about quick marriages.

Every one she reaches demands weeks she doesn't have. He calls a priest, who tells him the Church requires six months preparation, not like when he was a kid and a girl was pregnant.

They finally find two places in the yellow pages advertising "instant weddings." One's down the coast a ways, where he leaves a message on a lady's voice machine.

At the other, an old man says he can marry them in the morning in his office, not too far away. But the baby lets her know he won't wait that long.

He tries the lady down the coast again. This time she's in and tells him she can marry them at their home—and be there in under an hour.

He calls his grown son, to leave a message not retrieved in time. Her family, and his daughter—all on the other coast—can offer only telephone support.

He calls, then pages when he isn't in, one of the only friends they know they can rely on, who shows up not long after with white roses for the bride.

She has everything arranged the way she wants it by the time the lady minister arrives—candles lit, lights down, chanting monks on the CD player.

The lady puts on priest robes for the ceremony that they have out on their patio, where they can hear the ocean—and their hearts—beating in the dark.

The lady reads a passage from the Bible, about how love is never jealous or possessive or any selfish thing. Their friend reads from *The Prophet* something equally inspiring.

Their baby lets her know he's ready. She feels the mild pre-labor contractions as their son's blessing when they say "I do," and then kiss as if they were alone.

Later in bed, they both agree it was the best way to get married as they fall asleep happy. But she wakes up when she hears a pop and thinks something's gone wrong.

Until she stands and feels the water. She gets him up and tells him it's started. He calls the midwife, who says not to worry, she'll be there in the morning.

But the contractions come too fast and hard, so he calls the midwife back and she comes over right away. His bride is in more pain than she expected.

There's no relief between contractions like they promised. Her back aches so badly, *no* position gives her comfort. She quickly dilates seven centimeters and then gets stuck for hours.

In the morning the midwife has a class she says she can't miss and leaves, as a strange one comes to take her place and chat with her assistant while his wife's complaints are joked away.

He does what he can to comfort her, like they taught in birthing class. But his wife dismisses his help, even hitting him, as he was warned she might

Until she pulls him down to look him in the eye and whisper "I don't feel safe here anymore." He calls the hospital and tells them they're on their way.

The strange midwife tries to talk them out of going. She says things will only be worse there. He agrees the medical establishment can be dangerous.

But, he says, the midwives' help is obviously useless in this situation, and *their* promises were just as full of shit as any doctor's fear based trips.

By the time they get there, she's dilated two more centimeters, and is on her way to giving birth. A shot relieves the back pain, so she can concentrate on her contractions.

Soon their son's head's sticking out of her like she's some ancient icon, his eyes wide open as he looks around so calmly it would be humorous—if it wasn't so unexpected and profound.

She's asked to hold him there while they remove the cord wrapped round his head and arm in such a way that had his elbow jabbed into her vertebrae all night and half the morning.

It's the hardest thing she has to do, until they finally ask for one last push, and the rest of their son squeezes out. His father cries a little, awestruck at the wonder of it all.

He holds him after she does, whispering their love and gratitude for his miraculous appearance in their lives. The baby takes it in as if it's all natural. Because it is.

He only yells when nurses clean and poke and measure him. But by the time they bring him back to his mother, he's calmly observing everything again.

His father shares his tired—but totally contented—wife's temporary hospital bed, as their son nurses like he's been doing it all his life. And now he has.

They take him home as soon as the hospital will let them and climb into "the family bed" she's chosen over cradles, cribs, and bassinets.

The baby sleeps half the night on his chest, the other half on her breasts. They sleep together like that every night and wake up every morning grateful and amazed at their good fortune.

Others joke about their lack of sleep throughout the days and weeks that follow. But they compare it to when lovers first spend nights together.

Who misses sleep then? Only those who don't honor love in all its forms—or accept its consequences. But they do and will continue to.

Because they know that they have secretly believed they don't deserve it, and that others still believe they don't. The same others who condemn them for the way they met, or for their ages.

Not the newlyweds and their guru baby boy, who teaches them to live each day as if it's a blessing and each night as though it were their right to be as happy as they knew they'd be.

Whether others see them as an old cliché—or worse—they know what they created with their truth is far more real and lasting. And they also know people were hurt.

They feel remorse and sadness for the pain they've caused, and accept others' disappointment with their choices—but are glad they made them.

Including moving back to Jersey, where they come from, where neither's lived since each was in their teens—ten years for her, forty for him. People tell them that they're crazy, once again.

But giving up the Southern California sun—and smog and traffic and polluted water—isn't difficult for them. They know their happiness is where they are.

And they want their son to be around his huge extended family, and the trees and seasons and smells and sights and attitudes they grew up on and sorely missed.

They find a place not far from where the poet lived as a kid. Only minutes from her family's homes. They can't contain their joy as their son blossoms in this familiar atmosphere.

As they find God in the details of their son's development, with each day they give up any pretense of regret or guilt—or embarrassment—for what they did. It happened.

M*y life 2*

When I was 10,
I thought I was "Irish,"
even though I was
born in the USA.

When I was 20,
I thought I was "Black,"
even though my skin
is pink & freckled,
my hair is straight,
and I have no
African ancestry.

When I was 30,
I thought I was "queer,"
even though I was
married and had
two children, and
all my fantasies
& obsessions & com-
pulsions & attractions
were and had always
been about women.

When I was 40,
I thought I was a
"movie star," even
though the movies
were terrible, and
I was terrible in
them, and almost
no one knew them,
or who I might
have been in them.

When I was 50,
I thought I was

"enlightened," even
though I wasn't.

But of course I was
and am—enlightened,
as I was and still am
—an Irish-Black-
Queer-Movie-Star.

Printed November 1999 in Santa Barbara &
Ann Arbor for the Black Sparrow Press by
Mackintosh Typography & Edwards Brothers Inc.
Text set in Plantin by Words Worth.
Design by Barbara Martin.
This first edition is published in paper wrappers;
there are 200 hardcover trade copies;
100 hardcover copies have been numbered &
signed by the author; & 22 copies lettered A–V
have been handbound in boards by
Earle Gray & are signed by the author.

PHOTO: Robert Zuckerman